The State, Administration and the Individual

Michael Hill studied in his spare time for a degree in sociology
while he was a civil servant in the National Assistance Board.
After graduating he became a lecturer at Rutherford College of
Technology in Newcastle upon Tyne, and then at Reading University.
He then moved to the University of Oxford to work first on
a study of unemployment, and latterly as Deputy Director of
a study of field social work. He is the author of *The Sociology
of Public Administration* and co-author of *Community Action
and Race Relations* and *Men out of Work*. He has served as
a local councillor and has been active in community organizations.

Studies in Public Administration

This is a new series designed to introduce the reader to the study of the different aspects of public administration. Unlike most literature in this field the series will not be directly linked with the study of business administration. The readership foreseen for the series includes administrators, whether or not they are studying for professional exams, students of political science and related subjects, as well as the general reader seeking a more informed appreciation of the key role of the administrative process in political decision making.

The series is edited by F. F. Ridley, who has been Professor of Political Theory and Institutions in the University of Liverpool since 1964. He is Chairman of the Joint University Council for Social and Public Administration, has been Chairman of its Public Administration Committee, and is a founder member of the European Group of the International Institute of Administrative Science. He is also Chairman of Examiners in British Government and Politics with the Joint Matriculation Board. He is Editor of *Political Studies*, and his publications include *Public Adminstration in France* (with J. Blondel), *Specialists and Generalists: A Comparative Survey of Professional Civil Servants* (Editor), and *The Study of Government: Political Science and Public Administration* (in preparation).

Volumes published so far: *The Management of Welfare* – R. G. S. Brown; *Techniques and Public Administration* – Maurice Spiers; *Administering Britain* – Dr B. C. Smith and Jeffrey Stanyer; *Understanding Local Government* – Jeffrey Stanyer.

Forthcoming volumes are provisionally entitled: *The Study of Public Administration* – Professor David Murray; *The Policy Perspective* – Dr W. I. Jenkins and Dr G. K. Roberts; *Comparative Administration* – Professor F. F. Ridley; *Governmental Planning* – Professor P. Self.

Michael Hill

The State, Administration and the Individual

Martin Robertson

in association with Fontana/Collins

First published in association with Fontana 1976
by Martin Robertson & Co. Ltd, 17 Quick Street, London N1 8HL

ISBN 0 85520 141 X

Made and printed in Great Britain by
William Collins Sons and Co Ltd Glasgow

To the memory of
my mother

Acknowledgements

I am grateful to Professor Ridley, the series editor, for encouraging me to write this book and for commenting upon it. Many friends and colleagues have made helpful suggestions, or have commented on all or part of the manuscript. I would particularly like to thank Roger Britton, Christine Desborough, Bob Harrison, Ruth Issacharoff, Cherry Rowlings and Olive Stevenson for their comments. My wife Betty has played her usual valuable part in commenting on my ideas and in helping with the checking of the manuscript. Brenda Goodall and the staff of the Supercopy Typing Agency have typed successive versions of the book with great speed and accuracy despite my illegible handwriting. I would finally like to thank my colleagues on the Social Work Research Project, and particularly Olive Stevenson, for tolerating my preoccupation with this book at times when there have been so many other things I should be doing.

Contents

Chapter 1
Introduction

Many books have been written about the relationship between
the citizen and the State, yet few deal with the impact of public
administration upon ordinary people. Most are either in the
central tradition of political science, interested in the nature
and working of representative institutions, or they are by
administrative lawyers, concerned with the broad legal framework or with the judicial mechanisms available to secure the
redress of grievances.

Those books which are concerned with representative institutions look at citizens as voters, as political party activists and as
members of pressure groups. Yet ordinary people have a chance
to vote in a general election only every four or five years; and
then their choices are dictated primarily by traditional allegiance,
social class, and the successes of various parties in manipulating
'images'. When they vote in local elections, national considerations tend to determine their choices. Only a very small proportion of the population belongs to political parties, and a much
smaller minority of them are politically active. Even amongst
the activists very few really have any influence upon political
choices. Quite a large sector of the population belongs to one
kind of pressure group, a trade union. However, few union
members play significant political roles within their organization.
Public representation through other kinds of pressure groups
is almost as rare as active involvement in political parties.

That is a very abbreviated statement of what 'representative
government' implies for citizens. Involvement in politics in any
way is very slight. By contrast, everyone is engaged in a series
of often very active relationships with public administration.
We pay rates and taxes, apply for social security benefits, have
to take note of many administrative regulations, send our children

to school, make use of the National Health Service and so on. It would be interesting to see how many different interactions there were, on average, between citizens and public officials in the course of a year. We would surely find that they hugely out-numbered the occasions upon which people voted, attended a political meeting or made contact with a political representative. Of course, many of the interactions would be quite minor and uncontroversial, but quite a few would entail arguments about rights and obligations. Furthermore, many of these apparently quite 'minor' contacts between individuals and public employees have a crucial impact upon individual welfare. If you ask a sample of people about their relationships with the State, once you have explained your question – which will merely baffle many in the first instance – they will surely tell you about these kinds of contacts rather than about the matters that have been the traditional concerns of political scientists.

Within political science, public administration has developed into a separate subject at the same time as responsibilities delegated to administrators have grown in significance. One concern in the study of public administration has been the implications of this delegation for democracy. The focus, however, has generally been upon 'accountability' – the relation-ship between politicians and administrators, or upon the 'repre-sentative' character of the bureaucracy. Little consideration has been given to the impact of administrative activity upon the public, and to the possibility that the State may be made more responsive by attending to relationships at this level rather than to the control of administrators by politicians.

Part of this gap in the study of administration in the modern State has been filled by the administrative lawyers. Wade, in the introduction to his textbook on administrative law, presents control over the State as resting upon a combination of political mechanisms, deriving from Parliament, and legal control through the courts. Administrative law, he says, 'is the practical enforce-ment of the rule of law, meaning that the government must have legal warrant for what it does and that if it acts unlawfully the citizen has an effective remedy' (Wade, 1971: 1).

Happily, in recent years writers on British administration

have ceased to argue that Britain has no system of administrative law. Interest has grown in the various devices available to citizens to secure the redress of grievances, and scholars are engaged in studying ways to make these devices more effective. However, citizens very rarely see their grievances against the State as matters about which they can litigate. Sometimes they are wrong; recent studies have shown that citizens often do not recognize problems on which they could benefit from legal advice, and do not have easy access to people who could point them out, Often, however, the available legal remedies are too ponderous and expensive to be used by ordinary people. Moreover, citizens' grievances are more likely to be against biased uses of legitimate power than against the forms of maladministration that can be the subject of judicial remedies.

Increasingly important in British administration, however, is a growing area of quasi-legal jurisdiction where many citizens can seek adequate remedies for official acts which they regard as wrongful or unfair. Administrative tribunals exercise powers as checks upon public administration. Their importance has been recently recognized both by government committees and by academic students of law and administration. They will be discussed in this book. Their coverage is patchy, however, and we will see that many of the aspects of administration which we want to examine lie beyond the scope of these tribunals. Again, these 'remedies', too, are at their most effective in the comparatively rare cases of maladministration. They are not so effective where the factors which prevent the citizen receiving adequate attention are professional prerogatives, or stigma and ignorance, or discretionary powers.

The aim of this book, therefore, is to try to fill a gap which has been left largely disregarded by the study of politics and public administration. Its focus is British administration but its concern with the many ways in which the activities of the State impinge upon the public makes it of more general relevance. It looks at the kinds of relationships between the individual and the State which have developed as the State has increasingly tried to control its citizens, to provide benefits and services for them, and to plan on their behalf. It looks at problems which arise in the resulting relationships, and evaluates some of the solutions to those problems which are widely canvassed.

The subject which has perhaps contributed most here is social administration. This is a curiously pragmatic subject, developed in Britain, which is hard to define and lacking an equivalent in other countries. Its concern has been with the effectiveness of the so-called 'Welfare State' in meeting the needs of citizens. In many ways it has developed a discernible political ideology, a Fabian socialist concern to examine the success of the Welfare State, as an instrument for the further-ance of social equality. It is this which has given it a distinctive character, making it something more than a 'rag bag' of topics taught to students, such as intending social workers, who want to know something about the history, structure and working of the various social services. Its development has owed a great deal to the late Richard Titmuss, who led the way in the study of the effectiveness of the social services, tempering his passion-ate concern for the advancement of the Welfare State with a desire to bring sociology and economics to bear on the analysis of social policies and policy making.

This book has been very much influenced by studies con-ducted under this social administration rubric. They, more than other work, have been concerned with the actual impact of administration upon citizens. Yet it is illogical that those forms of public administration which are concerned with the social services should be singled out for special attention and that a subject should be developed separating issues in the administra-tion of these services from the study of other activities of public servants. In the first place, it is hard to determine the boundaries of the 'social services'; for example, some courses treat educa-tion as within their purview while others do not. In the second place, the distinction encourages the view that social administra-tion is different from economic administration, or the administra-tion of defence or scientific policy.

While the social services may be more actively involved with citizens on a day-to-day basis than other public services, it must not be forgotten that all the other services have social implica-tions. More seriously, the distinction encourages the view that the interaction between social and economic policy can be disregarded. There is a danger that the study of the social services is seen as 'applied sociology', while sociological insights on the character of organizations, or on the determinants of policy making or implementation, are disregarded in the study of other forms of public administration.

Many writers on the Welfare State have stressed the importance of public services and benefit-giving agencies, sometimes neglecting the fact that the State is also seen in a controlling role by many people. This book, therefore, starts with a chapter which, taking an historical look at the growth of State power, emphasizes this control element in relations between the State and its citizens.

When, in the following chapter, attention shifts to benefits provided by the State a central theme is the significance of 'rights' in this context. Governments today are concerned with elaborate mechanisms to take money from some people and to provide benefits for others. There is a complex web of State-enforced exchanges between citizens, so that it is often quite difficult for the individuals to work out whether, on balance, they gain or lose from the activities of the Welfare State. We readily recognize taxation as an encroachment upon individual rights; what are not so clearly acknowledged are rights to receive State aid. It will be argued that public, political and official attitudes to the possible rights on either side of these exchange relationships have a crucial impact upon the effective operation of the welfare system.

In order for the State to play so positive a role in society an elaborate administrative system has been developed. We talk of 'State bureaucracy', often giving that term a pejorative meaning. There is a need to consider whether it is inevitable that a system of government which does so much for citizens must also suffer from the 'bureaucratic disease' of 'red-tape'. A government of 'laws and not men' can provide 'rights' for its citizens, but can it do this in ways which avoid mindless inflexibility and disregard of 'individualized justice'? These are some of the issues which are given attention in Chapter 4.

Where the State sets out to provide specialized services for its citizens it often employs professionals, granting them a measure of autonomy so that they may use their expertise without undue constraints. This freedom raises further problems for the relationship between the individual and the State since it makes difficult the imposition of controls to ensure that professionals are responsive to public needs, and have regard to individual 'rights'. The readiness of professional groups to accept responsibility and enforce forms of 'professional accountability' is therefore of crucial importance. Yet there is a danger that professional values may become too inward-looking, concerned with the protection of the professional group rather than with the giving of a public service.

Another characteristic of the State-supported professional services – education, health and social services – is that practitioners cannot be responsible to their clients alone but must also acknowledge wider social responsibilities. Critics of State services have emphasized the 'social control' aspects of these responsibilities. The two chapters on professional services, 5 and 6, examine this view as well as exploring the issue outlined in the last paragraph.

Chapter 7 looks at the adequacy of the various procedures individuals may use to secure the redress of grievances. A significant new development here has been the growth of movements which aim to help people obtain benefits and contest official decisions. The last part of that chapter examines these 'welfare rights' movements and discusses some of the strategic dilemmas which they face.

In recent years much attention has been given to the development of planning activities by the State. Attempts have been made to set up a system of land use, or town and country planning. Increasingly there are demands that economic and social planning should be integrated with physical planning. At the same time many critics of planning have suggested that public needs and interests are disregarded by the present system. Two particular kinds of criticism are common. One is that planners are 'evangelistic bureaucrats' imposing their visions with total insensitivity to the needs of ordinary people. The other sees planners as limited by narrow class interests, working with the economically dominant groups in our society to maintain the *status quo*. Chapter 8 looks at the impact of planning upon people, and evaluates these two arguments.

The discussion of planning leads naturally to the final chapter on participation. Here the weaknesses of the Skeffington proposals for increased participation are examined. It will be suggested there are some intrinsic difficulties to securing greater participation. 'Community action' movements aim to give more power to hitherto unconsulted sections of the population. Do they simply create new pressure groups, perhaps further limiting the scope for effective or innovatory decisions? Or can they help to create new, more democratic, decision-making structures? To what extent can movements seeking greater participation replace the existing representative system by a more 'direct' form of democracy? The final chapter thus brings together some of the book's underlying themes and relates the study of the impact of administration upon citizens to the more central preoccupations of traditional political science and political philosophy.

Chapter 2
State Control over Citizens:
An Historical Perspective

Introduction

Two kinds of relationships between individuals and the State may logically be distinguished: those where the State provides something for, or protects, individuals, and those where the State takes something from, or controls, individuals. In very many cases these two kinds of relationships go together, the State taking from some to give to others. However, there are interactions in which the State plays a negative, controlling or taxing role without there being in any clear sense a reciprocal positive role. Situations of this kind have contributed considerably to the conceptions of the role of the State as a limiter of freedom. It was in the guise of a controller and taxer of individuals that the State first assumed significance.

Confusion has been introduced into much writing about the State by those who, for obvious reasons, have been eager to argue that the process of government is one in which the general will is realized. For them, society and the State are virtually synonymous. Against this view others have argued that the State is a vehicle for the exercise of power by a minority. Thus, for Marx and Engels 'the State is an organization of the possessing class for its protection against the non-possessing class'.

We should regard this question of the relation between the State and society as not so much one that can be resolved by the definition of concepts or by polemic as one that must be the subject of study. Societies will vary in their distribution of power and forms of government, dispersing or concentrating control of the State in varying ways. Mosca sets out the basic issues clearly:

. . . the state is nothing more than the organization of all social forces that have a political significance. In other words, it is the sum total of all the elements in a society that are suited to exercising political functions and have the ability and the will to participate in them.

(Mosca, 1939: 158)

In his own work Mosca gives insufficient attention to the major significance of *'ability' to participate*. As the modern State emerged some elements in society were very much more able to participate than others. Hence even Dicey, a liberal theorist hostile to the socialist ideas gathering strength around him at the beginning of the twentieth century, wrote:

. . . from the inspection of the laws of a country it is often possible to conjecture, and this without much hesitation, what is the class which holds, or has held, predominant power at a given time. No man could cast a glance at the laws and institutions of the Middle Ages without seeing that power then went with ownership of land. Wherever agriculturalists are predominant you will find laws favouring the cultivators of the soil, and if you discover laws passed for the special benefit of manufacturers or artisans, you may be certain that these classes, in some way or other, are or were of political weight.

(Dicey, 1905: 12-13)

The State before the nineteenth century

Government in simple, small-scale societies, such as many of the tribal societies studied by anthropologists, is largely a process of regulation of inter-personal relationships, without the employment of any mediating officials. The concern in this book is with units of government where the delegation of responsibilities to administrators is necessary. With the development of nation states came forms of indirect government. In medieval Europe, attempts were made to achieve a system of government which was a compromise between a decentralized 'tribal' system and centralized government through officials. Feudalism involved the delegation of governmental reponsibilities to local nobility tied to an overlord by an oath of loyalty and by some recognition of mutual inter-dependence. In some cases this system only arose because of the failure of attempts at more centralized government, probably due to the inadequacy of communications. Japanese feudalism is often cited as a particularly clear example of this but, equally, European feudalism emerged after the break-up of Charlemagne's empire. In other cases feudal institutions represented an attempt at a small degree of centralization in what were hitherto more or less tribal societies. Feudalism was inherently unstable; as kings found it more possible to exercise central control and as subjects, interested in developing trade, accepted the case for that control, it was bound to decline.

Hence there emerged in Europe after the Middle Ages, but before the rise of large-scale industry, a society in which the relations between individuals and the State had the following characteristics. Monarchs, or oligarchic groups, sought to maintain the integrity of the State. To do this without being able to depend upon feudal ties they required standing armies and perhaps navies. Equally, these forces might be required to maintain order within the State. Indeed, one strong pressure towards the elimination of feudalism lay in the need of the central ruler to try to secure a monopoly of force within the realm.

The maintenance of regal power, and particularly of an army, could not, at least as the political pattern became more stable, depend upon plunder alone. Hence there was a need for taxation. The first non-military royal officials were naturally therefore, apart from those with largely ceremonial roles, recruited to assist with the raising of revenue and monitoring of expenditure. In a society where a low overall level of resources was accompanied by a high degree of inequality, the royal need to raise revenues was not of direct consequence for the common man. It is important to remember that income tax was not introduced in Britain until the Napoleonic Wars, and did not really affect ordinary working people until the twentieth century. However, as far as the nobility at first, then later the landed aristocracy and, by the sixteenth and seventeenth century, the trading classes, were concerned, the revenue-raising activities of the Crown were of crucial importance in the political evolution of the State.

Controversy over the raising of revenue played a major part in the generation of many of the fundamental political conflicts in European history. The English Civil War and the French Revolution are but the most salient examples of this.

In these conflicts, administrators played but minor parts; the relationship between the individual and the State was being hammered out at the highest political level. Because the conflicts were at this level, it has often been forgotten that their indirect effects were often of much more pressing importance for the common people. They were affected by the fluctuating growth of the economy and the shifts in the power of the great magnates. The kings had little direct impact on the lives of their ordinary subjects, for whom the local nobility were the real rulers. Feudalism lived on, as decentralized low-level administration, long after it had ceased to determine the formal relationship between king and lords.

Alongside the development of a monopoly in the use of force to secure the nation state, a system of law evolved. To secure political stability an element of social consensus was required to ensure the maintenance of the monopoly of power. One of the sources of this consensus needed to be the people's confidence that they would receive 'justice' in their dealings with each other and with the king. Although we tend today to conceive of the administration of justice as separate from the administration of the State, and we express concern when these two aspects of administration are confused, an historical view of the evolution of the State makes it very clear that the system of justice emerged from the resolution of conflict between the king and his most powerful subjects. Hence, while the national legal system grew out of conflict between the powerful, that system which is of more direct concern to ordinary people developed out of a commitment to secure order, shared by monarch and aristocracy. Accordingly, in Britain until the nineteenth century both the local system of law and the local system of government was almost entirely in the hands of members of the local gentry, the Justices of the Peace.

Thus, those functions that were first recognized as functions of

the State were built upon a need to secure order, a need fundamental to the continued existence of the State. In performing
these functions the State was primarily the controller of its
citizens. This control had to be further extended by the need
to raise revenue to pay for this controlling function. To perform
these tasks the pattern of administration adopted in England, and
to a considerable extent in other western European countries,
was in many respects a derivative of the feudal system. The
maintenance of order, the administration of justice, and the
collection of revenue depended upon the compliance of a group
of the more powerful laity. These were the people who were
expected to play a crucial subordinate role in the government
of the State, rather than a corps of professional officials.

This low involvement of central government with society
was also under-pinned by a Church which undertook roles
which today are seen as belonging to the State. Religious charity
provided relief for the poor and sick, and the development of
education was almost wholly a clerical undertaking. The gradual
shift of responsibilities of this kind from Church to State between
the sixteenth and twentieth centuries must be an underlying
theme in any discussion of the growth of the Welfare State.

The picture that has been painted of a very limited relationship between State and individual is, though simplified, reasonably accurate for Britain between the Middle Ages and the
beginning of the nineteenth century. Yet, even in Britain, the
Crown and/or Parliament tried in various ways to exercise
a very much fuller control over citizens. Elsewhere in the world
there were at various times in history 'absolute rulers' who succeeded in doing this. Karl Wittfogel's classic book *Oriental
Despotism* explores the key examples of the exercise of absolute
power, by means of a bureaucratic machinery of government, in
societies of varying antiquity. His main examples are drawn from
China, Ancient Egypt and Mesopotamia, and pre-Columbian
Central America. He describes the elaborate mechanisms employed to secure the loyalty of bureaucratic officials whose very
distance from the centre must have continually endangered the
stability of the State. It is difficult to understand how such
systems survived in an age of such poor communications. One of

the important sources of stability would seem to be the fact that the prosperity of these kingdoms depended upon the co-ordinated control of water resources; hence subjects had an interest in the continuing stability of these 'hydraulic societies'. Thus Wittfogel argues:

> . . . too little or too much water does not necessarily lead to governmental water control: nor does governmental water control necessarily imply despotic methods of state-craft. It is only above the level of an extractive subsistence economy, beyond the influence of strong centres of rainfall agriculture, and below the level of a property-based industrial civilization that man, reacting specifically to the water-deficient landscape, moves to-wards a specific hydraulic order of life.
>
> *(Wittfogel, 1957: 12)*

It may well be asked why it is necessary to refer to Wittfogel's discussion of 'oriental despotism' in an account of the development of the relationship between the State, administration and the individual which is characteristic of Britain. The point is that the emphasis here has been upon the very limited extension of State power, backed by an insignificant administrative staff, in pre-industrial Britain. Yet this was not for want of absolutist aspirations on the part of the Tudors and Stuarts, nor for the lack of general belief in the role of the State as a regulator of trade which characterized eighteenth-century Parliaments as much as earlier monarchs. However, by comparison with the 'hydraulic societies', there was no economic force making centralized government desirable or necessary. Rather, in a society in which agricultural and trading prosperity could be built up, without either government protection or interference, the decentralized feudal society was transformed into one in which autonomous private property became of key significance. In what Wittfogel describes as 'the race between the growth of lordly (and burgher) power on the one hand and royal power on the other', economic forces tended to be in favour of the former.

Once monarchs felt able to try to develop a central administrative machinery they were confronted by subjects who were powerful enough to resist attacks on their autonomy. Without the apparatus to enforce its will, the central government had to compromise with its more powerful subjects. The consequence was that the laws that survived to the post-industrial revolution era in which Parliaments proudly proclaimed the doctrine of *laissez-faire*, were but a mixture of Acts depending upon local enforcement (like the Poor Laws), Acts that conformed with the interests of powerful groups in society (such as those providing for certain trading or professional monopolies), and Acts (such as many designed to protect employees from exploitation) that were more honoured in the breach than in the observance. The officials appointed to administer these Acts were, as Henry Parris has shown in his *Constitutional Bureaucracy*, no impartial group of servants of the Crown. Some were also in business themselves, others were landowners, and many owed their appointments to political patronage and were able to combine political activities with their administrative functions.

From the late medieval period onwards the English government was prepared to legislate to regulate wages, to control the movement of labour and apprenticeship arrangements and to provide poor relief. This legislation conformed with the characteristics of early State involvement with the individual which have been stressed already. It was motivated primarily by a concern with order and it depended for its enforcement upon quasi-autonomous local functionaries.

A number of writers have stressed how poor relief systems emerged as a response to problems of social order. Piven and Cloward have suggested that poor relief schemes in Europe originated from concern about the threats to social order which occurred in the period of transition from feudalism to capitalism. The population began to grow rapidly, whilst economic growth was patchy and erratic. Hence there was an increase in the number of people lacking a clear place in society, and a stable source of income. These people were forced to migrate in search of work, or to resort to begging or perhaps banditry. Piven and Cloward point out that many localities enacted severe penalities against vagrancy. But:

. . . penalties alone did not deter begging, especially when economic distress was severe and the numbers affected were large. Subsequently, some localities began to augment punishment with provisions for the relief of the vagrant poor.

(Piven and Cloward, 1972: 8)

The main body of British legislation for dealing with the problems of poverty and vagrancy was the Act of Settlement of 1662 and the two Poor Law Acts of 1598 and 1601. This 'Elizabethan Poor Law' lasted until 1834. It was administered by the Justices of the Peace in each parish. They were empowered to levy a 'poor rate' to support their activities. Inevitably there were enormous variations in the way these Acts were administered, at different times and in different places, in response to local needs, local unrest and the dispositions of the individual magistrates.

The nineteenth-century extension of State control

Britain, in the nineteenth century, saw a remarkable series of extensions of State intervention in society. Not only were many Acts of Parliament passed which were intended to have a major impact upon the behaviour of individual citizens, but means were devised to enforce these Acts much more effectively than had ever been the case before. The basis of the modern civil service was laid, local government was reformed and a variety of effective *ad hoc* bodies were created.

Many of the key reforms of this period involved compromises with the older system of decentralized government. To enforce new laws without radically altering the administrative machinery, agencies were set up to inspect and supervise the activities of local organizations. The Poor Law Act of 1834, for example, set up a Poor Law Commission to supervise the activities of the local Guardians of the Poor and to organize them into Unions of parishes. Then, gradually through the century, the extent of central intervention increased. The Commission was transformed into the Poor Law Board and then, in 1871, into the Local Government Board, with a Cabinet Minister as Chairman.

The relationship between citizen and administration, as far as the recipients of poor relief were concerned, remained a local one. But even at this level it was increasingly the case that the administrators were full-time officials, while the lay Guardians faded into the background. The lash of State control was felt by the more prosperous, who were forced to contribute to increasing levels of 'poor rates' as the Guardians were forced by the government to raise standards.

A similarly indirect pattern of relationships between the State and citizens developed in the public health field. Here the initial legislation was largely permissive. Then, as this was seen to be ineffective, local agencies were required to take prescribed steps to curb dangers to public health. Yet local initiatives were not absent, the comparatively indiscriminate incidence of infectious diseases in the new towns forcing the wealthy and powerful to pay attention to public health problems. In this area too, a corps of professionals began to be built up, operating at both local and national level to deal with, and draw attention to, public health problems: the medical officers.

Public health legislation was one of the most significant nineteenth-century contributions to the extension of the coercive power of the State; it's key characteristic was the prevention of actions that might harm others. Factory legislation had similar characteristics. To be effective, such legislation had to bring in its wake a most significant extension of State bureaucracy. A new kind of policing role had to be played by officials appointed to ensure that legislation of this kind was carried out. An important Victorian addition to the apparatus of the State was, therefore, the government inspector. Capitalists were to be free to pursue profits. They were to be involved in decentralized government through the local authorities and the various *ad hoc* bodies, but were to operate in both these spheres within a framework of rules and restrictions laid down by central government and enforced by a cadre of inspectors.

Dicey characterized the early part of the Victorian age, or more precisely the period from 1825 to 1870, as the great period of 'Benthamism or individualism'. This he contrasted with the sixteenth and seventeenth centuries, which he saw as a period of 'confidence in the authority of the State', and the period after 1870 which he described, writing in 1905, as the 'period of collectivism'. While not disputing Dicey's account of the dominant ideas in each of these periods, contemporary historians have pointed out that the period of 'individualism' was in fact an era when the foundations of the modern collectivist State were laid. The interesting question is then, why was it the case that at a time when influential men were firmly wedded to *laissez-faire* there was nevertheless this widespread espousal of State control over the activities of individuals? Fraser, in his account of the evolution of the Welfare State, looks at this issue and discusses the reasons for the discrepancy between ideals and practice during the mid-nineteenth century.

The first of the reasons Fraser gives is perhaps the most important. He argues that 'while men held genuinely to a belief that *laissez-faire* was at least the best answer, they had to accept that the problems posed by urban industrial society of necessity enlarged the practical activities of the State' (Fraser, 1973: 103). While many Victorians regarded the capitalist mode of economic organization as the most satisfactory way of achieving the general good, we do not today treat this as so self-evident. Some of the critical problems Victorian legislators had to face arose from the consequences of unrestrained capitalist enterprise. As Parris's study of the Railway Acts shows, for example, there was as early as the 1830s 'a widespread recognition that railways were monopolies, not subject to the restraint of competition. Thus the normal arguments against public regulation did not apply'. Some of the early public health legislation stemmed from the discovery that unrestrained competition had consequences that were destructive of the general good. Finally, even so committed an individualist as Dicey recognized that there are anomalies in the doctrine of minimal restraint on individual freedom, using as his example the problems of freedom of association which continue to worry politicians and political philosophers, of both Right and Left, to this day. The problem is that the freedom of the citizens to 'combine together by agreement . . . for the attainment of a common purpose' may at the same time greatly restrict the freedom of other individuals. The very process of upholding *laissez-faire* may require State action to restrict individual freedom.

Fraser links with the impact of the need for the State to cope with the problems of the age, two related reasons for the gap between political theory and political practice. One of these is that the dominant, Benthamite ideology combined with its belief in freedom a commitment to the attainment of 'the greatest happiness of the greatest number'. Where the 'hidden hand' of economic freedom seemed unable to attain the general good, 'rational social engineering' could be carried out as an alternative means to that end. Bentham, and the other Utilitarian philosophers, tended to make a distinction between economic and social affairs, expecting *laissez-faire* to prevail in the former but not the latter. Of course, this is a false distinction, yet practical politicians, whatever the strength of their commitment to economic individualism, find it hard to resist demands for intervention wherever special, appealing cases of hardship arise. The 'hard case' is the 'Trojan Horse' for State intervention in the economy. In the middle of the nineteenth century perhaps the most significant exception to the general acceptance of *laissez-faire* was a recognition of a need to protect women and children. Hence, as Dicey pointed out, 'Individualists of every school were only too keenly alive to the danger that the sinister interest of a class should work evil to the weak and helpless' (Dicey, 1905: 220).

Yet the early Factory Acts provided powerful precedents for future legislation. They opened up the evils of the factory system to the gaze of an inspectorate. Moreover, the practical effect of limiting the hours of women and children was often that employers were forced to limit the hours of men too.

This 'Trojan Horse' explanation appears again in a theory developed from the work of two students of nineteenth-century policy making, MacDonagh and Roberts. MacDonagh provides an account of the evolution of control over passenger shipping in his *A Pattern of Government Growth*, while Roberts's *Victorian Origins of the British Welfare State* is primarily concerned with the activities of government inspectors.

Fraser reports the theory developed by these historians as involving a five-stage model of Government growth.

The first stage was the discovery of some 'intolerable' evil, such as the exploitation of child labour. Legislation was passed to prevent this. In the second stage, however, it was discovered that the legislation was ineffective. New legislation was passed with stronger provisions and inspectors were employed to ensure enforcement. Third, many of the new groups of professionals recruited to enforce legislation themselves became lobbyists for increases in the powers of their agencies. Fourth, this growing corps of professional experts made legislators aware 'that the problems could not be swept away by some magnificent all-embracing gesture but would require continuous slow regulation and re-regulation' (Fraser, 1973: 106). Finally, therefore, a quite elaborate framework of law was developed with a complex bureaucratic machine to enforce it. The professionals helped to transform the administrative system into a major organization with extensive powers, almost without Parliament realizing it.

An interesting aspect of this theory is the role which is attributed to groups of public employees as individuals with interests in, and commitments to, extensions of State activity. The studies of Roberts and MacDonagh have attracted wide interest and more recently Paulus has shown how public analysts, and Carson how factory inspectors, similarly played important parts in extending State control over individuals. Paulus describes these public servants as 'moral provocateurs', individuals who 'try to achieve change by laying claim to a higher morality for their actions'. Yet in many cases the 'higher morality' is, he acknowledges, reinforced by self interest. The public analyst, for example, stood to gain from further legislation against impure food:

> ... any proposed actions had a direct effect upon their prestige and chances for lucrative employment. Their collective goals to achieve a well-fed and undefrauded working-class population were compounded by divergent personal goals to secure professional advantages.
>
> *(Paulus, 1974: 25)*

Clearly the theory developed by MacDonagh and Roberts is important, but to give it full force it needs to be linked with other social and political changes of the age. The country 'grew smaller', as railways speeded up communications and roads were improved. Not only were social evils more readily brought to the attention of legislators, but processes of enforcement could be more effective. Political corruption was gradually eliminated; one important aspect of this was the creation of an impartial career civil service. Hence legislative enforcement became more feasible. The administration and research to back up this enforcement began to become a more systematic process. The professional expertise, though to a considerable extent the creation of dedicated public servants, rested upon a growing body of knowledge and a rising level of education. Men could believe in rational policy enforcement because they had the skills to make it possible.

Another interpretation of the gap between political philosophy and policy in the mid-Victorian period is that the initiatives taken were pragmatic responses to a growing unrest amongst the working classes and to demands for social reform. Certainly, some of the measures of the earlier period, before and after the beginning of the century, have been seen in this light – a combination of attempts to quell unrest with extension of poor relief to conciliate the working class. Similarly at the end of the nineteenth century the ruling classes were aware of a need for policies which 'bought off' the restless urban working class and undermined the growing socialist movement. The political programmes of people like Joseph Chamberlain and Lord Randolph Churchill were evidence of this. Indeed, in 1895 Balfour, one of the leaders of the Conservative Party, made it very clear:

> Social legislation, as I conceive it, is not merely to be distinguished from Socialist legislation but it is its most direct opposite and its most effective antidote. Socialism will never get possession of the great body of public opinion . . . among the working class or any other class if those who wield the collective forces of the community show themselves desirous to ameliorate every legitimate grievance and to put Society upon a proper and more solid basis.

Perhaps it was because the salient mass movement in the middle period of the nineteenth century was Chartism, which was directed largely at electoral reform, that historians have found less evidence in this period of social legislation as a direct response to working-class unrest. Yet clearly the police legislation of the period stemmed from a recognition of a need to control the people; surely some of the more reformist legislation must also have been influenced by the recognition of a need to conciliate. Certainly there was a mass movement seeking factory legislation. The 'Tory Humanitarianism' of Shaftesbury and the concern of Disraeli to unite the 'Two Nations', both of which Dicey saw as contributing to the triumph of 'collectivism' over 'individualism', are in a direct line of descent to the more calculated 'social imperialism' of the Conservative and Unionist Party at the turn of the century. This Tory involvement in social reform, moreover, was also a reaction of the weakening 'landed interest' against the urban bourgeoisie, dominant in the Liberal Party. An alliance with newly enfranchised working-class 'householders' provided a means to 'dish the Whigs'.

The twentieth century

By the end of the nineteenth century, in the view of Dicey, the 'collectivist state' was truly established. Yet Victorian legislation primarily aimed at the control of the worst abuses of industrial capitalism. Little had been done, except in the field of elementary education, to provide services *for* people; the emphasis had been upon preventing things being done *to* them.

Social security provision was still severely limited by the stern rules of the Poor Law. Health services were also either hedged around by Poor Law restrictions or only available on a charitable basis. The scale of provision of public housing was insignificant.

Victorian planning, except in a few far-sighted municipalities, was largely negative. It was directed at removing or preventing 'nuisances', mainly dangers to public health, and not at the positive control of the environment. Hence, in this field too the relationship between the individual and the State was to be transformed very much more in the twentieth century.

Before the twentieth century the people of Britain had had no experience of mass mobilization by the State for the purpose of waging war. This experience, fundamental for the transformation of the relationship between the State and the individual, was still to come. Equally, apart from a limited range of municipal enterprises (the 'gas and water socialism' of the Webbs), people had no experience of large-scale public undertakings. These were to emerge both as social service organizations and in spheres that the Victorians had regarded as entirely the province of private enterprise.

It is not intended to give a comprehensive account of twentieth-century developments in administration, nor will attention be given here to the State as a provider of benefits and services or as a planning agency, as these topics are covered in later chapters. Attention will be confined to advancing the theme developed in the earlier part of this chapter, the role of the State as a controller of individual citizens.

Victorian intervention by the State involved, as has been said, primarily curbing the activities of capitalists to protect their employees or the public. Twentieth-century legislation has continued to increase these curbs. One public interest that has been given increased attention is that of the consumer, which has been a special feature of more recent legislation. The State has added to its responsibilities for the protection of the public from dangerous or impure commodities a concern with misleading advertising and labelling, and is beginning to assume a more general watchdog role over products offered for sale. The policing of these areas of life raises considerable problems for public officials who have to exercise extensive powers of supervision over activities of which they have little direct personal experience. It is significant that one of the recent official exposures of civil service inadequacy concerned a failure to protect the public adequately from an insecure car insurance firm, the Vehicle and General Company. Similarly, the administration has been criticized for its failure to anticipate the collapse of a travel firm offering package holidays. These complex cases are a far cry from the cases of adulterated flour or inadequate disposal of refuse which provoked State response in the mid-nineteenth century.

In an account of the development of labour law during the twentieth century written by Professor Kahn-Freund in 1958, it was stated that 'few branches of the law have been less changed in their fundamentals since Dicey's day' (Kahn-Freund, 1958: 215). When he wrote it appeared to be the case that union bargaining rights had been clearly established and that British labour law was dominated by the principle of free bargaining between unions and employers. There had been legislative interventions in this field, notably the Trade Disputes Act of 1913, but the primary intentions of these were to clarify the bargaining rights of unions without involving the State in the process. The war periods, and particularly the Second World War, saw greater State intrusion into this area of life. But after the wars everyone seemed eager to return to normal free bargaining. Indeed, the disputes that had emerged in wartime – notably on Clydeside in the First World War, and a miners' strike in Kent in the Second, during which the imprisonment of law-breaking strikers was shown to be a crude and ineffective weapon for the enforcement of State 'will' – confirmed the advantages of the 'normal system'.

However, after 1958 the position began to change as governments became increasingly concerned to manage the economy and to protect the 'general interest' from specific bargains *between* employers and employees. This concern with a national incomes policy introduces quite a new dimension into the relations between the individual and the State. Here it is an overall planning concern which motivates State intervention, and the actual effects of such activities on individuals are varied, confused, and often unpredictable.

While this book was being written a Conservative Government vacillated on the extent to which it wanted to involve the State in control over the activities of trade unionists. Its Industrial Relations Act set up a new, partly judicial, partly administrative agency, the Industrial Relations Court, which became engaged in a series of battles with unions, a situation which the Government found increasingly embarrassing. This embarrassment arose as it shifted its economic strategy from one of encouraging free bargaining, contained (it hoped) within a rather stricter code of trade union law, to the development of an incomes policy. This new policy required the co-operation of the unions to be successful, co-operation which the Conservatives failed to win. Eventually they lost an election in 1974 in the middle of a debilitating trial of strength with the National Union of Mineworkers.

In February 1974 a Labour Government came to power, jettisoning the coercive parts of the Industrial Relations Act and seeking to avoid any fettering of free bargaining on wages. To do this without undermining the management of the economy, and in particular trying to prevent very serious inflation, it attempted to rely on the 'special relationship' between the Labour Party and the Trade Unions to maintain a voluntary 'social contract'. Inflation remained high and the social contract guidelines, which political necessity required to be very vague, were increasingly broken. The future choices were seen as lying between another attempt at 'incomes policy' and monetary policies which would initially create high unemployment and by that means break the power of the unions. By summer 1975 fiscal measures had led to a situation in which unemployment was rising fast but inflation was still not contained. A new voluntary incomes policy, backed by the threat of statutory enforcement, was adopted. This was a compromise, necessary because of Labour's dependence upon union support, a statutory incomes policy dressed up to appear voluntary and presented as a temporary expedient.

The conflict between the demand for the maintenance of free bargaining between powerful agencies, likely to put the short-term needs of their members before all other considerations, and the need for tight State control over the economy in an increasingly unstable international economic climate, raises problems for the relationship between the State and individuals which cannot be easily solved. In the last resort the enforcement of the will of the State in a struggle with a union must involve punitive action against individuals. This area of relations between citizens and the State will not be considered very fully in this book. To cover it adequately would require detailed examination of the role of the State in the management of the economy. This is a separate, and rather specialized area of public administration, requiring a book in its own right.

There is, however, another area of State interference with individuals that has many of the characteristics of the nineteenth-century concern to curb some citizens in order to protect others and which involves restrictions on a much higher proportion of citizens than was ever the case with restrictions upon entrepreneurs. This is State intervention to control motoring. There are over fifteen million vehicles in Britain, and control over their use involves a substantial body of public servants who license vehicles, test drivers, supervise safety standards, check on the activities of car insurance firms, plan roads, and organize systems of traffic signs and signals. The administration of the law relating to the motorist has given an enormous new responsibility to the police force. The individual citizen is more likely to fall foul of the laws relating to motoring than to offend against the law in any other way.

William Plowden has provided in his *The Motor Car and Politics in Britain* a fascinating account of the development of political responses to the problems posed by motor vehicles. Interestingly, when only a minute proportion of the population were motorists the responses of the State were excessively restrictive. The first relevant Act was passed in 1896, limiting speeds to 14 miles per hour and imposing an excise duty on motor vehicles. The speed limit was put up to 20 m.p.h in 1904 but remained at that level for the next 27 years. Plowden argues that 'the peculiar position of motorists as a very small minority group, distinguished by their ownership of an expensive technical novelty, was important in defining their role as a political force' (Plowden, 1971:23).

Then, in the inter-war period, the use of the car spread to a substantial proportion of the middle classes and the motorists' lobby (and in particular the AA and the RAC) grew in political influence. The overall speed limit was abolished in 1930. It was restored in 1934, in urban areas only, because of widespread public concern about accidents. The tendency from the thirties until very recently has been for governments to be very nervous of the motoring lobby and sensitive, latterly, to the electoral effect of restrictive attitudes to motorists. Now this era of *laissez-faire* is waning. Concern to limit individual freedom to drive a dangerous machine has brought the 70 m.p.h. speed limit and the breathalyser. Motor cyclists have even experienced, with the introduction of compulsory crash helmets, limitations on their own freedom to kill or maim themselves. It is only a matter of time before a similar compulsion applies to seat belts for car drivers.

Yet the most dramatic policy development in this area has come as the car numbers have built up to levels at which congestion on roads and in parking places has become intolerable. Faced with the impossibility of unlimited public provision for road and car park building, the government has had to begin to restrict, and, more particularly, allow local authorities to restrict, the use and parking of cars in various places. With such a high proportion of the population using cars, this restriction of individuals for the very 'non-specific' general good raises considerable political problems. The police and parking meter attendants have a role to play as enforcers of the law that is in many respects more difficult than any 'control' task yet required of public servants. Furthermore, Plowden argues that in due course the restrictions on the use of the car will have to be extended further in ways which must threaten the rights of some citizens to own or use cars. The various ways government may do this raise problems of distributive justice, between rationing by cost and rationing by other means, which may become critical issues comparable to the issues of distribution of benefits by the State which are the concern of the next chapter.

It is indicative of the rate of change of government responses in this field of policy that, since the first draft of this chapter was completed, a new reason for government intervention arose – the fuel crisis which led to the imposition of more restrictive speed limits. The promise of North Sea oil seems to have tempered British responses to this crisis, but undoubtedly the next few years will see the development of debates about whether governments should try to limit fuel consumption by taxation to affect its price, or whether new kinds of intervention may be appropriate. The height of the crisis saw traffic-free Sundays in a number of European countries. It may be wondered whether the future will bring similar attempts to limit motoring, and what consequences such measures will have upon relations between citizens and the State if they are resisted.

The next chapter will examine how the State has become increasingly involved in the provision of social security benefits. What requires consideration here, however, is the way in which schemes of this kind have extended the control of the State over individuals. As was made clear by the aristocratic ladies who protested in 1911 against Lloyd George's requirement that they should buy insurance stamps for their servants, a compulsory scheme in which both employers and employees must pay towards an insurance contribution inevitably involves an element of 'control'. While contemporary opinion lays more stress upon what the social security legislation *provides* than upon this aspect, this scheme introduces many complications in the affairs of small businessmen and the self-employed. Over the years, National Insurance charges have increased, graduated contributions have been introduced and the system as a whole has become more complex. At the same time other forms of taxation, notably Value Added Tax, have made business administration more difficult. The small businessmen's organizations point out that the government requires them to be unpaid tax collectors.

Another form of benefit which has developed from State concern to limit the free play of economic forces is Industrial Injury Benefit. The Workmen's Compensation Act, passed as far back as 1896, supplemented the common law right of an injured workman to sue for damages where his employers could be deemed to be responsible for an accident. Under the Act, employers were required to pay compensation to injured workmen regardless of 'fault'. To obtain this workers had to waive their common law rights to damages.

This system was replaced in 1948 by an insurance scheme; hence the State changed from enforcing compensation payments from employers to requiring insurance payments. Qualification for Industrial Injury Benefits does not prevent common law action in addition.

Industrial accidents are but one variety of accident. It has been argued that the State should become more actively involved in other forms of accident insurance, since litigation for damages is a slow, expensive and hazardous business. The State does require individuals engaged in a variety of dangerous activities, of which motoring is the most significant, to take out 'third party' insurance. But here the State is not itself the insurer. The many anomalies in the law relating to civil liability led in 1974 to the setting up of a Royal Commission under the chairmanship of Lord Pearson. Its report may well stimulate debate about the extention of State involvement in accident insurance.

Some recent writers on social security legislation have stressed the role of social security benefits as an extension of social control by the State. Their concern about 'control' is rather different to that discussed above. Piven and Cloward, in their *Regulating the Poor*, argue that relief policies must be seen in terms of the roles they play in the wider 'economic and political' order. These policies, they suggest, are cyclical according to the problems of order that governments face at various times. They suggest that:

> relief arrangements are initiated or expanded during the occasional outbreaks of civil disorder produced by mass unemployment, and are then abolished or contracted when political stability is restored . . . expansive relief policies are designed to mute civil disorder, and restrictive ones to reinforce work norms.
>
> *(Piven and Cloward, 1972: xiii)*

Piven and Cloward are Americans and much of their book is concerned with the discussion of social policies in the United States, but similar views to theirs have been expounded in polemic form in Britain, by Jordan in his book *Paupers* and by Kincaid in *Poverty and Social Security in Britain*. But the most scholarly treatment of this theme with regard to Britain occurs in Gilbert's book *British Social Policy 1914-1939*. By drawing on Cabinet minutes and Secret Service reports that have now been made public, Gilbert shows how the extraordinarily erratic treatment of the provisions for unemployment insurance in the early years after the First World War were heavily influenced by reports of dangers of civil unrest.

In evaluating this thesis we obviously have not the benefit of access to more contemporary records. We should also note that, erratic though the growth of the British Welfare State may have been, there does seem to have been a more distinct pattern of growth than that perceived in the United States by Piven and Cloward. But we should beware of treating a pattern of legislative growth as evidence of a similarly consistent growth in the value of benefits to the poor. This value is naturally influenced by changes in the cost of living; fluctuations in the real value of benefits during this century have inevitably been marked. To evaluate the Piven and Cloward thesis fully we still need a systematic study in which movement of benefit levels relative to the cost of living is related to political and social events.

The importance of Piven and Cloward's book is in providing an attack on the naive view that advances in social security provision depend simply upon a growth of humanitarianism, a growth of a 'caring' Welfare State. Where Piven and Cloward are at their weakest is in treating as broadly similar forces towards change, social unrest perceived as a danger by ruling élites and social discontent reflected in electoral movements. The fact that a long line of Conservative and Liberal politicians – Disraeli, the Chamberlains, Balfour, Lloyd George, Churchill and Macmillan – were eager to 'steal the clothes' of radical and socialist movements should not be treated as an élite response comparable to the nervous concessions of the founders of the Elizabethan Poor Law or the politicians of the Napoleonic period. It should be counted as one of the successes of the British Left that it has been so easily able to get conservative politicians to make concessions to the working class. Of course, 'welfare capitalism' has come about partly because the capitalists have gradually and reluctantly made concessions to the working classes, for fear of worse alternatives. But it is equally the boast of democratic socialists that this is the road to social transformation which they have chosen. Peaceful change in our society has, moreover, also been facilitated by the extent to which more egalitarian ideas, and conceptions of the role of the State as an active protector of its citizens, have entered into the general philosophy of the age.

Clearly it is arguable that progress has been inadequate or indeed that it is bound to be inadequate, but this is not the same as arguing that no change has occurred. It may be accepted, therefore, that one of the reasons why individuals have secured State intervention to provide social security is that ruling élites have been mindful of the consequences of refusing to make such concessions, without going all the way to argue that those benefits are *merely* 'social control' devices designed to prevent revolution.

The development of the health service – through the shift of responsibility for the Poor Law health services to the local authorities, the organization of the 'panel doctor' scheme for working men under the 1911 Insurance Act, and the evolution of the municipal hospital, to the National Health Service, founded in 1946 – is one of the extensions of State activity in which a 'social control' aspect is least evident. However, this has not prevented some writers seeing the mental health service in this way. This is a topic that will be taken up on pages 138 to 143. The lack of an overall 'social control' aspect should not lead us into regarding the development of a free health service as motivated solely by humanitarian concerns. Not only was the development of such a service a central concern to leaders of the Labour movement in the twentieth century, but the improvement of a nation's health, as the sanitary reformers of the nineteenth century discovered, bestows benefits that reach beyond those who are the direct recipients of the service. Medical examinations for the Boer War revealed that the physical standard of Britain's potential soldiers, and thus of course of its workforce, could be considerably improved. The two World Wars contributed enormously to the recognition of a need for the more efficient organization of the nation's medical resources, and the system eventually achieved, for all its shortcomings, made possible the advancement of medicine on a broad front to the benefit of all. This development has brought with it some control over the activities of doctors, but Aneurin

Bevan was prepared to minimize this when he set up the service by giving a high degree of autonomy to general practitioners and considerable self-government to the hospital doctors.

State intervention in the housing field has had two very distinctive twentieth-century characteristics: control over rents and security of tenure in the private sector, and the evolution of a large public sector. The latter development has brought much sound and reasonably priced housing as an amenity for tenants. At the same time, however, it also brought about a substantial accretion of power to public agencies. The power the private landlord possessed in earlier times to evict tenants and to determine rent levels in the face of excess demand for accommodation, has been reduced by State regulation. Yet local authorities are now large landlords with powers of this kind which are really only limited by the extent to which they possess a sense of responsibility and a sensitivity to public opinion.

Planning is an interesting case in relation to this discussion of the extension of State control over the individual. There was little development of the basic nineteenth-century arrangements for land use and development control until the Second World War, after which, under government supervision, local authorities acquired extensive planning powers. Economic planning is also a recent phenomenon to develop. After the economic failures of the thirties and the Keynesian revolution in economic theory, the government began to try to control both the overall health of the economy and the allocation of resources within it.

The point about planning is that controls over individuals are intended to produce public benefits. The difficulty is that most people perceive only the individual controls, and so imperfect is our knowledge of the social mechanisms involved in a planning process that intended public benefits often are not achieved. Planning is bedevilled by 'unintended consequences'. Simple physical controls are the easiest to operate to impose some order upon the environment, but most land-use planners today aspire to do much more than that. Their aim is to influence the social environment. A later chapter will deal much more fully with the impact of this kind of planning upon the individual; the point here is to emphasize that to individuals such planning must appear as negative and controlling.

Economic planning is slowly and painfully beginning to transform the interest of the State in those areas which Dicey recognized as posing problems for the individualistic philosophy. Associations of employees, amalgamations of companies and similar activities were allowed to proceed with but little interference from the State other than sporadic attempts to mitigate the worst effects of monopoly or oligopoly. Now, however, these private institutions have such a major impact upon the economy that the State has had to seek to work with them to secure some measure of control. Although governments now try to prevent the working of the economy having an uncontrolled impact upon our lives, much of their concern is at a general and high level at which specific effects on specific individuals are hard to control. Ironically, the more governments try to control our society, the less easy the individual finds it to relate their actions to his own life. When we do try to relate to such activities we tend to see the Chancellor's efforts to stimulate demand here and restrict it there as so many pence on this tax and off that one. Budgets are evaluated in terms of what they do for us, not what they do for the economy.

The occurrence in the twentieth century of two wars, on a vastly greater scale than ever before, inevitably had a major impact upon the relationship between the State and the citizen. The only simple way to describe this impact is to say that both wars, and particularly the second, involved the mobilization of citizens in the pursuance of the war effort. In the Second World War not only were young able-bodied men conscripted but the State also assumed control over the working lives of all men below pension age and of all women without dependent children. A similar control was exercised over resources to provide a form of planning more total than the peacetime efforts, described above. In the later stages of the First World War and throughout the Second (and for several years afterwards) rationing imposed upon consumers a rigorous form of State control unknown before. Under this system, as the jokes of the period make very clear, citizens became deeply aware of some of the problems of intense State control, with queues and the black market ever-present evidence of bureaucratic disfunctions. Hughes has argued that the 'spivs' who flourished under this system contributed to the undermining of the relationship between the individual and the State:

> The spivs, flashily displaying all the suppressed energies of the back streets, were an unconscious, dramatic protest, a form of civil disobedience that millions of English people found endearing and which, since the Government found no affable or challenging way of dealing with it, survived beyond that Government.
>
> (*Hughes, 1963, 99-100*)

He suggests that the legacy of this era is still with us in the expense-accounts in high places, the lack of restraint in wage-bargaining and industrial relations, a belief 'that work has no virtue or purpose, that money should be easy-come easy-go, and that the individual must look after himself, if necessary at the expense of others' (Hughes, ibid).

Certainly while the nineteen-forties saw a great growth in the power of the State there also developed a great readiness to question that power. The role played by the State in Nazi Germany heightened this concern, as did the growing understanding of the true character of the Soviet State. Nevertheless the growth in the controlling power of the British State was no more than momentarily checked, if that, in the nineteen-fifties.

It is easy to chronicle the innovations in State control over the individual which occurred during the wars, less easy to isolate the ways in which permanent changes in this system can be attributed to the impact of wars on society. Clearly, politicians and civil servants gained experience of more total forms of government and the public learned to accept some forms of State control. The high participation required by all classes in war led to the diminution of some of the major barriers to understanding between individuals and brought concessions by political leaders that led to extension of the Welfare State. Yet over the period that Britain advanced to a so-called Welfare State with strong economic controls and extensive welfare policies, so did Sweden without the 'benefit' of a war!

Another characteristic twentieth-century development in the relationship between the individual and the State has been the emergence of the 'public enterprise'. First, the 'gas and water socialism' of the early years of the century produced a variety of enterprises to provide water, gas, electricity and transport in many areas under direct or indirect local authority control. Then in the inter-war period a number of public corporations were set up to deal with new tasks which were seen as likely to be monopolies or near-monopolies: broadcasting and air transport, for example. To them were added the nationalized industries set up in the forties to take out of private hands coal mining, steel manufacture and the railways, and out of the mixture of private and local government control, gas, electricity and road transport. Some of these nationalized industries were subsequently denationalized, and the history of nationalization since the forties has involved a complicated mixture of this with re-nationalization and the nationalization of individual enterprises. These details need not detain us here.

The State enterprises have not had a fundamental impact on individual/State relations. As far as relations between employers and employees and between producers and customers are concerned, few changes have occurred which enable the individual to distinguish the nationalized industries from private enterprise. There are, for some of the industries, consumer councils – committees of citizens selected by an arbitrary and secret process to represent the public interest – but these bodies have little impact. There have been some experiments in joint-consultation between management and workers, but these differ little from similar practices in private enterprise. Latterly, there have been some moves towards the appointment of worker-directors but these too, perhaps not surprisingly, have had little impact.

In general this tendency for the nationalized enterprises to differ little from private enterprise has been encouraged by a commitment, in respect of which the politicians in both major parties differ but little, to ensure that the nationalized industries are judged in terms of profitability. Government subsidies have been given fitfully and grudgingly and the nationalized industries have been expected to 'stand on their own feet'. While this policy has perhaps made sense as far as steel is concerned, it has led to often senseless competition between gas and electricity, and to a disastrous running down of the railways in face of competition from the roads. The individual citizen has watched this process as confused and helpless as he has watched the activities of the property speculator or the transformation of the shops in his high street.

In the early part of this chapter it was shown that as monarchs became more ambitious they had to raise revenues and thus draw into government those wealthy citizens able to pay taxes. In a similar way the enormous growth of State activity has made taxation the concern of every citizen. Even that minority who do not pay direct taxes are taxed in indirect ways as consumers.

There are two important complications in the relationships between the individual and the State that have come about as a result of the all-embracing impact of taxation. One of these is that the taxing activities of the government have a critical impact upon the economy as a whole. Governments have become committed to manipulating the economy by changing the pattern of State revenue-raising and expenditure. The consequences of this for the individual have already been mentioned.

The other complication is that a government that taxes on such a wide scale inevitably, whether it wants to or not, manipulates the relative distribution of income and wealth between different citizens. This unavoidable consequence has stimulated political interest in using the taxation system to deliberately influence the distribution of resources. Using the taxation system for raising revenue, managing the economy and redistributing resources at the same time, raises problems for politicians which are not always adequately appreciated by the public, who tend only to perceive the last-named role of the budget.

In the next chapter attention will be specifically concentrated on the role of the State as a distributor of financial benefits. Although emphasis will be primarily upon social security benefits, where a quite explicit relation between each individual and the State exists, it is important not to forget that when the government manipulates the taxation system it may also be said to be giving benefits, directly or indirectly. Some of the most difficult problems confronting those who want to influence social policy today – be they politicians, administrators, pressure groups or isolated members of the public – lie in the fact that redistributive policies are affected as much by the system of taxation as by the more benefit-giving systems. Nowhere is that brought out more clearly than by the example of the 'poverty-trap' where individuals find that as their incomes rise they, at one and the same time, lose means-tested benefits and become increasingly subject to income tax. The consequence may be that in practice, although they still have very low incomes, they lose all, or almost all, of their increased earnings.

Conclusions

In this chapter the evolution of State involvement with the citizen has been loosely traced from that period when the 'State' first achieved an effective identity to the present day. The emphasis has been upon the State as the controller of individuals. The pre-modern image of the State was essentially as a controller, and this is still the way many individuals perceive it. An alternative way of perceiving it places more emphasis upon its role as a provider of services. It is necessary to recognize that the State as controller is an ever present reality, even when it is providing services. Where, later in this book, the service role of the State is given particular attention this must not be forgotten. The protection of some individuals depends upon the reallocation (and sometimes redistribution) of resources, and planning depends upon control of many individuals in an endeavour to contribute to the more general good.

Chapter 3
Access to Benefits
in the Welfare State

Introduction
The purpose of the next two chapters is to explore some of the basic issues that arise in relation to contacts between individuals and public departments when those contacts arise from a quest for personal benefits in cash or kind. However, many of the points that will be made will be applicable to almost any kind of situation in which dealings might occur between citizens and public agencies, and there are some additional issues to be examined when what is at stake are personal services or decisions that have a collective impact, or where the government is the initiator of the contact because it is seeking to control the behaviour of individuals.

The main material benefits which the State may provide for individuals fall into a number of categories: social security benefits, housing, the reduction of taxes and charges, and assistance to entrepreneurs.

Social security benefits
Social security provision has its origins in the Poor Law. In the sixteenth century the decline in the role of the Church as a charitable institution, together with the economic changes of the age, led to State concern about vagrancy and unrest amongst the poor. We have seen that the characteristic features of the Poor Law until 1834, and in some respects until well into the twentieth century, were laid down by two Acts of Parliament at the end of the reign of Elizabeth the First, in 1598 and 1601. These placed a responsibility upon local magistrates to levy 'poor rates'

on property so that they could provide institutional care for the 'impotent poor' and 'houses of correction' (or 'workhouses') for the able-bodied poor.

In implementing these Acts during the next two centuries, some parishes, finding difficulties in securing sufficient institutional places, provided 'outdoor relief', in cash and kind, for the poor. At the end of the eighteenth century, when large numbers of people were affected by the economic dislocation of the early 'agricultural' and 'industrial revolutions', this outdoor relief had become much more widespread. In some areas a system of subsidies for agricultural wages was developed, the Speenhamland system. One of the aims of the Poor Law Act of 1834 was to curb the giving of outdoor relief, and particularly the sub-sidization of 'able-bodied' labourers. The parishes were amal-gamated into Poor Law Unions. They were required then to revert to a strict version of the Elizabethan principles. Closer central government supervision was imposed to try to enforce this. Relief was only to be given within the strict regime of the 'workhouse' and it was intended that anyone who secured aid should be worse off than the poorest class of workers. In this way the system was designed to encourage 'self-help' and reduce the numbers of people dependent on the Poor Law.

Like the Elizabethan Poor Law, this system failed to be adopted in its full rigour throughout the country. Moreover, as the nineteenth century wore on, 'involuntary' causes of poverty were increasingly recognized. Medical advances began to lead to a recognition that the care of the sick poor was under-mined by a too vigorous enforcement of Poor Law principles. Hence, some (or some parts) of the workhouse began to evolve into poor law hospitals and, increasingly, outdoor relief was paid to the sick.

At the end of the nineteenth century, dramatic evidence was provided on conditions amongst the poor by the systematic investigations of Booth and Rowntree and by the more journal-istic publications of Mayhew, Mearns and W. T. Stead. Poli-ticians began to recognize a need to set up some more com-prehensive forms of social security alongside the Poor Law. The first such innovation was the Old Age Pension Act of 1908, providing a small non-contributory pension for the over-70s. This was subject to a means test and evidence of good character. The former was much less rigorous than that imposed by the Poor Law and the latter was soon abandoned.

Then in 1911, influenced by earlier German innovations, Lloyd George introduced compulsory insurance schemes to cover sickness and unemployment amongst certain groups of employees. In the inter-war period these schemes were extended.

By the outbreak of the Second World War the old Poor Law powers had been given to the local authorities (in 1929) and a national agency had been set up to operate a means-tested relief scheme for the unemployed unable to obtain any, or sufficient, insurance benefit (the Unemployment Assistance Board). During the war the latter agency became the Assistance Board, taking over the Poor Law's responsibilities for outdoor relief to the elderly but operating a less harsh means test.

.During the war William Beveridge was asked to prepare plans for post-war social security. His report, published in 1942, had an enormous impact. In it he advocated the extension of the insurance principle to provide a near-universal service for the old, the sick, the unemployed, widows and expectant mothers. He advocated that his scheme should be supplemented by universal family allowances, and underpinned by an 'assistance board' providing a 'safety net' for those inadequately covered by the insurance scheme.

In the immediate post-war years the government implemented Beveridge's scheme with the Family Allowance Act in 1945, the National Insurance Act in 1946, and the National Assistance Act in 1948. Yet in practice the National Insurance scheme provided far less than comprehensive coverage. Quite apart from the fact that it did not deal with single-parent families, a group whom Beveridge had left out of his scheme, it also tended to give insufficient provision for those in the scheme who lacked private resources to supplement their benefits. The government had disregarded Beveridge's advice to bring in the pension scheme gradually so that pensions could be based on contributions. It thus committed itself to heavy expenditure out of taxation. This tacit disregard of the insurance principle, together with high inflation, faced future governments with grave problems in sustaining adequate benefit rates. The consequence was that millions of insurance beneficiaries (and particularly the elderly) had to apply for means-tested 'assistance' to supplement their benefits.

There have been a number of modern responses to this situation. Attempts are being made to provide more comprehensive pensions for the old by adding more realistic contributory benefits to the basic scheme. However, today's pensioners benefit but little from any of the elaborations of the scheme which have occurred so far. The sickness and unemployment schemes have, on the other hand, been substantially altered by the introduction in 1966 of 'earnings-related supplements' which raise the incomes of many well above the 'basic' levels during the first six months of a spell of sickness or unemployment.

Finally, it is appropriate to mention, if only to avoid confusion over terminology, that the National Assistance Board was replaced in 1966 by a Supplementary Benefits Commission, whose officials are all within the Department of Health and Social Security instead of being the employees of a separate State agency. Some minor modifications of the means test were made at the same time, but the main aim of the reform was to try to eliminate the stigma of 'Assistance'. This was attempted by a change of name, and by combining the social security agencies to facilitate integrated services (such as the issue of joint weekly order books for 'insurance' and 'supplementary' benefits). However, the many differences between the insurance scheme and the supplementary benefit system have made the integration of staff from these two sides of the social security system difficult. The public find that even where they can go to the same building for both benefits, they have to deal with different people on different floors who often do not act in a particularly co-ordinated way. The position is further complicated by the fact that both the insurance and supplementary benefits schemes for unemployed people are administered by Employment Services Agency officials on behalf of the Department of Health and Social Security.

Housing

Since the nineteenth century, governments have intervened in housing in ways that provide benefits both for owner-occupiers and for tenants of private landlords, and it has created a third housing group, local authority tenants. This third sector's origins lie way back in an Act passed in 1875 which empowered local authorities to replace insanitary dwellings, and in the Housing of the Working Classes Act passed in 1890 to help authorities obtain loans for this purpose. However, very little local authority housing was provided until after the First World War. An Act of Parliament passed in 1919 made subsidies available to local authorities to enable them to provide cheap houses for the working classes. During the inter-war period several housing Acts were passed with developed the subsidization of municipal housing in various ways. In the twenties the emphasis was upon remedying the deficiency in the stock of cheap housing left by the war and exacerbated by rent control. In the thirties attention shifted to slum clearance.

In the Second World War the problems created by the cessation of house building were worsened by bomb damage. After the war, therefore, another great housing effort was required. The 1945-51 Labour Government concentrated this effort upon the council housing sector. In the fifties the Conservatives shifted the balance a little towards the building of houses for owner-occupiers but their awareness of a need for slum clearance, as the problems of gross deficiency lessened a little, led them to continue to encourage local authority efforts with subsidies. In recent years the balance between private and public housing, and the most appropriate approach to subsidizing the latter, have become politically controversial. Only one detail of this controversy concerns us. This is that there has been a shift, encouraged by the Conservatives' Housing Finance Act of 1972, from the subsidization of houses to the subsidization of poor tenants by means of rent rebates.

In the nineteenth century, the only government involvement with the private rented housing sector was public health legislation to prevent the worst slum conditions. Then, as part of the government's effort to control the rise in the cost of living during the First World War, rent control was established. After the war, although the rigid control adopted during the hostilities was terminated, some of the private sector remained under public control. Strict rent control was reimposed in the Second World War and remained until 1957 for unfurnished lettings, while furnished tenancies were brought under a measure of control by Rent Tribunals, with discretionary powers to fix rents and give limited security of tenure.

The 1957 Rent Act took some unfurnished tenancies out of control, and modified the system for others. The Labour Party at this time committed itself to bringing back full rent control. This they did in 1965, but in so doing they moved away from the former rigid system of control, with rent levels determined by the gross values calculated for rating purposes, to a system which creates a large new area of administrative discretion. Rent officers are required to determine appropriate rent levels on the basis of a curious principle which involves estimating what the market rent for a house would be if there were no 'scarcity'. There is a procedure for appeal against these decisions by either tenants or landlords. In 1974, furnished tenancies, where landlords are not resident in the same premises, were brought into this system of control, so that this group of tenants could obtain the security of tenure denied them by the existing Rent Tribunal scheme.

This system of rent control has been mentioned since by controlling rents governments can be said to be providing 'benefits' for tenants at the expense of landlords. However, the Housing Finance Act took the principle of subsidization of private tenants a step further by extending rent rebates and rent allowances, assessed on the basis of a test of means, to tenants in this sector.

It will come as a surprise to many readers that it was suggested at the beginning of this section that governments also provide benefits for owner-occupiers. This is done in two ways at present, and we may well see further forms of subsidy for this group of people in the near future. First, income tax payers receive relief on their payments of mortgage interest. Initially this was not a sizable concession because interest rates were very low until the 1960s. Furthermore it was really a way of reducing, for those who did not fully 'own' their houses, tax that had to be paid on owner-occupied property (Schedule 'A' tax). But this tax was abolished in 1963. Today, therefore, very considerable amounts of tax relief are given on the basis of a concession which has lost its original rationale. The difficulty for any government which sought to abolish this relief would be that without it many house buyers would find it difficult to maintain their mortgage repayments. There is a clear sense in which governments 'give' benefits when they provide relief from taxation or any other charges. House buyers are being protected from the full rigours of the open money market by what are, in effect, subsidized interest rates. It was recognition of this that led in 1968 to the adoption of an 'option mortgage scheme' to enable people whose incomes were so low that they did not benefit from the tax relief to obtain mortgages at directly subsidized rates of interest.

The other form of benefit which owner-occupiers may obtain is also available to tenants. This is the rate rebate, introduced in 1966, to enable poor householders to pay lower rates if they qualify under a means test. This was designed to counterbalance the fact that local authority rates are an often regressive form of taxation in an age in which the relationship between means and housing standard has become a very crude one. Furthermore rates are continually growing in importance as a form of taxation, from the minimal 'poor rates' levied when the Poor Law was the only substantial local 'enterprise' to the high levels associated with the heavy commitments of local authorities today. Again, subsidizing people like this was seen as a new way, as with rent rebates, to concentrate upon the poorest in the community some of the benefits from the high central government grants to the local authorities.

The demand for government subsidies in the housing field continues. Government intervention to influence the price of land, which has taken various forms since 1945 and may well grow in importance, clearly brings benefits for various groups in the housing market. Political commitments are emerging which aim at controlling mortgage interest rates in various ways. The distribution of housing costs in Britain has been so distorted by government intervention that is is very hard even to estimate where the benefits and costs of this intervention really fall. If this section has given the impression that nearly everyone gets benefits, then clearly this is misleading because the costs must be paid somewhere. Yet it is important to recognize that benefits *appear* to be given to all groups. It must not be assumed that the most obvious forms of benefits – subsidies for council houses – are necessarily the only real benefits given.

The actual effects of all this government intervention are so obscure that it is really futile to get into arguments about the ways in which the system deviates from the 'natural' order that would prevail in a market free of interference. It is better to concentrate political discussion upon the way any further change proposed will shift the burden of costs and benefits, and will affect the housing market. What is important is not to assume that any further innovation to provide benefits – say for example a subsidy to prevent a rise in the mortgage interest rate – will carry no costs for any other segment of the population. Very little actual debate about housing is concerned with the over-all redistributive effects of policy changes.

Reduction in taxes and charges

Reductions in taxes and charges range from the very considerable number of income tax allowances to a multiplicity of separate circumstances under which local authorities can remit charges for social and other services. Between these extremes important examples are those that have already been mentioned in connection with housing, together with refund of health service charges, free school meals and legal aid.

There is little point in providing an historical accout of these. While some of them developed from a late-nineteenth-century or early-twentieth-century concern to enable the poor to benefit from newly emerging services, it is only recently that awareness has grown of the complexity of the processes of income redistribution that go on in this way.

It was necessary for taxation to rise to a high level, and to have a universal impact, for it to be recognized that decisions about it have a crucial impact upon the pattern of redistribution of income or wealth. Traditionally, taxation was concerned with the raising of the relatively small amount of money needed for government from a minority of rich people. The debate about Lloyd George's extension of taxation in 1909-11 seems to have been crucial in bringing recognition of the redistributive potential of government budgeting into the centre of the political arena.

Situations in which the government gives benefits and situations in which it refrains from imposing full taxes and charges may be regarded as broadly similar. The argument for doing this was put by Professor Titmuss in an influential essay on 'The Social Division of Welfare', published in his *Essays on the Welfare State*. Titmuss criticized the ways in which government accounting does not identify as 'social service' expenditure allowances and relief from income tax, although they are 'providing similar benefits and expressing a similar purpose'. He argued that both the recognized social security expenditure and the income tax reliefs 'are manifestations of social policies in favour of identified groups in the population and both reflect changes in public opinion in regard to the relationship between the State, the individual and the family' (Titmuss, 1958: 45).

It is argued, against Titmuss's view, that tax reliefs cannot be considered 'benefits', since the State is merely allowing people to keep some of their own income! This view rests upon a perspective on the relationship between State and society in which our income is regarded as something to which we have a natural right and the State is seen as an external and alien agency which limits our freedom. If, however, government is seen as legitimately concerned to regulate the social and economic order then, when it chooses between increasing social security benefits, altering tax allowances, or even intervening more directly to influence incomes, it will be seen as merely selecting alternative modes of redistributing 'benefits' in society. The aim here is not to persuade readers to accept a particular, perhaps ideologically charged, definition of the concept of 'benefit'. Rather it is to stress that governments which wish to redistribute resources, whether in the direction of more or less equality, may well do this in ways which do not involve the alterations of those State payments which we all readily recognize as 'benefits'. Indeed, it must also be pointed out that governments which take actions which reduce or increase the rate of inflation also manipulate, though generally not wilfully, the distribution of 'benefits'. Inflation alters the real value of social security benefits, tax rates, tax concessions and benefits in kind and thus alters the balance of gains and losses which individuals make from these various State attempts to manipulate our resources.

Of course, we have varying attitudes to the different ways in which the State influences our incomes. These attitudes affect the kinds of relationships which we have with public officials. We see ourselves as having, and are seen as having, different 'rights' in respect of the various kinds of possible additions to, or deductions from, our incomes.

Benefits for entrepreneurs

The final category of benefits to individuals to be distinguished is assistance to individuals as entrepreneurs. These also come both in the form of direct subsidies, to farmers for example, and in the form of tax reliefs, for example the wide variety of tax concessions and other arrangements to enable manufacturers in marginal areas or industries to obtain supplies or land cheaply. One of the difficulties in dealing with this category of benefits is that they are largely given to corporate enterprises rather than directly to individuals. Another difficulty is the almost total absence of evidence on the relationship between such recipients and government departments. This is made all the more surprising by the fact that a high proportion of the theorizing and philosophizing about the relationship between the State and the individual has come from the defenders of the rights of entrepreneurs and the opponents of State intervention in the economy and not from people concerned, for example, about the rights of welfare recipients. Equally, simply because the cost of common law remedies against the State tends to limit litigation to entrepreneurs or companies, a high proportion of the case law on the relation between the individual and the State also comes from this source.

Rights to benefits: some general considerations

It is necessary to look at the extent to which the individual benefits with which this chapter is concerned are 'rights' and at the meaning of 'rights' in this context. Essentially, this is a legal issue: has Parliament given *statutory force* to particular rights for individuals who fall into particular categories, or has it given *discretion* to administrative agencies to decide whether or not benefits should be given, without reference to clear rules? But in practice the subject is more complex because the rules/discretion distinction is not so much a dichotomy as a continuum. Moreover, attitudes towards rules have a powerful impact upon the extent of their enforcement.

It is possible to identify a number of points along the rules/discretion continuum. The following are some of the most important of these:

1. Situations in which the establishment of membership of a category entitled to benefit is straightforward. For example, as long as one pays income tax one can claim a basic personal allowance.

2. Situations which are generally straightforward, but where complications may sometimes arise. For example, proof of the existence of a wife is sufficient to obtain an income tax allowance in respect of her, and proof that you have two children who are living with you will secure you a Family Allowance. Yet awkward marginal cases will arise where the statuses of wives or children are in dispute.

3. Cases in which ambiguities over status of the kind described above assume a much greater significance. Subject to complex but relatively unambiguous contribution rules, persons who are sick or unemployed may qualify for National Insurance benefits. Yet officials have responsibilities to examine individuals' claims to be unfit or workless. Unemployment benefit can be disallowed where persons are considered to be not genuinely seeking work, or to have refused suitable employment, or to have become un-

employed in circumstances in which they were 'at fault'. Doctors can refuse to certify sickness and individual claims to be sick can be tested by an examination by official doctors.

4. Discretion plays a much more significant part in curtailing rights when public agencies are given powers to depart from normal practices in exceptional circumstances. The most widely discussed example of this is provided by the regulations relating to supplementary benefits (formerly National Assistance). Under Schedule 2 of the 1966 Ministry of Social Security Act, the following clause qualified a number of specific rules about rights:

> Where there are exceptional circumstances:
> (a) benefit may be awarded at any amount exceeding that (if any) calculated in accordance with the preceding paragraphs;
> (b) a supplementary allowance may be reduced below the amount so calculated or may be withheld; as may be appropriate to take account of these circumstances.

There is little attempt to define 'exceptional circumstances' elsewhere in the Act; this is largely left to the discretion of the Supplementary Benefits Commission and its staff. The implementation of sub-paragraph (b) involves a discretionary judgement that exceptional circumstances justify a departure from the general right to benefit set out in the earlier part of the Act. Moreover even the provision for the giving of additional benefits under the terms of sub-paragraph (a) implies a recognition of differing rights to help. In this case, discretionary judgements have to be made which favour some but not all applicants for benefits.

5. Where Parliament has delegated to local authorities the power to make decisions about claims to benefit even less fettered discretion occurs. Three rather different situations can be found,

> (a) those in which Parliament has laid down a basic framework of rules which it requires local authorities to fill out in operation (for example, rent rebate schemes under the 1972 Housing Finance Act);
> (b) those in which local authorities are able to make their own

rules, though these have no statutory force (points schemes for council house allocation, or rules for dealing with applications for discretionary education grants, for example);
(c) those in which local authorities choose to operate in such a way that their committees or officials have almost total discretionary freedom (many operate their money-giving powers under the 1963 Children and Young Persons Act in this way, and a few authorities still allocate council houses on this basis).

These variations in the forms discretion takes are further complicated by variations (a) in the extent to which attempts are made to develop a rationale for such decisions, (b) in the degree to which individuals perceive what the lawyers call 'procedural due process' to be occurring in the consideration of their claims, and (c) in the levels within hierarchies at which responsibilities for decision making are placed.

Decisions upon entitlement to benefits, then, involve a variety of combinations of rules and discretion. To further understand the complexity of the rules/discretion dichotomy we need to look at another dichotomy given considerable attention by students of the Welfare State, the distinction between universal and selective benefits. This distinction has caused confusion. Universal benefits are those for which people qualify automatically if they fall into certain broad categories; as Townsend has put it: ' "Universality" in social policy is the principle of allocating services or benefits to the population or a group in the population irrespective of income'. Selectivity involves the use of means tests which enormously complicate the decision-making process. The British welfare system involves a group of universal benefits given as 'of right', supplemented by selected services to cover needs unmet by those benefits. The consequence is that selective services tend to be administered separately, with benefits conditional upon 'a body of rather opaque administrative rules and conventions governing behaviour' (Townsend, 1973: 3). The needy person is placed in the role of supplicant facing civil servants with powers to determine whether he conforms to complicated requirements.
Discretionary powers may or may not be significant in

these circumstances, but at the least there is likely to be uncertainty about rights. Application procedures are necessary in which unofficial practices may complicate individual access to benefits. Exceptionally, selective benefit schemes can avoid most of these problems. At least one current form of selective benefit, university maintenance grants, is administered without these problems arising to any great extent. Furthermore, one significant extension of selectivity which has been discussed, 'tax credits', a form of negative income tax, could be organized in such a way that stigma and official discretion were minimized.

Clearly, it is not simply that 'rights' to benefits are undermined by the rules which hedge in and restrict them. Of crucial importance in determining the form 'rights' take and the way they are distributed are social and political attitudes. Richard White, in an interesting essay 'Lawyers and the Enforcement of Rights', has suggested three models of society which can provide reference points for a discussion of this kind. The first model is a 'consensus' one, 'where society is seen as basically unitary' with legislators representing the common interest and the law equal to all, so that there is no fundamental conflict between the individual and the State. White's second model is the direct opposite to this. Society is 'seen as in a state of dichotomous conflict between those with power, wealth and authority and those without it'. The Marxist model of capitalist society is of this kind, but such a conflict model may apply to relations between races even within a society where the consensus model may describe the situation *within* races. White describes his third model as an 'open' model: 'a society which recognizes a continuing multiple conflict of interests and values taking place; within an accepted over-arching structure of a more or less fluid or dynamic nature'. This is a society in which there are many conflicts but some degree of consensus over means for resolving them.

There is, of course, nothing fundamentally original about White's typology. Students of sociological or political theory will readily recognize some of the sources of his models. However his valuable contribution is to suggest ways in which models of society may be related to different conceptions of rights.

White argues that no one of his three models provides an 'accurate description of English society'. There is no need to take issue with him on that since the point here is that each model represents points of view held within our society. The views of our social structure held by administrators and by applicants for benefits influence the way they behave in situations where 'rights' are at stake.

White argues that in his first model 'rights' will be seen as generally unnecessary and in any case potentially contentious and divisive. Those who hold this view of society will expect discretionary powers to work on a basis in which those with administrative responsibilities will be glad to help those in need whilst recipients will be grateful for what they receive. In such a system disagreements will be rare, and will be resolvable by mechanisms which help contending parties to understand each other's point of view.

In the second model White says that rights will be meaningless. Benefits will be grudgingly given as social control devices, concessions from the powerful to stave off revolution. Where those with power hold this view of social order they will be unlikely to reveal it, preferring rather to damp down unrest by propagating a consensual view of society. By contrast, those amongst the powerless who perceive the system in this way will want to win the support of those who have accepted a consensual view for a general assault upon the 'system'. However, the powerless face a critical dilemma. The pursuit of revolution, by uncovering what they see as the hypocrisies of the 'system', may well come into conflict with efforts to obtain benefits for the needy, where what is required is skilful 'working of the system'.

White's third, 'open' view of society is accordingly popular with many welfare rights advocates since it evades this dilemma. He argues that the 'open' society is one in which a 'strong concept of *rights* is essential . . . they are the crucial means by which individuals and groups enter the arena'. However, the case for taking the third model seriously does not rest solely upon the fact that it entails a compromise position between the other two, and therefore provides a model for anti-revolutionary radicals. There are various reasons for regarding the other two models as over-simplifications. British society is neither as harmonious nor as polarized as the other models imply. Therefore, as far as the general pattern of attitudes to, and conflicts over, State benefits is concerned, the open model fits best with reality. But where there are universal benefits claimed widely by all classes (income tax reliefs and pensions for example) the consensus model may be perhaps more applicable. Conversely, where the benefits at stake are typically paid to a minority often regarded as deviants (as is the case with supplementary benefits for unsupported mothers and long-term unemployed men) the polarized conflict model may be of more relevance.

Evidence on under-claiming of benefits

If individuals have rights to benefits, then evidence on under-claiming must give cause for concern. Over the past few years a number of studies have attempted to estimate the extent to which individuals' incomes fall below minimum 'supplementary benefits standards' and have shown that this is very often a result of failure to obtain specific benefits to which they are entitled. People with incomes below supplementary benefit levels will of course be a mixture of people who have failed to qualify for benefits, or whose benefits have been refused or reduced (as a result of discretionary decisions, or official malpractice, or perhaps just because of muddle within a public agency). Thus, in *Men Out of Work*, the present author and his colleagues showed that in three British urban areas, when the most cautious assumptions had been made to avoid exaggeration, about 18 per cent of unemployed married male householders who had been out of work over a month had incomes of more than £1 below supplementary benefit levels. About half of these men were below those levels because of failure to obtain supplementary benefits, but the others had these low incomes *in spite* of the fact that they were getting supplementary benefit.

It is only possible to guess at the factors that might have led to non-claiming amongst the first group, while the explanation for the second group is even more elusive. It is important not to jump to any uni-causal explanation, whether in terms of the impact of disqualifying rules, or malpractice, or ignorance, or bureaucratic inefficiency. The author's experience within a National Assistance office suggests (see Hill, 1969) that each of these factors will have had some impact, but it is difficult to assess their relative importance. Furthermore, these different factors interact. For example, individuals accept discretionary decisions, or even incorrect decisions, as indications of irreversible rules and refrain from applying for help when they are next in similar situations. Sinfield found, when studying unemployed men in North Shields in 1963-64, that a considerable number in his sample did not know what were the correct levels for payments, or about the possibility of special grants or about their appeal rights. Some of the unemployed men '. . . thought they knew and were spreading wildly inaccurate rumours; a few boasted of their knowledge while not realizing that their grants were being paid at a reduced level' (Sinfield, 1970: 232).

Important evidence on the extent of underclaiming has been provided by studies of poverty amongst families whose breadwinner is in full-time work. The demonstration by Abel-Smith and Townsend in *The Poor and the Poorest* that in 1965 about a quarter of the two million people living below the basic national assistance level were in households where the key problem was not inadequate or unclaimed benefits but low earnings, helped to lead to the founding of the Child Poverty Action Group, and to the beginning of a campaign to obtain substantial increases in Family Allowances. The main issue here was not under-claiming of benefit, since there were no benefits available to solve their problems. Nevertheless very many people within this group would have been better off if they had claimed everything to which they were entitled. The 'universal' benefit, Family Allowance, is the only one that is taken up by almost all the poor. By contrast, many of the wide range of selective benefits available are seriously underclaimed.

In 1967 the Government's survey of the *Circumstances of Families* revealed some relevant evidence of underclaiming by families with a father in full-time work. Here, it was estimated

that while 60 per cent of children entitled to free school meals
had them, only 34 per cent of the eligible children whose
fathers were in full-time work did so. This report also stated that
'very few families with fathers in full-time work were receiving
free welfare milk'. Similarly there seems little doubt that few
low-wage earners claim rate rebates, and some of the other
allowances paid by the education authorities to the parents
of school children have in general a very low 'take up'.

In an attempt to do something about the problem of families
supported by wage earners but nevertheless below supplementary
benefits standards the Government introduced a new means-
tested benefit in 1971, Family Income Supplement (FIS). The
'take up' of this benefit has remained persistently low. According to answers to a Parliamentary question, quoted in Ruth
Lister's useful pamphlet *Take Up of Means-Tested Benefits*, the
official view is that only half of the families entitled to FIS
actually claim it.

A number of factors have been identified as having an
impact upon the use wage earners make of selective benefits.
The general problem of ignorance is compounded by the fact
that each of the special forms of benefit discussed above has its
own distinct means test. To be able to work out whether or not
it is worth his while to apply for aid, the wage earner has to be
able to relate the facts about his own income and family
circumstances to a variety of schemes operated by a variety of
authorities. He does not have the advantage possessed by the
supplementary benefits recipient of finding that his SB entitlement provides a 'passport' to other selective benefits, and that
SB officers may explain to him some of the other benefits he may
be able to secure.

Furthermore, many low wage earners do not have steady
weekly incomes at specific levels which can be readily related to
means tests, their earnings fluctuating quite considerably. One
special problem that has been observed in relation to changing
earnings is that the various thresholds applying to selective
benefits can produce a 'surtax' effect for low wage earners whose
incomes rise. Peter Townsend gives the following example:

Late in 1972 a man earning £20 per week with a wife and two children, and therefore entitled to an extra 90p as a family allowance, was subject to the following deductions if he earned an additional £1 :

Loss of Family Income Supplement	50p
Loss of free school meal for one child	60p
Income Tax	10p
Loss of Rate Rebate	14p
Loss of Rent Rebate	8p
Increased National Insurance Contribution	4p
Total	146p

(*Townsend, 1973: 13*)

The widespread ignorance of benefits available ensures that a situation like this rarely occurs in practice. But this makes it less surprising that people are unprepared to try to seek all the benefits to which they are entitled. They may well realize that lengthy form filling and enquiries into their means often yield but little gain, and the fluctuations in income make them vulnerable to losses of benefits, or to prosecution and demands for repayment if they forget to keep the authorities informed of changes.

Another group amongst the poor who face considerable difficulties in ensuring that they secure all the help to which they are entitled are unsupported mothers. For this group Marsden has quoted, in his book *Mothers Alone*, several sources of under-claiming. Again lack of knowledge of available help is of considerable significance, a problem exacerbated for this group by previous dependence upon husbands who knew how to cope with such issues or by a lack, immediately after being abandoned, of anyone to turn to for advice. Many were, moreover, very reluctant to seek help. (This raises the problem of 'stigma' which will be discussed later in the chapter.)

Underclaiming of benefits by pensioners is a subject that has been given wider attention in recent years than the examples considered so far. Politicians and the public are more willing to treat this as a matter of key social concern and more effective steps have been taken to overcome it. Perhaps the most important evidence of underclaiming of national assistance by old people was provided in Cole and Utting's *The Economic Circum-stances of Old People*, published in 1962. As a check on this evidence the government carried out their own survey. This study, *Financial and other circumstances of Retirement Pen-sioners*, published in 1966, showed that over 850,000 were failing to obtain national assistance to which they were entitled. It was with a view to correcting this situation that the govern-ment replaced national assistance by supplementary pensions, giving pensioners' rights, to a prescribed minimum, statutory force. At the same time the Ministry of Social Security set out to find the 'missing' pensioners, with an advertising campaign and instructions to staff to try to improve the 'take up' rate. To try to deal with reluctance to acknowledge dependence upon a means-tested benefit national insurance and supplementary pensions were paid on a single book order, thus eliminating the recognizable book. Yet, Atkinson, in *Poverty in Britain and the Reform of Social Security*, estimated that despite all this the increase in the number of pensioners receiving supplemen-tary pensions between 1965 and 1968 was very largely attribut-able to the changes that were made by the 1966 Act and subse-quent regulations in the basic rates of benefits and the rules about the calculation of resources. He suggested that the increase in recipients 'not explained by the higher assistance scale amounts only to some 100,000-200,000'.

Two concepts which may explain underclaiming of benefits, ignorance and stigma, have been widely discussed. These will now be examined to reveal their implications, and to throw light upon the efforts that have been, or might be made to over-come them.

Ignorance of benefits

Radical critics of the social security system argue that the obscurity of some of the benefit provisions and the absence of official publicity about rights can be directly explained by a desire to reduce demand for benefits. It is, not surprisingly, extremely difficult to prove that inhibition of demand is deliberate. However, this proposition may be put another way as a much less rapidly convertible statement about the function of ignorance. If individuals are not made fully aware of benefits available the practical outcome, whatever the intention of officials, will be the denial of rights. Do not governments, therefore, have an obligation to ensure that persons entitled to public benefits or services know about them?

There are marked variations in the ways in which public services are publicized. It is difficult to say what represents a reasonable minimum of publicity for any particular service. It would be naive to fail to recognize that there are cost constraints which prevent central or local government making absolutely sure that no one remains in ignorance of benefits available.

Nevertheless there has been no lack of evidence in recent years of absence of adequate information about benefits. The most extreme cases of this involve an almost total failure to provide information even on request. It is hard to see how this sort of behaviour can be explained except in terms of a wilful desire to restrict demand. It seems to have come particularly from those bodies which are most aware of a need to ration scarce resources, the local authorities. Thus Rosalind Brooke has written about local authority administration of benefit schemes:

> Some will not publish information about scale rates for welfare benefits, for example one county borough in the Midlands does not divulge information about its educational welfare benefits. Others will not make available leaflets and forms to agencies endeavouring to publicize benefits.
>
> *(Brooke, 1972: 252)*

There are many leaflets available about the various benefit schemes run by the government. Yet the difficulties for potential benefit claimants in obtaining useful explanatory leaflets are considerable. Post offices are the main sources of such leaflets. The reader who wishes to test the allegations made here should try going into one or two post offices to find, for example, a leaflet about supplementary benefits and a leaflet about prescription charge refunds. If that post office is a small sub-post office, few leaflets will be clearly or tidily displayed. Enquiries to counter staff may well be no help in such a situation. Indeed, the author's attempt to get a basic information leaflet about supplementary benefits scale rates from a local sub-post office caused considerable delays for other customers while the clerk riffled through a pile of papers, loudly protesting that he was sent too many different kinds of leaflets. A really needy person might well have left the office in embarrassment. Surveys of post offices have revealed considerable numbers which were simply out of stocks of relevant forms.

Once he has obtained a form the individual may find difficulties in working out whether or not it is worth his while to make a claim for help. As an example of this problem David Bull has quoted a leaflet about entitlement to free welfare foods:

> . . . so designed that the supplementary benefit scale rates catch the eye, and any low-paid worker who wonders whether he can earn more and still qualify must read the small print carefully. Even if he does this, he will not discover that 'income' excludes tax, insurance and other deductions, as well as fares to work; that the first £2 of his income is disregarded; or that HP commitments are deductable expenses.
>
> *(Bull, 1969: 12)*

Of course, problems of this kind arise as much out of the complexity of the scheme as out of bad design of forms. Part of the general case against selective benefits is that in order for them to be at all sophisticated there must be complex rules about entitlement. These maximize the possibility that persons who are qualified to obtain benefits will remain in ignorance of that fact. Such is the complexity of the supplementary benefits rules that an attempt to explain them in a handbook has produced a lengthy document which, even if its circulation were not to some degree limited by price, is unlikely to be used by the poor themselves, but only by their advisers. Yet the handbook is only a very abbreviated version of the internal rule books, Codes, used by Supplementary Benefits Commission officials to help them with their decision making.

Hence officials who are eager to find ways of publicizing benefits are faced by a dilemma. If they try to represent accurately the numbers of forms of benefit, and to do justice to the complexity of the rules relating to them, they must expect to overload small post offices, confuse potential clients, and deter applicants simply by the complexity of the information they impart. If on the other hand they design simple forms, and use advertising media such as television where a straightforward message is essential, they will be condemned for arousing unrealistic expectations.

During 1971 the government launched an advertising campaign to try to increase awareness of benefits. This was an advance on some of the more half-hearted efforts made in the past. Yet still the 'take up' of 'selective' benefits, like Family Income Supplement and refund of prescription charges, fell below the government's own targets. This failure can be contrasted with official success in securing 'take up' of 'universal' benefits. For example, when the government introduced pensions for those persons over 80 who were not already in receipt of one, it estimated that 150,000 persons would qualify but found that within a few months of the passing of the Act 156,000 awards had been made. Part of the explanation for this differing degree of success must be in terms of the variable impact of stigma. Nevertheless an announcement that anyone over 80 can obtain a pension, if he or she does not have one already, is so much less ambiguous than the complex statements necessary for means-tested schemes.

A more efficient way of finding out about entitlement to a particular benefit than trying to decipher an official leaflet, is to go to the authority concerned and seek advice or make an application. Whether or not individuals take that course of action must depend enormously upon the treatment they expect to receive if they do so. However, whether or not the agency is itself able to play a role in dispelling ignorance about its services will be influenced by its physical accessibility and by its officials' personal approachability. Hence the tendency in Britain today for large agencies to be set up to maximize 'efficiency' may be a cause of some concern wherever economies of scale require offices to cover large, widely spread, populations. Potential applicants for local authority benefits may be deterred by the fact that the new large authorities often have very distant headquarters offices. If these authorities do not develop local contact points, people without telephones and unaccustomed to letter writing will find it hard to secure information about services. A similar problem is arising from the replacement of small supplementary benefits offices by fewer large, integrated, social security offices. Public offices are also tending to restrict the hours they are open to the public, and in particular to eliminate opening on Saturday mornings. Such trends need to be counterbalanced by a great deal of advertising and public relations work, and above all by efforts to make agencies more approachable, if they are not to reduce access to benefits by the least well-informed and most readily deterred member of the public.

One characteristic of the universal/selective distinction in British social policy is that the greater an individual's deprivation the more likely it is that he will have to apply for selective benefits. This follows from the way in which the system provides low basic rates of universal benefits. These have to be supplemented by selective benefits if social security dependence is prolonged, or private resources are absent. The consequence of this is that people who have most to do with the complex selective services are those who are likely to be least well equipped to deal with them. Sjoberg has expressed the key argument on this point in his essay 'Bureaucracy and the Lower Class':

> . . . the lower-class person simply lacks knowledge of the rules of the game. Middle-class persons generally learn how to manipulate bureaucratic rules to their advantage and even to acquire special 'favours' by working through the 'private' or 'backstage' (as opposed to the 'public') sector of the bureaucratic organization. Middle-class parents teach by example as they intervene with various officials . . . the lower-class person stands in awe of bureaucratic regulations and frequently is unaware that he has a legal and moral claim to certain rights and privileges.
>
> *(Sjoberg et al., 1966: 332)*

The point made here can be amplified in two ways. Sjoberg runs together two concepts, 'inhibition' and 'ignorance'. The lower classes are less likely to know what they can obtain, and may be inhibited by awe of bureaucratic systems from taking steps to find out. Second, while Sjoberg adopts a two-class dichotomy between middle and lower class, it is important to recognize that the concept of a social continuum is perhaps more applicable. At one end of that continuum are upper-class persons who are able to pay advisers – such as accountants and lawyers – to secure their 'rights' in income tax relief, the reduction of rates, or home improvement grants. At the other end of the continuum are persons whose deprivation is compounded by illiteracy, who face the gravest difficulties in securing even the most basic benefits. At one extreme is found lack of needs, maximum knowledge stemming from education and socialization, and ease of access to advisers. At the other extreme chronic needs are compounded by both a lack of knowledge and an absence of advisers.

Today Claimants' Unions attempt to propagate knowledge of the system amongst the poor, and a variety of welfare rights advisers offer their services. Yet, it seems improbable that these weak groups (see discussion on pp. 175-6) will develop to the point where they can make generally available a knowledge-base such as is accessible to the well-to-do, when they tangle with the bureaucratic State. Such a change could only accompany the elimination of the poor; when they can manipulate the system as well as the rich they will be poor no more.

Ignorance may protect a service with scarce resources from heavy demand, thus providing what may be described as a crude form of rationing. For example, many local authorities will provide houses for some people in extreme need who do not qualify for council houses under their routinized 'points schemes'. In allocating these houses they may take note of requests from health authorities, or social service departments, or even from councillors, but they are most unlikely to give any publicity to these special routes to housing aid. Much the same applies to the allocation of temporary accommodation, despite, as Shelter's *Grief Report* pointed out, local authorities' apparent statutory obligations. *The Grief Report* suggested that the responsible government department and the local authorities had converted a statutory responsibility into a discretionary one, making the actual situation for the homeless extremely uncertain. Homeless persons cannot have any idea under what circumstances they will get help from a local authority, and any authority which was bold enough to declare its admissions policy might run the risk of being overwhelmed by homeless people moving from its less forthcoming neighbours.

Stigma

Ignorance and stigma powerfully reinforce each other as sources of underclaiming of benefits. Individuals who feel that they are likely to be stigmatized for claiming certain benefits, or even for simply revealing their needs, are likely to fail to take steps to overcome their ignorance of their rights. Equally, when governments do not make clear the facts about rights to benefits, individuals may conclude that it is in some sense discreditable to claim such benefits. They will be particularly likely to do this when those rights are new, deriving from measures to benefit people who were not previously considered to be deserving of public aid.

The general observation has been made that the most deprived tend to be the most ignorant of their rights. However, deprivation in itself tends to lower individuals' capacities to seek out their rights. In societies where the poor have to subsist on very low resources, with a poor diet and a total absence of anything to lift the individual above survival level, the association between deprivation and apathy can be largely explained in biological terms. In countries like Britain, where official subsistence levels are comparatively high, other factors need to be considered in the explanation of the apathy of the deprived. In particular, attention needs to be given to the stigma, the impact of a dependent condition upon an individual's sense of his own worth.

Several writers have referred to the way in which unemployed men become apathetic if worklessness is prolonged (Bakke;

Johada *et al.;* Sinfield). While this may be partly explained in terms of the impact of a lack of purposeful activity, many men make it clear that they see unemployment as undermining their sense of their own worth and that they feel themselves to be stigmatized by people around them. There are sentiments, widespread in a society like ours, which reinforce the work ethic, encouraging children from an early age to earn benefits and privileges, and stimulating many adults to be prepared to take any kind of work largely regardless of rewards. Accordingly, those who do not go to work are likely to feel that they are in some sense inadequate citizens. Even if they consider that there are good reasons why they are workless, they may feel that people who do not know their circumstances are judging them, and talking about them behind their backs.

Similarly, Marsden reports that unsupported mothers feel that they are failures who have been unable to live up to the expectations of society because they have not maintained an intact marriage or prevented an unwanted pregnancy. He says 'our society defends the institution of marriage by stigmatizing them'. Some experience ostracism from former friends or neighbours. People see them as having failed or misbehaved. We more readily identify the female members of a broken relationship, left with children to bring up, than their former male partners.

People like unemployed men or unsupported mothers are forced to seek State aid. They must acknowledge their dependent and vulnerable condition, and supply personal information to establish their need for help. Three-quarters of the mothers interviewed by Marsden said they felt embarrassed when they applied for Assistance. Much of their discomfort in social relationships, Marsden argued, stemmed from sensitivity about their dependence upon Assistance. He went on:

. . . it would appear that mothers' hardships and feelings about the inferior status accorded to fatherless families were deepened by the stress placed by neighbours and friends upon their dependence. Mothers were liable to be told, 'It's us that's keeping such as you'.

(Marsden, 1973: 239)

Underclaiming of benefits may be attributable, Marsden suggests, to stigma arising out of public attitudes to (a) being deviant in the sense of being out of work or a deserted wife or an unmarried mother, and (b) being dependent upon public aid whilst in that condition. The state of being dependent may be stigmatizing, or believed to be stigmatizing by the individual concerned, even when the reason for that dependence is not in itself seen as a source of stigma.

Some discussions of the underclaiming of social security benefits lay emphasis upon the legacy of the Poor Law, stressing that people, particularly old people, keep alive outdated and no longer relevant attitudes to State assistance. The widespread incidence of selectivity, together with the continuing suspicion of some dependent groups by politicians, officials and the public alike, do however preserve the 'Poor Law legacy' regardless of changes of name and, the elimination of the worst abuses of that system. Accordingly, too much stress should not be laid upon long memories and the *legacy* of the past. The Poor Law legacy theory has been particularly adduced to explain the continuing tendency of old people to see the receipt of supplementary benefits as stigmatizing. But there is another explanation which must also be considered; this is that old people are reminded both of the Poor Law and their dependent status when they observe that the agency that pays their supplementary pensions also has to deal with widely stigmatized deviant groups within our society. Hence the problem is what Olive Stevenson has called 'stigma by association'. This she explains particularly by reference to the callers at local SB offices, amongst whom there are inevitably some

> . . . whose appearance and behaviour mark them out as socially
> unacceptable to most people in society. In local offices one must
> expect to see itinerants, alcoholics, drug addicts, prostitutes and so
> on. It would be naïve to suppose that improved office conditions
> could remove the sense of stigma-by-association that many people
> feel . . .
>
> *(Stevenson, 1973: 21)*

Certainly many claimants for benefits are disturbed by some of the people with whom they rub shoulders when they visit a social security office. Yet it is also the case that the physical conditions of the offices leave a great deal to be desired. Low standards in such places are a recognition that some of the people who use them are aggressive and dirty. The low priority given to the improvement of social security offices, on both sides of the counter it must be added, is a reflection of social attitudes to their clientele. The Employment Service has been concerned in recent years to get 'away from the dole queue images'. It has manifested this concern as much in a commitment to serving better qualified manpower in new premises away from the ordinary run of unemployed people, as in a drive to eliminate the old style employment exchanges.

It is suggested, then, that the sense of stigma aroused by use of a State benefit agency is the result of a complex of factors. Conditions in these public offices, the company found there, and even the way people behave while they are there, are all both reflections of, and factors which contribute to, societal attitudes to dependent groups. No change in the treatment of applicants for benefits would, of itself, solve the problem of stigma-by-association. Yet it arises from labelling processes which mark out and stigmatize deviants in our society, and it must be recognized that public agencies play important roles in those processes. Crucial here is the character of the benefit provided. If it involves a payment, secured after a detailed and sometimes disturbing personal interview and conditional upon the fulfilment of emphasized 'conditions', as is the case with supplementary benefits, this will tend to be stigmatizing. Similarly if it is quite clearly a provision well below normal standards, as is the case with much of the squalid accommodation provided for homeless families, then recipients will be clearly reminded of their dependent status.

Stigmatization as an inherent aspect of the 'benefit' has a quite fundamental deterrent impact upon the individual pursuit of help. The many 'strings' attached to benefits are seen as designed to prevent abuse. The Fisher Committee on the 'Abuse of

Social Security Benefits' rightly recognized a conflict between 'measures taken to prevent and detect abuse' and 'prompt and sympathetic dealing with claims'. What they failed to acknowledge was that when measures to prevent abuse are built in as clear conditions of service they must tend to stigmatize the recipients of that service. A contrast can be seen here between the procedure adopted by the income tax authorities who accept most claims without proof and confine the detection of abuse to checks on a minority, and that adopted by the supplementary benefits authorities who expect all applicants to document their own claims fully and employ visiting staff to check those claims.

The sources of stigma identified here will be reinforced if the officials who deal with claimants for help fail to treat them with normal courtesy or in any sense go out of their way to remind them of their dependent situation. Where there are widespread social prejudices against certain kinds of applicants for aid it will not be surprising if some officials share those prejudices, and are not particularly careful to conceal their own attitudes. Some of the factors which influence official behaviour will be examined in the next chapter.

Conclusions

Concern in this chapter has been to give an account of some of the general issues affecting the access of individuals to benefits provided by the State, either directly or through local authorities. At many points in the discussion reference has been made to the way the factors examined inter-relate. The views of the government, its officials and members of the general public on the extent to which specific welfare 'rights' exist will have a critical impact upon the 'take up' of benefits. Many of the problems of access to benefit stem from a lack of social and political consensus about rights to State aid for deprived or dependent groups in the population.

Specific measures to make benefits more readily accessible need to be seen in this general context. Of course, a great deal can be done to publicize benefits in such a way that the public are more aware of what is available and what they may be entitled to receive. However, the complexity of many of the benefit schemes, itself a product of the political compromises that were required to bring them into being, weakens the impact of simple and direct advertisements. Measures designed to increase awareness of benefits and combat stigma need to be accompanied by efforts to ensure that staff who can explore the details of schemes with the public are readily available.

Such staff need to be approachable and ready to adopt a positive stance of helping people to secure their rights. They may be expected to treat potential customers with tact and courtesy, to an extent which is often not typical of junior employees in other organizations. It may be questioned whether it is reasonable to expect officials, who as receptionists and other 'front-line' counter staff have a largely routine function to perform, to treat members of the public with the consideration that is often only required of highly motivated professionals. This point raises problems about the powers and motivation of employees of bureaucratic organizations which are the concern of the next chapter.

Chapter 4
Bureaucracy and the Public

The complex range of benefits and services provided by the modern State depend crucially upon very complex forms of organization. While we may yearn for a more simple social order, we are forced to agree with Perrow's double-edged comment that: 'Without this form of social technology, the industrialized countries of the West could not have reached the heights of extravagance, wealth and pollution that they currently enjoy' (Perrow, 1972: 5).

The critical contemporary problem is to harness the strengths of formal organization to enable large-scale complex co-ordinated activity whilst mitigating its worst effects. Consideration of this problem has taken the form, in sociology and political science, of a debate about the characteristics of bureacracy. The term bureaucracy has been used as almost synonymous with 'complex organization', to describe a formal organization with such characteristics as:

Division of labour
Organization in a hierarchy of some form
Impersonal rules governing activities
Written records to ensure continuity and consistency
Separation of formal organizational rules from other aspects of employees' personal lives
Prescribed conditions of service for employees

The elaboration of a concept of bureaucracy along these lines comes from a classic discussion of the characteristics of modern society by Max Weber. Yet the term bureaucracy has come to be widely used in a pejorative sense, to define all that is disliked about the way complex organizations relate to individuals. How do we relate these two very different concepts of bureaucracy? Are they really quite divergent usages of the word? Or do they involve an assertion that bureacracy is a necessary evil in the modern world?

In this discussion neither of these positions will be taken. It will be shown that the main characteristics of complex administrative organizations involve both advantages and disadvantages for members of the public. Some of the main criticisms of bureaucracy will be examined, and it will be shown that the features they condemn can be seen from other perspectives as points in favour of this form of organization.

A most popular indictment of bureaucracy is that it is insensitive to individual needs. Politicians, journalists and humourists regularly point out examples of situations in which individuals are refused help by an organization on the grounds that their particular circumstances do not fall within the categories prescribed by the rules which govern its services. However, critics of such decisions rarely go on to make clear whether they would argue that the rules in question should be amended, or whether exceptions should be made to the rules. Naturally, in the process of raising special cases it is much easier to deride existing rules than to formulate alternative ones. The public can thus readily be deluded into believing that complex political problems have easy solutions if only 'common sense' instead of 'bureaucratic pig-headedness' prevails.

Opposition to bureaucratic rules is often expressed in a way which implies a need for a widening of discretion, a greater responsiveness to special cases. While it is the case that systems of rules cannot entirely eliminate discretion, (see the discussion on pages 93 to 100, it is important to recognize that actually widening the discretionary powers of public servants may have consequences that may be judged social evils, comparable to or worse than the evils of bureaucratic rigidity that they are supposed to eliminate. Rules about civil service recruitment have been developed to eliminate patronage, nepotism and corruption. The rights discussed in the last chapter depend upon effective rules. Rules about entitlement to social benefits came into being to eliminate relief systems under which help for the poor was administered at best with paternalism, at worst with the degradation and stigmatization of needy citizens. Various procedural rules within organizations are designed to secure equality of service to all citizens without regard to race, creed or sex. Individuals should thereby receive adequate treatment whether or not they are personally congenial to the clerks who administer the services. Hierarchical control within organizations is intended to enforce such rules.

Where official behaviour is governed by rules it becomes predictable to the individual member of the public. He is likely to know in advance whether he will be qualified for a particular service. If he has wrongly expected something, officials will be able to explain to him how he has been misinformed about, or misunderstood, the rules relating to his case. Bureaucratic organizations are often criticized as slow to take decisions. The problem is that much of this slowness stems from rule following, from ensuring that all relevant rules and precedents are considered.

Studies by Blau and by Francis and Stone show how service to clients may be facilitated by the evasion or modification of rules. With examples like these it is only too easy to fall into the trap of seeing rules in general as obstructing efficient service to the public. In fact before such a mistake is made the perhaps rather obvious points must be made that there are both satisfactory and unsatisfactory rules, and that some rules *are* unnecessary. It must also be recognized that rules may exist both to facilitate and to inhibit service to the public. Furthermore, rules that may have been promulgated to promote a service may sometimes be capable of manipulation by officials in order to undermine it. A sporting example makes this point very clearly: where in association or rugby football a referee applies the rules about foul play very rigidly he may undermine the very purpose of those rules, which is to ensure that the game flows smoothly and fairly. Actually he will have failed to apply another rule, the 'advantage rule', which is in fact an injunction to him to use his discretion in certain circumstances. When bureaucracy is attacked for 'red-tape', therefore, it is important to distinguish between this as an attack on the existence of rules and as an attack on specific kinds of, or uses of, rules.

It has been argued that the salience of rule following within bureaucracies means that operative roles within such organizations are occupied by people (whether as a result of differential recruitment or socialization within the roles is immaterial) who respond in rigid ways to special public needs or novel situations. This hypothesis was advanced by R. K. Merton in an influential essay, 'Bureaucratic Structure and Personality'. It has, however, been widely contested. It has been argued that Merton exaggerated the rigidity of bureaucratic institutions, that strong rule-structures provide individuals with security within which they can give rein to their own personality characteristics, and that dependence on a framework of rules reduces the tension in authority relationships. The last point is of some importance here, for it may well be the case that the relationship between a junior government official and a member of the public can take a much more relaxed and egalitarian form when the issue is 'let us examine where you stand in relation to the rules' than when it is 'let me see what I can do for you'.

Even if there is some evidence for the 'bureaucratic personality' hypothesis, there is nevertheless a need to consider the following question. Is it better to be confronted by polite and sympathetic officials with a great deal of power over one, or by rude and rigid ones who have no alternative but to provide a statutorily prescribed service if you qualify for it? The answer to this question is likely to be, it depends upon the service. In particular it may depend upon the extent to which a discretionary element is inescapable within it. What we require of post office counter clerks differs from what we need from our doctors. It therefore follows that it would be unwise to take an absolute stand for or against bureaucracy on the basis of Merton's theory.

Similar considerations apply to a further point often linked with the bureaucratic personality theory. This is that bureaucracies do not easily adapt to new needs or new situations. Of course, this implication follows from Merton's emphasis upon the rigid personalities of bureaucrats, but since there are grounds for scepticism about Merton's theory perhaps a more sound hypothesis about bureaucratic rigidity focuses upon structural rather than individual inflexibility. Some research by Burns and

Stalker into problems of implementing change in industrial organizations, reported in their book *The Management of Innovation*, has led to widespread acceptance of their distinction between 'mechanistic' and 'organismic' management systems. Burns and Stalker showed that mechanistic systems, which can be loosely equated with the bureaucratic model outlined by Weber, respond weakly when faced by a need to change whilst organismic systems – in which roles, authority, and communications are but loosely structured – are much more responsive.

Sociologists have tended to seize on this theory as offering another argument for the case against bureaucracy. Yet there is a need for caution in applying this too enthusiastically to public administration. Two characteristics which political scientists have often regarded as important in civil services in modern democratic states have been control from the top (from politicians), and the capacity of officials to modify extreme initiatives from that source. These two characteristics, though obviously in tension with each other, are not necessarily incompatible. They are *both* moreover key characteristics of bureaucracy. Anyone who attempts to explore the great volume of twentieth-century writing on this subject will be bewildered by the fact that while some theorists stress the extent to which bureaucracy provides an instrument in the hands of those at the top (for example Neumann, Mills and Mosca), others emphasize the inherently conservative impact of the dispersion of power within it (for example Selznick, Michels and Blau).

The Burns and Stalker theory rather confuses the issue on this point. The 'organismic' structure shows a strong capacity to handle innovation generated within the organization, yet it is clearly not particularly susceptible to hierarchical control. Such a structure may be appropriate where change may be expected to come about because of the sensitivity of middle and lower ranking officials to changing needs, and where it is regarded as desirable that the power of expertise should transform directives from the top. In a later chapter examples of professional services will be discussed where this may well be the case. On the other hand, a mechanistic structure may facilitate processes of change imposed from the top, where hierarchical discipline will ensure compliance even when junior officials do not particularly like the new policies.

Furthermore, where the organization is required to provide a stable but flexible service a greater degree of predictability of hierarchical response may facilitate this. An absence of rules, and therefore of certainty about hierarchical requirement, creates a situation in which individual officials do nothing or refer more than is necessary to their superiors for decision.

It is only too easy to provide examples of the weaknesses of the bureaucratic form of administration; in the remainder of this chapter some will inevitably be cited. This introduction has been concerned to point out that simplistic critiques of bureaucratic government may well disregard the many strengths of this sort of administration. A great deal of criticism of bureaucratic rules should be recognized as really an attack upon bad rules, and not upon the notion that administrative behaviour should be markedly constrained by rules. However, it is important to recognize that situations of over-regulation can arise in which the intentions of rule-makers are undermined by their excessive zeal in promulgating rules. Furthermore, rules are used as weapons in the power struggles surrounding organizations. In this sense individuals often try to manipulate rules to their own advantage.

All work roles can be seen as involving a combination of rules and discretion. Therefore the problem for those responsible for creating or modifying bureaucratic institutions is to determine to what extent officials, at any level, should have their activities constrained by rules and to what extent they should be left with discretionary freedom. The complexity of the activities involved in many cases makes generalization difficult. A variety of different constraints may be applied. In some cases it may be useful to distinguish between substantive rules, determining what may or may not be done, with procedural rules, specifying the ways in which officials should operate. It is the latter rules which particularly attract criticism, yet the regulation of procedures helps to control action when there is difficulty in specifying substantive controls.

To some extent the problem of achieving a balance between

rules and discretion can be solved by examining results. The 'right' structure must depend upon the ends desired. A value choice may be required, as to whether the 'evils' stemming from bureaucratization are greater than the 'evils' which are consequences of insufficiently fettered discretion. In private industry the choice between mechanistic and organismic forms can be seen as depending upon the nature of the task to be performed, judging the correctness of that choice ultimately in terms of its contribution to profitability. But in public administration such a choice cannot be made so easily. One pattern of organization may benefit some parties but not others, and the number of parties is large indeed. Even to list the broad categories here – employees, clients, taxpayers – is insufficient, since within these groups some individuals will gain from particular forms of organization whilst others will lose. The extent to which making administration more flexible, speeding it up, allowing it to give more attention to special cases, or enabling it to change more easily, will benefit or penalize specific individuals will depend upon where they stand in relation to the services involved.

Such is the complexity of the issues at stake that it is not surprising that public opinion, at least as reflected in the Press, appears to oscillate erratically in relation to the choice between bureaucratization or de-bureaucratization. When there appears to be negligence by a hospital or a social services department, when a motor insurance company or a travel agent goes bankrupt or when racketeering landlords or shopkeepers are exposed, the demand is for more controls, more supervision or more rules. Yet when an apparently deserving case for a pension or disablement allowance fails to come within the rules, when a company is prosecuted for what seems to be a technical breach of the law, or when delays occur in processing claims for benefits or subsidies, an equally vociferous cry is heard for more flexibility, fewer rules or less 'red-tape'.

The point of contact

An application to a public agency for any form of benefit has to be received by someone who checks that all relevant information is available and despatches it on the appropriate route through the administrative system. Many applications come in by post, but some individuals, and this particularly applies to the less literate, prefer to present themselves in person. However, to meet the requirements of a complex bureaucratic apparatus, and indeed to facilitate its control, personal applications normally have to be translated into documents that can be passed through the system. Sometimes personal applications are required; where this is the case the interaction between applicant and official may assume a greater importance for the eventual decision, but it will still normally involve the translation of the interaction into a written application accompanied, perhaps, by official observations.

Most agencies get enquiries from members of the public which should have been directed to other organizations, enquiries that can be dealt with by routine procedures and enquiries that they cannot (or will not) deal with immediately. There is a task to be performed at the boundaries of an organization which March and Simon call 'uncertainty absorption'. When there is an input of information from outside there is a need for someone to fit what is received to the categories and concepts with which the organization customarily operates.. As Perrow suggests:

> . . . a body of information must be edited and summarized in order to make it fit into the conceptual scheme – to make it understandable. The inferences from the material rather than the material itself are transmitted. The recipient can disbelieve the 'facts' that are transmitted to him, but he can rarely check their accuracy unless he himself undertakes the summarization and assessment.
>
> *(Perrow, 1972: 152)*

Consequently those who receive information may have considerable influence upon the way the organization operates. Yet, since these tasks apparently involve not so much the taking of decisions as the sorting of information for the formal decision-makers they are often performed by comparatively low-level officials.

The apparently simple role of receiving communications may

be developed in various ways. The official may do this on his own initiative or at the implicit, or explicit, behest of his superior. He may then come to play a crucial role 'protecting' an agency from certain kinds of contact. This protective role may operate to provide a crude kind of rationing scheme for the benefit or service a department has to offer, as the flow of requests for help is checked or slowed down at reception. The recognition that these 'gatekeeper' roles may have such a crucial impact upon the service provided by an agency has led to a considerable interest in the activities of receptionists in recent years, but similar observations may be made about the roles played by secretaries and telephonists.

An influential American study by Peter Blau, *The Dynamics of Bureaucracy*, examined the behaviour of receptionists in a public employment agency. While these officials had fairly clear rules to operate in deciding whether or not applicants should be turned away or sent through for employment interviews, they inevitably had an element of discretion in marginal cases. They were also influenced by a dislike of turning eager clients away. On examination of the actual pattern of decision, it was found that an ethnic bias existed, white receptionists being more ready than black receptionists to turn away Negro clients.

Similarly, another American study, Deutscher's 'The Gatekeeper in Public Housing', shows how the receptionist in a housing agency was able to enlarge her responsibilities in such a way that her prejudices against integrated housing projects and against unmarried mothers could be ventilated and thus distort agency policy.

In Britain, Anthony Hall has studied the behaviour of receptionists in social service agencies. The group he examined had far less clearly defined rules than Blau's officials but they were similarly largely unqualified people. He found that they played crucial roles as buffers between the public and social workers in the agencies, and thus had a considerable influence on the services provided.

Hall's study shows how receptionists tend to enlarge their roles to increase their interest in their job. But he also suggests that the extent to which receptionists take on responsibilities beyond their competence is crucially influenced by the extent to which they are able to refer cases smoothly to more qualified personnel. He suggests ways in which social service departments can minimize the intervention of receptionists, by ensuring that social workers are available on call. However, in at least one of his case studies the enlargement of responsibilities of the receptionists arose as much from social workers' desire for 'protection' from the public as from the receptionists' desire to take on wider responsibilities. This use of 'gatekeepers' derives, Hall suggests, from 'the absence of a systematic approach to defining priorities which provides a rational basis for alloca-tion of resources – accepting, rejecting, and closing cases' (Hall, 1974: 139).

Members of the public do not always realize, when they are dealing with receptionists, that they are facing junior officials with few powers and limited discretion. Hence receptionists may make decisions which are not recognized as open to challenge, give opinions that are wrongly accepted as authoritative, and convey an impression of the agency's interest in the clients' needs which is quite misleading – hostile or sympathetic. If an agency's services are in heavy demand, pressure will be very apparent at the reception point. Then receptionists will be more prone to give hasty and ill-tempered replies to enquiries, and if applicants have already been annoyed by a long wait an angry exchange may develop. Once again therefore the reception func-tion may assume an importance out of all proportion to the actual task involved.

Where, as is particularly the case in social security agencies, the primary task is to make large numbers of decisions on closely similar applications for benefits, it is probable that at the next stage beyond reception the official whom the applicant meets will also be a junior one. This official's role will be to establish, and probably check, the full facts in support of the application and then to report them to a more senior official. Where he has responsibility to take decisions he will be confined to the more routine and non-controversial cases. Thus, for example, all supplementary benefit decisions have to be made by Executive Officers (EOs) and not by Clerical Officers (COs) who do much of the routine fact-collecting work, whereas in many National Insurance cases where the facts are straightforward and the applicant's right to benefit is not in doubt the decision is taken by the lower grade official.

However, once again the applicant does not often know what grade of official he is talking to. Furthermore, as Olive Stevenson has argued about supplementary benefit decision making in her book *Claimant or Client?*

> ... the EO, if he has not seen the claimant himself, is dependent upon the CO, not only for the accuracy of information upon which to base a recommendation, but also in more subtle ways, when discretionary powers are involved. It is obvious that the way a request from a claimant is presented by a CO, for example the amount of supporting evidence that is produced, may have an effect on the EO's decision.
>
> *(Stevenson, 1973: 21)*

Finally, having taken a decision, the higher official may well require the junior to present it to the client. This may be a result of a necessary division of labour under pressure, or it may more cynically be regarded as a means by which the decision-maker preserves a quiet life. However, the preservation of a layer of officialdom between the decision-makers and the person affected by that decision helps not only to reduce conflict but also to ensure impartial decision making.

What are regarded as fairly routine processes of assessment of facts about applicants for benefits, to be carried out by but slightly trained officials, can in fact involve decision making that will have a crucial impact upon the benefits received. Elizabeth Burney in her book *Housing on Trial* showed that the visitors who see potential local authority tenants prior to re-housing, to check the facts about their needs, are often also required to assess housekeeping standards. Their reports then influence the kinds of houses offered:

> The principle is simple: a clean person gets a clean house and a dirty person gets a dirty house. In between are all kinds of subtle gradings which are the everyday material of housing manage-

ment. Quiet, clean, steady-earning families with not more than three children are highly prized because they make life easy for management and their neighbours. They are usually repaid by being put near other 'good' families in better houses. The most unsatisfactory tenants may only get old terraced property awaiting demolition, or rehabilitated as part of the council's permanent stock; or simply one of the shabbier inter-war houses.

(Burney, 1967: 71)

Burney's observation here is similar to that made by Deutscher in his American study of the public housing 'gatekeeper':

The person's dress, speech, manners, attitudes and whatever he is able to present about himself during the interview situation are all taken into account by the gatekeeper in her determination of desirability.

(Deutscher, 1968: 46)

Burney was particularly concerned to point out that this approach to the establishment of facts about future tenants led to discrimination when visitors were faced with people of unfamiliar cultures and ways of life. However, the Cullingworth Committee, in their report *Council Housing Purposes, Procedures and Priorities,* condemned the general way in which this sort of assessment introduced moral considerations into the selection of tenants. Sometimes housing authorities had quite deliberately done this. They were satisfied to let the prejudices of their officials guide their decisions. But in other cases the introduction of moral judgements was a much less intentional consequence of the visiting of prospective tenants.

It is indeed difficult to distinguish those cases where the prejudices of junior officials have led them to enlarge their responsibilities, by taking it upon themselves to discourage claimants or give them an unsatisfactory service, and those where they have been encouraged by their superiors to play such roles. The reality may be very ambiguous, as I suggested in a study of the National Assistance Board (Hill, 1969: 84-85). A double standard may be allowed to develop in which officials are unofficially encouraged to behave in this way, or at least not resolutely prevented from doing so, while their superiors will nevertheless refuse to endorse their actions when a member of the public complains about his treatment.

Control and morale in relation to contacts between officials and the public

Even if the discretionary powers of junior officials, responsible for much of the face to face contact with the public, are severely limited, the inevitable absence of total control over personal interactions means that personal grievances, prejudices and values will influence the treatment received by the public. Informal practices (see Chapter 3 of the author's *The Sociology of Public Administration*) will develop in defiance of rules and often to the detriment of the public's needs and interests.

In a welfare system where benefits are not totally limited by the Poor Law principle of less eligibility, it is likely that there will be occasions on which officials are giving out benefits which seem to compare favourably with their own circumstances. Social security clerks will compare cash benefits with their own salaries, and housing officials may live in accommodation inferior to that they are offering to tenants. In a contribution to *Poverty* an official of one of the civil service unions pointed out that the income of many social security clerks was low compared to benefit rates, and accordingly ended his article with an angry diatribe against

> . . . people who are physically and mentally capable of working, who live in high employment areas, but who prefer to collect their 'wages' from Employment Exchanges rather than do an honest day's work.
>
> *(Poverty 8 1968: 11)*

Writing this section twenty or thirty years ago, reference might have been made to class differences between officials and clients, and it might have been suggested that class-conscious judgements were being made by middle-class officials who condemned without understanding the behaviour of the working-class people with whom they dealt. Today, however, many junior officials are drawn from a social group not dissimilar to that of many of their clients. Indeed, many social security offices, particularly in the inner-city areas, regularly recruit staff from their unemployed clientele. Of course, older, more permanent staff may still have the prejudices against their clientele described above, and this may be heightened by an awareness that the gap btween them and their clients, in both material and social terms, has narrowed. But today it is far from uncommon for clients who remark 'you don't know what it's like on this side of the counter' to be met with the reply 'yes I do, I was there only a few weeks ago'.

The question is therefore: does being in a situation in which their welfare is influenced by the judgement of their peers contribute to the understanding of clients' predicaments or the reverse? The 'you don't know what it's like' view is commonly expressed; indeed, several of a sample of unemployed men who were asked about attitudes of social security and unemployment officials expressed this opinion. Yet it is sadly the case that once people have escaped from a particular predicament they are often unsympathetically disposed to those they have left behind. 'There but for the grace of God go I' is replaced by 'Thanks to my superior efforts, I have avoided this situation'. What is more, even people belonging to dependent groups widely condemned in society tend to join in the general condemnation, simply explaining their own membership of the group by citing their exceptional circumstances. Thus, Herron says of a sample of redundant shipyard workers he studied in the Glasgow area:

> Many of the men expressing contempt for the 'regulars' had experienced considerable difficulty in getting back into work and were often again unemployed when interviewed. This, one might have thought, would have persuaded them to see other unemployed men in a different light . . . (but) it was their concern with 'layabouts' which they chose to emphasize.
>
> (*Herron, 1974: 142*)

It is obviously difficult to generalize here. Whether officials who are socially close to their clients will identify with them or reject them must be influenced by personality factors. It must also be influenced by the extent of value dissensus within society, within the agency, and between society and the agency. If the existing agency staff strongly condemns a particular group of clients then any new recruit, even if drawn from the stigmatized group, will come under strong pressure to adjust his values. If, even when he belongs to the stigmatized group, the new recruit was ashamed of that fact little value change will even be necessary. However, if both outside and inside the agency there is a diversity of views the impact of change of status on the recruit will be much less clear.

Writing about the National Assistance Board, I took the view that the values of junior officials will probably correspond to those of a cross-section of the social groups from which they are drawn. This is no more than a common-sense statement of the likelihood, other things being equal. Yet there are some important factors which disturb this *ceteris paribus* clause in bureaucratic employment in public service.

First, organizations do not recruit at random from the general public, or even from that part of the public with specific qualifications. They both select and are selected. The more it is the case that an occupation makes unusual demands upon people, the more it is likely that recruits will have special interests, commitments and values that may distinguish them from other people. Such an observation can, for example, surely be applied to the police. When stressing the opportunities for service to the public provided by administrative roles, it is also necessary to bear in mind John Vaizey's remark that 'institutions give inadequate people what they want – power' (Vaizey, 1959: 7).

A number of social scientists have argued, along lines similar to that adopted by Merton, that bureaucracies recruit individuals who are rigidly conformist, ready to accept and exercise authority. A general objection to this is that we are nearly all employed in bureaucracies these days. Nevertheless it may be the case that roles with low discretion, but apparent high power over others, tend to be occupied by people of this kind. The more flexible recruits to the lower ranks of organizations may be removed relatively quickly by promotion, while in many cases the more able join bureaucracies above the basic levels.

Second, even if recruitment to a public organization yields a comparatively undifferentiated cross-section of the population, promotion and wastage will sort these people out in non-random ways. While at best differential wastage will eliminate those least fitted to the organization, in practice differences in alternative opportunities available to dissatisfied staff may limit the extent to which some 'square pegs' move elsewhere. If promotion is removing from the lower ranks the most able amongst those satisfied with the organization, and wastage is removing the able but dissatisfied, the consequences will be that those remaining in basic grades may include a high proportion of people who are ill-fitted to the organization in terms of either commitment or understanding or both.

Third, public organizations may be overtly or recognizably committed to certain ideals or goals. If they are then able to control their own recruitment processes, they may ensure that newcomers have compatible values. Kaufman in his book *The Forest Ranger* provides a very clear example of a public agency in the United States where shared commitments to the development of the forest service contribute considerably to solidarity and morale. Political differences, civil service commitment to neutrality, and central recruiting policies limit the extent to which the staff of British central government agencies develop such explicit commitments. Nevertheless, the new recruit to the civil service, who is given a chance to express preferences for particular departments, recognizes that different departments have different objectives. Some of the problems of public relations with the benefit granting agencies may stem from the fact that they have many unwilling recruits among their ranks, who would much prefer to be employed elsewhere in the civil service, together with locally recruited people who have joined the public service for want of a job. A contrast may be made here with local authority social work where basic grade recruits enter with a high commitment to many of the tasks they are to perform.

Fourth, it may be that the strong hierarchical control existing in many public bureaucracies provides an opportunity to influence value orientations. Training programmes exist to inculcate organizational values, and these are likely to be supplemented by a steady flow of exhortations. Two problems exist, however, with this form of organizational influence. One of these has been mentioned already in connection with recruitment, the tradition of civil service neutrality and the consequent avoidance of political controversy. The result, as I argued with reference to the National Assistance Board, is that the message which reaches junior officials from the top is often ambiguous and equivocal. Hence, a failure effectively to counter-balance prejudices against some classes of benefit claimants helps to reinforce those public prejudices which senior officials insist, for political reasons, cannot be disregarded.

The other problem with the use of intra-organizational influence to change value-orientations at the bottom of a hierarchy is that high wastage is common at this level. This means that a continual process of education has to occur, yet at the same time heavy investment in training may be wasteful since recruits do not stay long enough. In 1970 over 11 per cent of the Clerical Officer staff in posts at the beginning of the year left the civil service during the year.

Where hierarchical influence upon the values of junior staff is not possible, it may be argued that the key to the problem of undesired behaviour must lie in hierarchical control. This introduces the subjects of the extent of discretion and the problems entailed in minimizing it, which are the concern of the next section. Here, however, one critical dilemma must be pointed out. Writers on industrial relations, such as Alan Fox in his *Beyond Contract: Work, Power and Trust Relations*, have stressed that high morale, job satisfaction and reliable task performance are often encouraged by high discretion. The problem, then, for public administration, is that if hierarchical control is used to stamp out wide variations in the use of discretion (as, for example, Hall suggests in his study of receptionists) it may produce a lack of interest and application to their task on the part of officials which is just as damaging to the interests of the public. In extreme circumstances, indeed, this lack of freedom may actually lead to malpractice, with officials breaking rules to increase their influence. In this writer's view this is a risk that sometimes has to be taken, to limit democracy within the organization in favour of wider 'political' democracy, and put the client's interest before the official's. But, since the elimination of all discretion is impossible, it is wise to be on the lookout for unintended consequences when such action is taken. Informal practices may be as much a consequence of unenforceable rules as of deviant values.

Discretion

Writing about work roles, Jacques has made a distinction between 'prescribed' and 'discretionary' work, stressing that all tasks are a combination of both. Fox has used this distinction to develop an analysis of work roles in terms of their discretionary content. Both writers stress that just as no job is without some prescription, so no job is without some discretion. To illustrate the latter, Jacques quotes as an example an adding-machine operator:

> He himself controls the way he sits, the movement of his arms, hands and fingers, how hard he strikes the keys, the number of times and the way he refers to the columns of figures he is transcribing, his sizing up of how much work there is to be done, his adjustment of his pace of work . . .
>
> *(Jacques, 1967: 60)*

This usage of the concept of discretion in industrial sociology has been quoted because it is important to recognize that discretion in administration consists of very much more than the exercise of delegated power, under explicit statutory provisions. Discretion exists wherever rules to govern the activities of a public servant are absent. Davis has pointed out that administrators exercise discretion in a multitude of ways, in the course of:

> Initiating, investigating, prosecuting, negotiating, settling, contracting, dealing, advising, threatening, publicizing, concealing, planning, recommending, supervising. Often the most important discretionary decisions are the negative ones, such as not to initiate, not to prosecute, not to deal . . .
>
> *(Davis, 1969: 22)*

Thus, while in my previous writings on this subject (Hill, 1972: Chapter 4) I have been particularly concerned with situations in which legislation quite clearly states that officials are to exercise their discretion, I want to stress here that these are probably but a minority of the cases in which discretionary decisions occur.

In very many cases discretionary freedom is accorded to officials not because of a careful decision by the law-makers that this is the best way to deal with a particular kind of situation, but either because that situation has not been fully anticipated or because it had not proved possible to draw up rules to deal with it. In the former case experience of administration can lead to the discovery of means of limiting the areas of discretion which remain. The latter case, however, raises much more fundamental difficulties. The quotation from Jacques includes some trivial but in fact quite fundamental examples of uncontrollable discretion. These can be paralleled in the public administration field by kindred examples of interviewing style and timing, selective perception, and care over matters of detail which may have a critical impact upon the service received by the public.

Perhaps the area of discretion which has received most attention is that possessed by the police 'on the beat'. The most straightforward justification for police discretion is that were policemen to arrest all who break the law a gigantic police force would be necessary, the courts would be hopelessly overstrained, and the prisons filled many times over. The police need therefore to choose where they operate, where they concentrate their attention, and where efficiency is enhanced by turning a blind eye. Choice is particularly necessary in respect of what are often called 'crimes without victims' – drug and alcohol offences, gambling, and of course traffic offences not involving accidents – where the police cannot depend upon reports of crimes and yet still require public co-operation in law enforcement.

The police are, of course, not the only law enforcement agents in our society. Tax officials, public health inspectors, and factory inspectors, for example, have to operate in a similar way. Paulus has shown how the enforcement of the laws against the adulteration of food developed from a battle between public health authorities and the powerful food manufacturers and grocers in which convictions were hard to obtain, to a more voluntaristic but effective system in which the inspectors use extensive discretion to maintain standards with a minimal use of the prosecution weapon. The case for discretion in these examples rests not so much upon an argument that it is impractical to regulate the behaviour of law-enforcement officials, as upon a view that the ends of the system will not be effectively achieved by undue rigidity.

Discretion in law enforcement raises considerable problems, however. The combination of differential enforcement, the absence of complainants and, probably, a lack of public consensus about the immorality of the acts involved, provides considerable scope for corruption, favouritism or vendettas against particular segments of the population. While Paulus has suggested that public health inspectors have developed an effective relationship with manufacturers and traders, enabling them to enforce the law without undue formality, Gunningham argues that the Alkali Inspectorate enjoys too close a relationship with the manufacturers it polices. He argues that the Inspectorate is a weak agent against polluting manufacturers, operating as 'a self-conceived partner of industry, not as an independent judge, and . . . caught between serving industry and serving the public' (Gunningham, 1974: 65).

Davis, in his influential book *Discretionary Justice* rightly points out that some of the problems of differential enforcement, particularly in the United States, arise from the over-eagerness of legislators to try to regulate behaviour. The classic example of this was Prohibition. Similarly many States have on their statute books laws which proscribe all forms of gambling from the large-scale rackets to church hall bingo. Davis rightly argues that many forms of discretion can therefore be confined if the laws are more realistic. However, he also suggests that where selective enforcement is to occur the police should make explicit and public the working rules they are adopting. This is a strange view to take, since one essential characteristic of selective enforcement would seem to be that it should be unpredictable. For example, if the police decide, and make public their intention, to ignore speeding less than 10 miles per hour in excess of the speed limit, does this not, in effect, repeal the existing limit and replace it by a higher one! Similarly, customs officials could hardly make public the criteria they use in deciding which travellers, who pass through the 'nothing to declare' gates, should be stopped and searched.

Lying behind some of the legislation which creates differential and partial law enforcement is a concern to prevent dangerous driving, to ensure that food is *pure*, and that factories are *safe*. The provision of clear cut rules to define what is safe or dangerous, pure or polluted, is often difficult. It may be that legislators need the help of experts who are to enforce the law to provide some specific rules. In this sense discretion may be limited at a later date when experience of enforcement enables explicit rules to be devised. It may be that conflict over the legislation has led to the blurring of the issues, and that legislators have evaded their responsibility to make more explicit rules. But it may be the case that the translation of 'standards' into explicit rules is so difficult as to be practically impossible.

Jeffrey Jowell provides a valuable discussion of the problems of fettering discretion where concern is with the enforcement of standards. He argues that standards may be rendered more precise by 'criteria', facts that are to be taken into account. However, he argues that 'the feature of standards that distinguishes them from rules is their flexibility and susceptibility to change over time' (Jowell, 1973: 204). Very often, too, standards involve questions of individual taste or values. Jowell similarly suggests that situations in which unlike things have to be compared, or which are unique and non-recurring, cannot be regulated by reference to a clearly specified standard. He argues:

> It is not difficult to appreciate that it would be asking too much of the English football selectors to decide after a public hearing and with due representation, to state reasons why the national

interest would be served by having X rather than Z to play centre forward in the coming match.

(ibid., pp. 206).

Need, Jowell suggests, can be regarded as a standard. In the system of supplementary benefits, with its minimum basic income that has to be supplemented for many people by 'exceptional needs payments', it is easy to find examples of 'needs' about which it is hard to prescribe general rules. A good example is provided by an electric razor which would be accepted widely as a luxury for a young man, but can be seen as a necessity for an old man with shaky hands. Writing about legalization in the context of our present supplementary benefits system it was not difficult, therefore, for Titmuss to argue in his 'Welfare Rights, Law and Discretion', in favour of 'flexible individualized justice' through the maintenance of discretion.

However there are two ways of eliminating discretion where decisions about needs are concerned. One of these is to provide an elaborate catalogue of rules about needs. This is an approach that has been adopted by some relief administrations in the United States. It was attacked by Titmuss, in the article just cited, as requiring a most elaborate checking of individual items of need:

> in New York City in 1968 . . . a man had a 'right' to possess one pair of winter trousers at $7.50 (regular sizes); the household had a right to possess in the kitchen one can-opener at 35 cents and, in the lavatory, one toilet tissue holder at 75 cents 'but only if your landlord does not have to give you one'. And so on and so on through hundreds of itemized entitlements from scrub brushes to panties.

This implies in practice, however, a great deal of hidden discretion, in ascertaining the adequacy of individual items. A ponderous bureaucratic decision-making procedure is necessary if claimants are not trusted. Trust implies giving officials considerable discretion to decide on isolated cases where, like the customs officials cited above, they should check carefully. Where trust is absent, procedural rules are elaborated. In the New York welfare system, for example:

The major premise of all welfare interviewing is that 'mere un-substantiated assertions of need' are never sufficient to establish eligibility . . .

Applicants were not permitted to certify to their pauper status but had to prove it repeatedly by completing elaborate forms, by providing such documentation as birth and marriage certificates, records of prior residences, and places of prior employment. Afterwards there were long waiting periods during which, presumably, further investigations were going forward, including the questioning of neighbours and relatives.

(Piven and Cloward, 1972: 154)

The other way to eliminate discretion in relation to benefits is to define categories of people in need, and allowances appropriate to those needs, in such a way that neither precise rules nor on-the-spot discretionary decision making is necessary. This is one of the advantages of universal as against selective benefit systems (see the discussion in the last chapter pages 55-60).

The following is an example of a situation where only a new approach to the definition of a category of people in need would eliminate discretion. In order to prevent women who are living with men securing supplementary benefits for themselves and their children, there exists what is known as 'the cohabitation rule'. The enforcement of this rule requires some difficult discretionary decision making. Cases arise where women say they are living alone, or that there is no regular male breadwinner in the household, but SBC officials consider they have evidence to the contrary. To try to curb the amount of hardship and unpleasantness associated with these cases, attempts have been made to tighten up the definition of cohabitation. This only produces confusion between the various ingredients of the situation: sexual relations, co-residence, and the sharing of household costs. Elaborate guidelines have been provided for SBC officers but the core problem of discretion has not been eliminated. Indeed, the move away from moral judgements raises the problem that, in fact, financial intercourse is more difficult to detect than sexual intercourse!

Another suggestion that has been made to eliminate discretion here has been the removal of decision-making responsibility to appeal tribunals. But this only replaces official discretion by tribunal discretion, a change that has some advantages but which cannot be seen as providing for the elimination of the problem, as will be shown in Chapter 7.

One reform, widely canvassed, that would definitely eliminate discretion would be an instruction to SBC officials to disregard undisclosed cohabitation. But this could be seen as an unsatisfactory formal position, unfair to the honest. In practice, surely, SBC officers would be likely to impose a range of informal pressures where they suspected cohabitation. Again, a degree of trust is required which is, at present, not characteristic of social security administration.

The other form of discretion with regard to benefits, decisions about exceptional circumstances or exceptional needs which justify increases in the basic allowance or single special payments, can be eliminated in a way that can be simply described, by raising basic allowances to the point where they will cover any unusual need. Yet a rise in basic allowances would have to be very large to eliminate a minority of very exceptional cases requiring discretionary decisions – claims for help by employed persons alleging temporary needs as a result of flood or theft or loss of a wallet, for example.

Much of the stress so far has been upon discretion as a necessary evil. First, it has been acknowledged that all work tasks contain a discretionary element, hence it is not possible to eradicate it in relations between officials and the public. Second, reference has been made to limitations on the possibility of providing rules for all occasions. Third, even where the elimination of discretion is theoretically feasible, politicians may have to make decisions to achieve that end which are so radical as to be unlikely. For example, the best way to eradicate the 'cohabitation rule' is to alter the way resources are distributed in our society so that women who stay at home to work as mothers and housekeepers are not forced to be the dependants of male earners. Finally, there is a need to consider the view that discretion is not only necessary but desirable. Such a position was taken, for example, by Lambert in his discussion of police discretion in *Crime, Police and Race Relations*:

> This discretion is a valued aspect of the policeman's work for it encourages individuality of response to situations where advice and persuasion are more effective instruments than orders and demands.
>
> *(Lambert, 1970: 142)*

Equally, in their writings on social security Richard Titmuss and Olive Stevenson have stressed the value of discretion in providing flexibility in administration and in facilitating the adaptation of rules to human circumstances.

Conclusions

So the subject matter of this chapter is brought full circle. It began by discussing the weaknesses of rule-bound bureaucracies, it ends by citing those who stress the virtues of discretion. We are presented with choices in which, according to the service or benefits involved, and according to our values, we may elect for rules and discretion in different combinations. The nature of the choices involved can be illustrated by citing two extreme models, or ideal types – on the one hand an organization that is largely rule-bound, on the other an organization where officials have a very high degree of discretion – and examining the advantages and disadvantages of each 'model' for the citizen who goes to an organization of that kind for a benefit or service.

The advantages of a comparatively rigid, rule-bound organization are that the public are provided with a predictable service, there is a lack of scope for favouritism or corruption, and stigma and patronage are minimized. The disadvantages are that service may be slow and responses to exceptional situations may be unsatisfactory. Furthermore, in some circumstances the advantages cited above may be dissipated because low staff morale leads to the breaking of rules, the exploitation of rules as a form of bullying, and the enlargement of minimal areas of discretion in such a way that malpractices develop. We still have a very inadequate idea of the circumstances under which the latter group of bureaucratic evils occur, but we may predict from the American studies of police malpractice that they will be very probable when the aims of the organization conflict seriously with widespread popular values and when respect for authority is insufficiently strong to override objections to organizational aims.

The contrasting organization to the rule-bound one would employ staff with wide discretionary freedom. Very often, groups given this kind of freedom to develop a public agency in ways which conform to their own ideals of service to the public are those with special skills we identify as 'professional'. The next two chapters will be much more concerned to explore the nature of professional service. The advantages of the comparatively rule-free organizational form are that it provides opportunities for the elaboration of services in conformity with professional ideals, and that its flexibility enables an effective response to exceptional circumstances and to rapidly changing situations. However, the weakness of this form is that policies may become unduly subservient to inward-looking concepts of professionalism, in which group protection for the professionals may be treated as more important than service to the public. Furthermore, where discretionary services are provided by a State agency the member of the public will be likely to find himself in a very unequal 'practitioner/client' relationship of an authoritarian or paternalistic kind. Finally, despite the considerable flexibility of such an organization, it may be the case that problems of 'trained incapacity' arise. Individuals trained to exercise high discretion may nevertheless have relatively narrow views of their skills and of the situation in which their services are applicable. Very high discretion generates uncertainty, and practitioners may accordingly find security by adopting relatively narrow definitions of their responsibilities.

Of course, neither of these 'models' corresponds with reality. Real organizations provide for a mixture of rules and discretion. But it is useful to look at the extreme cases to gain some idea of the implications of developments which lead in either direction. However, it is not merely questions about the best way to provide a particular public service which determine the mixture of rules and discretion attained in any organization. The shapes of public agencies are determined by a variety of political considerations.

The process of formulating rules to fetter discretion is that which Simon has described as providing 'premises' for decisions. Legislators provide statutory structures for the decision making of those who implement their policies. But the act of 'legislation' does not end with the activities of the legislators; senior personnel within an organization similarly set out to structure the decision making of their juniors in various ways. There may be several 'legislative' layers in this sense.

It is possible to argue that certain principles should govern this process of elaborating premises for low-level decision makers. It may be argued that the aim should be to reduce the area of uncertainty, and thus unpredictability for the public, as K.C. Davis does in his *Discretionary Justice*. It may be suggested, as Simon does, that legislators should resolve the 'value' questions, leaving their administrator subordinates to sort out the 'factual' elements necessary for taking a decision. But the reality is that legislation is seldom such a rational process, and that political expediency (both for the true politicians and for those senior administrators who so often act 'politically') frequently dictates the premises for low-level decisions. Davis suggests that (a) legislators seldom dig deeply into specialized subject matter, (b) the process of 'generalizing in advance', necessary to set decision-making premises, is very difficult and, most importantly, that (c) where the subject matter is still very controversial the process of achieving consensus will inhibit the resolution of critical 'legislative' problems.

The last of Davis's points concerned me when I was writing about unresolved value-dilemmas which had to be faced by officials exercising discretion in the National Assistance Board. In many ways the framers of the National Assistance Act failed to follow Simon's advice to politicians to deal with the main value problems at the policy-making stage. The traditional attitude to the poor had been to regard them, in the absence of unambiguous evidence to the contrary, as undeserving individuals on whom public money should be spent most sparingly. The National Assistance Act seemed to turn its back on this doctrine, yet it failed to jettison the view entirely and it failed to provide financial resources sufficient to enable the Board to avoid having to distinguish between the claims made by applicants, particularly regarding their more unusual needs. Consequently the onus of distinguishing between the 'deserving' and the 'undeserving' poor tended to fall upon the officer dealing with the applicant in the field, just as it has fallen upon the relieving officer in the past. While the politicians and administrators who framed the Act would not have wished to espouse the notion of the 'undeserving poor', they felt unwilling to risk the public criticism that would have resulted from an approach to poverty which ignored the potential waste on 'work-shy' and fraudulent applicants in order to meet the needs of the majority of applicants adequately. The value-dilemma described here is still unresolved today in the NAB's successor, the Supplementary Benefits Commission.

In recent years, the delegation of responsibilities of this kind to junior officials has been increasingly criticized. Yet there are many other social policy dilemmas which are similarly 'delegated'. Doctors, for example, play crucial roles as allocators of scarce resources, taking decisions that could be pre-empted at a 'legislative' level. Their responsibility for decisions about who should have kidney machines is perhaps the most striking example of this. Here, the value issue to be confronted is very difficult indeed and we are rather less inclined to condemn governments for delegating this kind of responsibility. Rudolf Klein has argued:

It may be that in some sensitive areas of policy it is better to diffuse the decision-making process; deliberately to leave it to individual doctors to decide, for example, whether or not to keep *spina bifida* children alive – although this is precisely the sort of decision which has non-medical consequences for society in general, and the use of the NHS resources in particular.

(Klein, 1974: 8)

This very sophisticated example of discretion provides an appropriate note on which to end this discussion of the factors which determine the rules/discretion division in public administration, and at the same time serves as an introduction to the discussion of professional services in the next two chapters.

Chapter 5
Professionals in the Personal Service Agencies

Professionalism

Many of the services provided by the State are largely taken for granted, either because they are so universal that we scarcely acknowledge their existence so long as nothing goes wrong (for example drainage and the public utilities) or because we only have need of them in rare and exceptional circumstances (as is the case with the fire and ambulance services).

Services which involve regular personal contacts between the State-supported personnel who supply them and the many members of the public who benefit from them are, by contrast, given considerable public attention. These are the health, education and social services. This chapter will be primarily concerned with these, together with one other professional service which, though so far at an embryonic stage as a State-supported service, promises to grow in importance and to provoke some new questions about the relationship between the State and the individual – the 'legal service'.

The key characteristic of this group of personal services is the provision of expertise for the benefit of individuals who are unable, or not regarded as able, to solve problems or tackle tasks unaided. They involve interactions between individuals and State employees in which a special form of authority relationship exists, based upon this expertise. Therefore, even if it is considered desirable in an egalitarian society to eliminate those other aspects of authority which tend to exist in State/individual relations, this kind of relationship may still imply an unequal balance of power between the parties.

Sociologists have suggested that authority based upon expertise tends to be linked with a wider social phenomenon, 'professionalism'. Professionalism has been seen as involving a number of linked ingredients, about which there has been some disagreement. Although readers should note that professionalism has various facets, and that the occupational groups which we regard as professions differ in the extent to which they possess various identifying characteristics, there is no point in developing a pedantic discussion of this problem of definition here. Greenwood has provided in an essay 'Attributes of a Profession' perhaps the most satisfactory succinct list of the characteristics of a profession. He says 'all professions seem to possess: (1) systematic theory, (2) authority, (3) community sanction, (4) ethical codes, and (5) a culture.' The crucial elements here are the expertise provided by what Greenwood calls 'systematic theory' and the 'community sanction' involved in the fact that the society or State accepts that the authority and discretion which will be exercised in practise can be left to a considerable degree under the control of the professional group. To satisfy the society and the State that it can fulfill this trust the profession develops an 'ethical code', and the process by which its members are bound together in a relationship involving both social support and social control entails the development of a 'culture'. This is the ideal for the relationship between professions and society, yet often professionals are unable to achieve the autonomy which they feel they merit; while at the other extreme the consolidation of professional power may reach a point at which there is some substance to Bernard Shaw's view of professions as 'conspiracies against the laity' or Illich's thesis that the medical profession is 'a major threat to health'.

The degree of professionalization of occupations can be seen as varying along a continuum. To some extent that continuum involves different degrees of discretion in the performance of tasks. But that oversimplifies the position since the key factor distinguishing professional discretion from the discretion which many non-professionals exercise is the existence of mechanisms maintained by the occupational group itself, to influence and control it. Training institutions lay down standards, professional organizations enforce ethical codes, and informal relationships between colleagues will constrain deviants. Hence, although professions at the highly autonomous end of the continuum entail high degrees of discretion, there are other high discretion tasks – at the top of managerial hierarchies for example – which are not professionalized.

Professional groups well down the autonomy continuum, often described as semi-professions, are those which aspire to a full professional form of organization but are not allowed to achieve comparable autonomy. In such a situation the interaction between the professional 'attributes', listed by Greenwood, is complex. The absence of autonomy may weaken professional organization and undermine the drive towards the development of a systematic theory; but equally those who deny the profession autonomy will refer to the absence of theory, or the incompleteness of professional organization, as reasons for this denial. The complexity of the inter-relationship involved here leads, of course, to inconsistencies between professions in their patterns and rates of development. Some have tried to form tight professional organizations but have still faced problems of recognition, others have secured high degrees of autonomy while their 'theory' base was still very fragile.

In a study of the 'semi-professions' Etzioni and his associates have singled out teaching, nursing and social work as key examples of aspiring professions with difficulties in achieving autonomy. These occupation groups are largely in public employment in Britain, playing crucial service roles for the general public under the supervision of the State. Some writers on the professions have suggested that bureaucratic employment inevitably curbs professional autonomy. They see as the true professions the ancient 'free' professions, serving individual members of the public on a private contractual basis. But others have pointed out that organizations provide professionals with insulation from their clients, freeing them from commercial pressures and giving them the resources to develop their professional skills. Certainly the doctors have found that it is possible to have a role within a State bureaucracy which retains a high degree of autonomy. Clearly any professional, whether salaried within a bureaucratic context or earning fees as a private practitioner, has had to convince someone that he has a special expertise which must be 'bought'. In rare cases 'free' professionals secure the best of both worlds, private practice and State guarantee of an inexhaustible supply of clients, as is the case with lawyers. But more typically private practice involves a high risk element; this is eliminated when a State bureaucracy steps in and provides a secure link between practitioners and clients. Where indispensability of expertise will guarantee clients for free practitioners it will also help to secure autonomy for bureaucratically employed professionals.

The position is further confused by the fact that there are two kinds of autonomy, individual autonomy and group autonomy. The traditional medical and legal model of professional autonomy involves discreet relationships between individual practitioners and clients. The professional/client relationship is seen as a private one. Other professions only interfere in this relationship when one or other of the parties complains about behaviour which goes beyond the ethical boundaries deemed to govern it. But where today professionals operate within organizations they have obligations to their employers. If they are in State organizations this obligation is also, in a sense, public. Then, while the professional may no longer be able to expect complete discretionary freedom, he may nevertheless demand that his actions should be judged, and his activities directed, only by other professionals. Group autonomy rather than individual autonomy will be expected, with the professional control mechanism, described earlier, being to a large extent built into the bureaucratic machine.

Hence, while in some of the examples to be discussed in this chapter, the client still has to relate primarily to an individual practitioner, in other cases his relationship is rather more with a 'professional organization'. Sometimes, even when the practitioner/client relationship is *prima facie* one between individuals, in practice the behaviour of the practitioner is heavily conditioned by his organizational role.

This exploration of the phenomenon of professionalism has set out some of the general issues which affect the relationships between professional practitioners and individual clients within the public services. The rest of this chapter will examine the three main contexts within which citizens encounter professionals responsible for the provision of services. The recent history of State activities in the fields of health, education and social services in Britain will be outlined very briefly, and the reader will be given some idea of the structural contexts of these services and of the kind of employee roles found within them. There will also be a brief note on the position with regard to legal services. These descriptive sections will thus introduce the analytical discussion of the issues and problems that arise in the course of encounters between individual citizens and the providers of services, which is the subject of the next chapter.

The Health Service

It is important to recognize that in the days before the State became involved in the provisions of medical facilities the level of medical knowledge was such that practically the only service activity possible was ensuring that the sick, and often the dying, were as comfortable as possible. For most people such a service was provided within their own homes. In medieval times the charitable activities of the Church supplemented this. This Church activity gradually passed to hospitals set up as charitable ventures, and to institutions run by Poor Law Guardians. It was only as medicine started to make advances and as the need to provide antiseptic environments for the sick, and isolation for sufferers from infectious diseases, began to be recognized in the middle of the nineteenth century that more sophisticated institutions were developed. Even in this period charity continued to take a substantial share of the burden of care. Public hospital provision developed in two different ways in the nineteenth century. The Poor Law infirmaries grew in importance, and gradually diminished the rigour with which the poverty test was applied to prospective inmates. Local authorities secured powers to build institutions to extend their capacities as public health authorities to deal with infections.

Doctors gave their services free within the charity hospitals, subsidizing this by using their prestige as 'consultants' to secure private patients and to train pupils. The public institutions employed their own salaried doctors. The bedside care of patients was developed by Florence Nightingale and her successors from a mere extension of domestic activity into an organized and disciplined semi-profession.

The care of the sick outside the hospitals developed in a haphazard way. For those unable to pay for the services of a doctor, the charitable hospitals developed out-patient clinics and the more far-sighted of the Poor Law Unions also began to develop out-patient care. The big advance was to come when Lloyd George's Insurance Act of 1911 provided a 'panel' system of out-patient medical care for some employees, though the service given to their families largely depended upon the readiness of individual doctors to accept less than normal fees in payment for treatment.

The inter-war period saw the gradual elaboration of these services. But there was a growing recognition that, as the possibilities of health care advanced, a system which had grown up in such an *ad hoc* way was moving towards breaking point. The only significant administrative change was the transfer, in 1929, of the health responsibilities of the Poor Law to the local authorities. This made possible the development of much more comprehensive local authority services. (They had also at various times since the beginning of the century acquired responsibilities in the fields of maternity and child health.) The local councils could now provide services without means tests, and comprehensive municipal hospitals could be developed. In fact, by the Second World War few authorities had yet made much of this opportunity.

This account of the historical background of the health service has been rather protracted because the process by which a profession, which developed as a group of free entrepreneurs serving wealthy clients, was gradually drawn into public service has had a crucial impact upon the relationships between doctor and patient which exist today. When he set up the National Health Service in 1946-47 Aneurin Bevan had to deal with three different patterns of medical organization. There were the consultants serving the voluntary hospitals free of charge, but with many private patients, some part-time contracts with municipal hospitals, and a dominant position in medical education. There were other doctors, largely organized hierarchically, working for the local authorities in the municipal hospitals and in the clinics of the maternity and child welfare services. There were the general practitioners, some largely dependent upon private practice, others primarily 'panel' doctors under the State insurance scheme. The whole mixture had been confused by the *ad hoc* wartime arrangements, which had further undermined the traditional distinctions and revealed that the system was badly in need of reorganization.

The National Health Service Act kept the tri-partite division described above, but in an altered form. A unified hospital system was created under national control but with regional boards and local hospital management committees, appointed by the Minister to deal with detailed management. Hospital doctors were put on a salaried basis, but could be part-timers devoting the rest of their time to private patients and making use of hospital facilities to enable them to do this. The particular hierarchical patterns of medical administration which had been developed in many local authority hospitals were eliminated; consultants secured considerable autonomy and were given generous representation on management bodies to protect their interests. Nursing hierarchies were maintained, and subsequent changes (the introduction of grades based on a report of Lord Salmon) strengthened them. Lay administrators were given widened responsibilities, but essentially on a basis of 'partnership' with their medical colleagues that many would consider subordination.

The 'panel system' for general practitioners was maintained, but now all had access to doctors without payment or membership of an insurance scheme. The GPs were allowed to be self-employed workers paid by the health service on a 'capitation' basis (i.e., a fixed sum for each patient on their list). Supervision of this service was by means of a network of Executive Councils, having limited powers over individual practitioners and a number of professionals as members. The other relevant

practitioners – dentists, opticians, and pharmacists – were similarly allowed to remain self-employed, but paid on a 'piece-work'
basis for work done. A critical issue in the general practitioner
services since the introduction of the NHS has been the extent
to which, in the interests of a sound service to patients, practitioners have been prepared to work together in group practices or health centres. Developments of this kind were initially
slow but have more recently speeded up, the Ministry using
some critical disputes over pay as opportunities to devise
incentives for the modernization of practices.

The local authority public health, and maternity and child
health responsibilities remained with them after 1947 and steps
were taken to move this part of the system slowly towards a more
comprehensive preventative health service. However, in 1974 a
further health service reorganization brought the local authority
services into the 'national' service. At the same time, changes
were made to integrate the general practitioners' services more
closely with the rest of the health service. Hence, there is now
simply a network of regional and area health authorities, but
with provision in the latter bodies for liaison with the still 'free'
general practitioners through Family Practitioner Committees.

The pattern of government adopted, first for the health
services outside the local government sector and now for the
whole of the personal health service, entails no intervention by
an elected body below the level of Parliament. In the new
system there are Regional Health Authorities, and Area Health
Authorities, on which members of the laity serve alongside
members drawn from the ranks of practitioners. The 1972
White Paper on the reorganization of the health service made it
clear that the Government saw Regional Health Authorities and
Area Health Authorities as having 'management' and not
'representative' functions.

For administrative purposes the larger Areas are subdivided
into Districts. In each District (or Area where no District
divisions exist) Community Health Councils have been set up to
perform 'representative' functions. Half of the members of these
councils are drawn from the local authorities in the area, the
rest are appointed by the Area Health Authority on nomination

from, or after consultation with, local voluntary bodies concerned with health matters. On the functions of these councils the White Paper on the National Health Service Reorganization had the following to say:

> The council's basic job will be to represent to the Area Health Authority the interests of the public in the health service in its district. It will be for each council to decide how best to go about this, but they will be expected to influence area policy by contributing their own ideas on how services should be operated and developed.
>
> *(NHS Reorganization, 1972: 28)*

The new Government reviewed these proposals, publishing a Consultative Document 'Democracy in the National Health Service in 1974'. This did not propose changing the representative system to any radical degree and at the time of writing no significant changes have stemmed from it.

The member of the public is free to pick his doctor, dentist and optician. Equally the practitioner is free to pick his client. Individual choice is obviously conditioned by accessibility, and where doctors or dentists are scarce people may have difficulty in securing treatment. It is possible for practitioners to strike people off their lists or to refuse to take them on. Hence 'black-listing' may occur where doctors have found patients particularly difficult, and the Family Practitioner Committees may be asked to help resolve such problems.

Except in emergencies, public access to hospital treatment is by way of general practitioner referral. Hence, variations exist in the circumstances under which people secure specialist attention. The effectiveness of the referral system is affected by the relations which exist between individual general practitioners and individual hospital specialists. So the patient who is fortunate in his selection of a general practitioner may equally enhance his chances of getting high quality or rapid attention from a hospital.

Contact between the member of the public and the community health services, recently taken over from the local authorities, occurs in rather different ways. In the course of motherhood a woman is likely to get in touch with midwives and with ante- and post-natal clinics coming under this part of the health service. Health visitors have particular responsibilities to make contact with pre-school children. Their concern for the under-fives is then followed by the 'school health service's' responsibilities for the five-to-sixteen age group. The community health services also supply district nurses for home care of the sick and such services as chiropody and family planning, and their health visitors are concerned with other groups 'at risk' such as the elderly and the disabled. Slowly the general practitioner and the community health services are becoming more integrated: health visitors and midwives are attached to GPs, for example. It would be irrelevant here to go into the wide range of ways in which the various services tend to be interlocked.

Education

The first State involvement with education in England and Wales came in 1833 when a small grant was given to the religious societies engaged in the education of poor children to assist them with school building. With further subsidies in the 1840s came the development of a State system of inspection in education. This was to be a significant force for growth and improvement. In 1870 an Act was passed to extend education by establishing elected School Boards in each area. These boards had powers to set up their own schools. In 1880 attendance was made compulsory for children between five and ten, though it took time for sufficient schools to be available to enforce this. In the years after 1880 fees were eliminated within the public sector for most pupils. All this early development was confined to what we now call 'primary education', but in the last years of the nineteenth century the School Boards began to develop some forms of secondary and further education. The Education Act of 1902 legitimized this development and shifted responsibility for education from the boards to the County Councils and County Borough Councils.

Much of this early effort in education was organized as a pupil teacher system, with older children taking the responsibility for much of the teaching under the supervision of a trained adult. In the years immediately before the First World War, however, a corps of trained teachers was built up, and the pupil teachers were gradually phased out.

In the inter-war period the secondary and further education systems were considerably consolidated. This development was inevitably patchy; the education costs which fell upon the parents of pupils in this sector varied considerably, much of the system requiring fees subject to a means test. The 1944 Education Act provided for free education for children between 5 and 15. It divided the system into a 'primary' sector (up to 11) and a 'secondary' sector (11-15 but with provision for further years after the normal leaving age).

Since 1944 the school leaving age has been raised to 16 and the educational opportunities between 16 and 18, and in the years after 18, have been considerably extended. Perhaps the most important controversy since the war has been about the organization of secondary education. The 1944 Act was not prescriptive about this, but the orthodox view at the time was that three kinds of school should be provided: the Grammar School for the academically able, the Technical School for those primarily fitted for middle-range vocational training, and the Secondary Modern School for those destined for manual occupations. It was believed that these three school types matched basic kinds of ability groups in the child population, and that equal provision or 'parity of esteem' could be achieved between the three types. The system should rest upon accurate selection at the age of eleven. Naturally discontent arose because the three types of school were not equal, either in their facilities or in public esteem. The selection system involved judgements, moreover, about the potential of children at a comparatively early age and was bound to be unpopular with those whose children were relegated to inferior schools on the basis of imperfect tests.

Little progress was made towards the organization of a complete system of Technical Schools, so the system rapidly became bi-partite. At the same time, however, an alternative emerged, to be championed by the Labour Party, the comprehensive secondary school providing facilities for all children. At the time of writing there is, therefore, a mixture of forms of secondary education. A few local authorities still run a fully selective bi-partite system but are under pressure from the Labour Government to 'go comprehensive'. Some authorities now have totally comprehensive systems. Many authorities are in transitional stages between the two, with mixtures of types of school and with schools that are compromising between the selective and the comprehensive ideal (particularly varying in the extent to which they are 'streamed'). Finally, one other change has come with the transition to comprehensive education, the elimination in some areas of the age of eleven as the crucial transfer age. Instead, some authorities have three-stage systems with middle schools, catering for age groups such as 9 to 13, between the primary and the secondary schools.

The twentieth century has also seen the development of a sizable higher and further education sector in Britain. University students are able to obtain means-tested grants to support them while they are studying; these are given by local authorities under a mandatory scheme laid down by central government. Also doing comparable work to the universities are local authority-administered Polytechnics, formed in the 1960s out of those technical and further education colleges where a high proportion of degree-level teaching was provided. Another important group is the Colleges of Education, providing courses – often up to degree level – for intending school teachers. Other further education colleges cover a wide range of activities, mostly below degree standard. The overall appearance in higher and further education is of an elaborate hierarchical system led by the universities with local colleges of further education at the bottom, differentiated not only in terms of prestige but also in terms of staff/student ratios, capital resources and building standards.

Some stress has been laid upon differentiation within the education system in terms of prestige and hierarchy because, although on the face of it the professional groups in education perform similar tasks, it is in fact the case that they can hardly be regarded as a uniform group. Teachers in universities, in local authority colleges and in schools each have separate pay structures and conditions of service. The division in the professional representation system is even more marked. Even the body on which school teachers' salaries are negotiated has represented on it four different organizations of rank-and-file teachers, drawing on slightly different constituencies affected by distinctions of interest between primary and secondary schools, grammar schools and secondary modern schools, boys' schools and girls' schools, and graduate and non-graduate teachers.

On the whole, the higher the prestige of the type of institution in which he teaches the greater the autonomy possessed by the teacher. But it is important to differentiate two kinds of autonomy. The last statement refers to the freedom of the teacher or lecturer from supervision by his department head or headmaster; the other kind of autonomy is the freedom of the education institution as a whole from interference by government, local authority, parents or pupils. As far as this kind of autonomy is concerned the difference between the institutions is probably not so great. The schools and local authority colleges experience an inspection system, from national and local levels, which the universities do not, but in general the impact of 'outsiders' (as defined above) on the nature and content of teaching is really very slight. It is interesting to note that many of the significant innovations in the involvement of parents in decisions about the education of their children have come from the primary sector. This seems to be a contradiction of the view that professional groups with relatively low status are likely to be the most defensive in the face of client groups, but may just be evidence that they are least able to resist demands for parent involvement. At the other end of the education system extensive demands for participation have been made by students. Many universities have made concessions to these demands but, significantly, many academics strongly resist the involvement of students in decision making about curriculum content.

The formal position with regard to lay influence over education is broadly as follows. Below the national government all public education, except in the universities, comes under the local authorities. These authorities have to maintain education committees consisting primarily of councillors but including representatives from the ranks of the professional educationalists. Schools and colleges also have governing bodies appointed by the relevant education committee(s) and sometimes including church representatives, university representatives, and, less often, representatives from groups of parents. Many schools also have parent/teacher committees, but formally these have no powers and in practice their activities are often confined to the raising of funds and the organization of social and sporting events. The formal powers of all these bodies are in any case severely limited. Tyrrell Burgess has put the position succinctly in his *Guide to English Schools*: 'Traditionally in Britain, the courses of instruction offered in a school, its organizations, ethos, and curriculum, are matters for the head teacher and staff' (Burgess, 1964: 64). It is more difficult to deal with the informal power of some of these bodies, or the indirect pressures which bodies of informed parents may put upon schools. Ultimately the 'output' of schools is people with various kinds of qualifications, together with references from teachers and perhaps the reputation of their school, upon which they depend to obtain jobs or further education. Hence the school is under considerable pressure to ensure that its 'output' conforms to the demands of parents and employers. These considerations must considerably curb experimentation within the schools, and thus the autonomy of the teachers. The examination boards here play a crucial role in mediating this 'pressure', helping to transform public demands into educational requirements.

The statutory position with regard to selection of schools by parents, is, according to section 76 of the 1944 Act, that:

> . . . the Minister and local education authorities shall have regard to the general principle that, so far as is compatible with the provision of efficient instruction and training and the avoidance of unreasonable public expenditure, pupils are to be educated in accordance with the wishes of their parents.

This is a good example of a statutory provision which, in

practice, gives a very high degree of administrative discretion. In this sense the key expressions are 'shall have regard', implying that parental choice is only *one* factor to take into account, and the other considerations which are given after 'so far as is compatible with'. This statement of parental rights, therefore, has not precluded secondary school selection, zoning of primary schools to provide geographical catchment areas, and the expulsion or exclusion of children whose delinquencies range from criminal or severely disruptive behaviour to failure to wear school uniform or get hair cut.

The Act also lays it down as the duty of parents to send their children to a school, though not necessarily a State one, or otherwise to provide him or her with an education which the authorities consider satisfactory. Failure to do this can lead to court proceedings, as can truancy on the part of children below the school leaving age.

This section has dealt fairly fully with some of the statutory arrangements affecting parental relations with schools. There is little point in setting out at similar lengths some of the rather complex statutory and governmental relationships in the higher education sector. A government-appointed University Grants Committee, its membership dominated by senior university staff, stands between the Department of Education and Science and the universities, though doubt is increasingly expressed about the effectiveness of its so-called 'buffer' role. This argument need not detain us, since one thing the committee manifestly is not is an organization to secure involvement of the general public in the government of this sector of the education system.

Each university has representatives of the outside laity, and in particular local authority nominees, within its governing bodies. Yet, on the whole, outsiders play but a minor role in university government. Some universities have recently taken steps to ensure that students are represented in their government, but both students and outsiders are heavily outnumbered by academics (mostly drawn from the ranks of the professoriate).

Social services

The heading 'social services' embraces most social work together with the provision of a great deal of practical and institutional help for handicapped and disadvantaged groups within our society. Thus, the latter includes homes and domiciliary services for the elderly or handicapped and home helps and services for the mentally handicapped. The account given here is of the system as it has developed in England and Wales. In Scotland and Northern Ireland the history and present structure is a little different.

It is hard to provide a clear historical picture of the growth of these services. To a large extent their nineteenth-century predecessors were provided sparingly, and under the rigid limitations of means tests and institutional relief, by the Poor Law. As that century progressed this meagre State provision was supplemented by a wide range of charities. One of the sources of social work as we know it today was the development (particularly by the Charity Organization Society) of personal case-work to prevent the indiscriminate giving of charity.

Children's services developed in the nineteenth century, again largely under the auspices of charitable societies, to try to cope, first with the need for institutional care outside the rigours of the Poor Law for the many orphaned and neglected children of that age and, second, with the problems raised by the ill-treatment of children. Societies like Barnardo's and the large organizations set up by the churches were prominent in the first activity, while the National Society for the Prevention of Cruelty to Children was pre-eminent in the latter field. Not until the local authorities took over responsibilities in these fields from the Poor Law did a State system of care and aid for children really develop, and even then the Government needed to give the whole service impetus by clarifying statutory responsibilities. This was done to some extent in the inter-war years, but the crucial codification of responsibilities did not come until the Children's Act of 1948.

Institutional provision for the elderly, handicapped, and homeless remained a Poor Law responsibility until its final demise in 1948. Then the National Assistance Act transferred the Poor Law institutions to the local authorities. Hence the process of eliminating the 'less eligibility' rules, which limited institutional care to the totally impoverished and provided an exceptionally spartan regime within the institutions, was only really begun in the 1940s. Once they had responsibilities for these institutions, the local authorities, aided by a widespread suspicion of institutional care (not surprising in view of the Poor Law legacy), began to recognize that the development of domiciliary services could reduce the use that had to be made of institutions which were bound to be costly if their standards were raised to an adequate level. Nevertheless the position in which local authorities have a clear duty to attend to the needs of the handicapped, outside the institutions, has only emerged very recently. Indeed, the Chronic Sick and Disabled Persons Act of 1970 is the crucial 'milestone' here.

With such a confusing range of functions, and with a legacy of Poor Law and charitable provision, under strict tests or an ideology of *noblesse oblige*, it is not surprising that the personal social services and particularly the main professional group within the services, the social workers, are struggling to achieve an adequate conception of role and sense of identity. In 1970 all the local authority social services in England and Wales (except the education welfare service) were brought by Act of Parliament into single Social Services Departments. After local government reorganization in 1974 these departments were all sited in the county councils, except in the metropolitan areas where the lower-tier boroughs were given this responsibility. This reorganization also removed from the health service to local government the social work services existing within the hospitals.

Hospital social work mainly developed from the service provided by almoners. These were a relatively well organized group of social workers who had set up their own training courses before the First World War. They were originally appointed to help assess the capacity of patients to pay for hospital services, and to ensure that efficient use was made of the various sources of monetary aid available. Within some of the psychiatric hospitals another group of social workers became established in the inter-war period. These were 'psychiatric social workers', practising 'case-work' in a comparatively sophisticated way under the influence of psychoanalysis and case-work theory emanating from the United States. The first training course for this group was set up in 1930. Today all are hospital social workers, the earlier disciplines having been abandoned. In the future the distinction between social workers in the community and those in hospital may also become blurred as a result of their integration within single local authority departments.

Apart from the small numbers in voluntary organizations, the only group of trained (or partly trained) social workers to remain outside the local authority departments are the probation officers who remain attached to the courts and prisons and under overall Home Office supervision. In Scotland, however, probation responsibilities are within the social work departments of the local authorities.

As a local authority responsibility for social services like education comes under a committee of councillors. This represents almost the sole avenue to lay involvement in the control of the services. The manifold powers and responsibilities of social service departments are not subject to specific appeal, or consultation mechanism, for the general public, except in so far as powers to bring children under local authority care come under the control of the courts. At the field level members of the public may be involved with social service departments as volunteers, but this activity largely consists of the performance of low-level, non-discretionary practical tasks.

It was hard to decide whether this discussion on social services should be included in the chapter describing individual benefits or in this chapter on personal services. The public may receive from these departments money or material aids, institutional care, routine services like those of a home help, or personal case-work. Individuals come into contact with social services departments in a variety of ways. Research by Glastonbury and his colleagues indicates that few people have a clear idea of what these departments have to offer. People find out that social services may supply things they need – home helps, day nursery places, free telephones and so on – so they get in touch. They may also be put in touch by other agencies – health visitors, doctors, schools and voluntary organizations.

But people may become involved with social service departments quite involuntarily. These departments have statutory responsibilities for the care and protection of children, which may lead them to intervene in situations where their help has not been sought. Similarly, they have mental health responsibilities and must be involved when compulsory admissions to hospital are contemplated. These roles take social workers into an area of activity where they may been seen as having rather more 'social control' than 'personal service' functions. This raises problems for their relations with the public which will be examined later on (see pages 138-143).

Working as they do in settings in which combinations of personal help and more material aid may be required by clients, social workers face a dilemma. To what extent should any request for help be taken at 'face value' and to what extent should it lead to a wider exploration of material, personal and psychological 'needs'? This issue has caused a great deal of controversy and anguish within social work ranks and will be discussed more fully later.

Legal services

Although the organization of the courts has been determined by Acts of Parliament, and although the systems of self-regulation adopted by the legal profession have depended upon statutory licence, the State cannot be said to provide a legal service for its citizens. The securing of any legal advice is costly and the pursuit of any case through the courts can be very expensive indeed. While the independence of lawyers may be seen as one of the bulwarks against tyranny, the cost of the law must tend to undermine equality before the law.

Of course, traditionally there has been a cheap system of law, if not justice, for the poor, provided by the magistrates' courts. Yet the growth of a sophisticated legal system has entailed the responsibility for serious crimes being given to higher courts in which advocacy is more or less monopolized by barristers. The development of civil courts requires a higher degree of legal expertise, and an overall increase in complexity which implies a need for legal aid and advice in a wide range of social situations (many of which are far removed from the courts). At various points governments have intervened to try to simplify the legal system and to ease the problems and costs of access faced by individual citizens; but since fees paid by clients have continued to be the key source of income for lawyers, these reforms have had little impact upon the cost of legal help for the citizen.

Accordingly the government has sought to reduce the cost of legal aid and advice to citizens by providing a system of financial support for clients. This is based upon a means test. Legal aid is generally available to defendants in criminal cases, but it is restricted for civil cases, both statutorily and by administrative discretion (exercised primarily by the Law Society, the governing body of the solicitor's profession), in ways which are intended to limit the scope for 'vexatious' litigation. Legal aid was introduced in 1949. Since then improvements have been made, particularly with a view to securing legal advice for people with problems which do not clearly require court action.

Individual access to the existing free or subsidized legal aid and advice services is very haphazard. Abel-Smith and his associates have shown that very many people face legal problems without securing any form of legal advice. Areas in which the poor live are under-supplied with solicitors, and the agencies which refer people to legal advice – the Citizens' Advice Bureau and the Law Centres – are thinly and erratically spaced. Many people with problems which lawyers might tackle, and for which legal aid is available, have no idea where to go for help. There is enormous scope for growth in the accessibility of legal services.

Recently some voluntary bodies and local authorities have set up law centres to provide initial legal advice on a more generally free basis. Rather like the doctors confronted by free charitable clinics at the end of the last century, many lawyers have shown concern that law centres may offer free advice and aid to people well able to pay. The present statutory position therefore limits the scope for these centres, and little money has been available to enable them to expand their services. But many of the radical lawyers associated with law centres advocate the extension of the service they provide, so that one day we may have a 'national legal service' providing free access for all to legal assistance and to the courts. If this happens it will offer an opportunity for the legal profession, which is sometimes condemned as narrowly self-interested, to demonstrate its capacity to provide a valuable service to members of the public who rarely seek its help.

If such a service develops the fact that many people will come for legal assistance with grievances against other State agencies will provide a particularly stringent test of professional autonomy and ethics. Indeed, the very notion of a publicly supported service dealing with such appeals and complaints presupposes a liberal political order, capable of accommodating conflicts and protecting the individual against the State. Many critics of contemporary pluralist democracy would predict that the system could not take that sort of strain, and that the independence of the legal system would be undermined. If a national legal service were successfully secured it would be a fairly remarkable achievement, unlikely to have counterparts elsewhere in the world.

Chapter 6
Professionals and the Public

Special problems of access to services

In Chapter 3 access to benefits was discussed very fully. Here concern is, therefore, with special problems of access to services, problems that are likely to be particularly acute where those services are provided by professionals. Of course, many of the problems of access which applied to benefits apply also to services and repetition will be avoided where this is likely to be fairly obvious.

However, some further attention must be given to the problem of ignorance, which is particularly salient where services are concerned. The very fact that professional services involve expertise makes it likely that clients will not always be aware of what is available to them. Ignorance may take the form of unawareness of services available, inability to find them (to which may be linked confusion between agencies), failure to recognize a need for help, and inability to persuade practitioners, or their 'gatekeepers' that a need exists. There are related problems of communication once a practitioner/client relationship is established, which will be considered in a later section.

It is important to recognize that the ignorance of clients is not always inevitable. Despite the necessary knowledge gap between practitioners and clients, there are clearly ways in which members of the public can be helped to achieve diagnostic skills sufficient to enable them to identify 'presenting problems'. The only general exception to this rule is the situation in which the client is deemed to require a service which he refuses to recognize as necessary. Then, as we shall see, the service agency is likely to be engaged in playing a social control role.

It was stressed in connection with benefits that the total

elimination of ignorance about available State aid implies a cost which may be deemed to be prohibitive. But it was also suggested that in some circumstances knowledge levels are deliberately kept low. Where professional services are concerned, there are several motives for this. First, the informal rationing that is achieved by deliberately inhibiting demand may seem to be particularly necessitated by short supply of professional practitioners. Second, experts' time is likely to be scarce and expensive. Hence, it is typically the case that lay, or less qualified, 'gatekeepers' are employed to screen the public to ensure that professional time is not wasted. This screening process will, with the best will in the world, tend to deter approaches from the public. However, it may sometimes be used quite deliberately to achieve this end. Members of the public may find receptionists hostile. They may be so protective of their professional employers or superiors that they come to be regarded as difficult people to convince. Appointment systems, particularly when waiting lists are long, will further deter people who are unsure about their needs and ready to abandon the quest for help if inconvenienced. (Some evidence on this last point was provided by Ann Cartwright in her study *Patients and their Doctors*.)

Third, it may be suggested that the very fact that a profession has gained power and influence because of its monopoly of expertise may deter it from seeking fully to equip the public with pre-diagnostic information. It may be feared that the undue spread of knowledge will not increase demand for service but will decrease it in favour of 'do-it-yourself' enterprises. Furthermore, even information that does not have this effect may nevertheless make more manifest the role played by the professional group and thereby reduce their professional prestige and influence. In relation to this the notion of varying degrees of professionalism, expounded in the last chapter, is important. The lesser the expertise upon which a profession is grounded, the greater the possibility that information about it will undermine its position.

Fourth, one of the characteristics of high professional prestige is deference. While it may be debated whether this is a universal accompaniment of professional prestige, there is little question that the professions are embedded in the British class structure in such a way that the more deferential of their working-class and lower-middle-class clients will regard them with awe, and even the less deferential are likely to see them as distant people with whom it is difficult to communicate. Clearly inaccessibility, formality of manners and imposing styles of clothing, for example, will encourage deferential attitudes in clients. This will help to protect professional power and autonomy. Several writers have pointed out how deference inhibits demand for, or use of, professional services. Thus, Ann Cartwright in her *Human Relations and Hospital Care* argues that patients meet doctors in hospital in circumstances in which the power and prestige of the latter are highlighted. She argues that:

> Doctors tend to underestimate both patients' desire for information and their ability to understand explanations. They often seem to discourage patients from asking questions and they sometimes use patients' feelings of respect and deference to evade discussion.
>
> *(Cartwright, 1964: 100)*

In an American study Friedson has drawn attention to the significance of social class differences in patients' relations with doctors:

> High social class was associated with a greater degree of sensitivity to social stimuli in the doctor-patient relationship, and with a critical and manipulative approach to medical care. In contrast, the lower classes were less sensitive about their status as patients and were rather more passive and uncritical in their approach to medical care.
>
> *(Friedson, 1961: 210-11)*

A number of studies have similarly drawn attention to the inhibitions of working-class parents in approaching school teachers about the educational problems and opportunities facing their children. Although in a compulsory education system this cannot reduce use of that system in the most basic sense, it will reduce the use of its more special resources. Jackson and Marsden wrote, in their *Education and the Working Class*, that

. . . parents badly wanted, needed and yet could not easily come by quite elementary information about the sixth form, specialization, college, university, careers. And yet . . . there were schools staffed with able and interested teachers most unlikely to refuse any clear demand for help. Still the gap was not crossed.

(Jackson and Marsden, 1962: 226-7)

The crossing of this gap is enormously influenced by the way in which public services are presented. McGeeney, in his book *Parents are Welcome*, quotes notices displayed inside school entrances which were clearly intended to discourage parents; for example, at one infants' schools:

As new school entrants are now settled down to school routine, parents are kindly requested to hand their children over at the gate, where a member of staff will be responsible for their safe conduct to the classroom at 9.10 a.m. There, the teachers take over. Children will be taken to the gate at 3.30 p.m. If and when necessary, parents may see the headmistress or class teachers *by appointment only*.

(McGeeney, 1969: 6)

There may be circumstances in which access to services can be totally prevented. In such situations the scope for redress of grievance is generally very limited, much more so than is the case with benefits. The difficulty is that professional practitioners giving an expert service are recognized as people who cannot be forced to accept clients against their wills. The most clear cut example of this is provided by general practitioners' power to refuse to accept people on their lists or to have people removed from their lists. Fortunately these are rare occurrences or there might be a hard core of 'blacklisted' patients. Doctors may also refuse to see their own patients but they do this at risk of complaints, or even legal action for negligence.

We have also observed that schools may expel or exclude pupils. Likewise, parents have no powers to compel schools to provide their children with specific kinds of education. Their only recourse in the face of recalcitrance in this respect is to move the child to another school, if that is possible.

Many other failures to provide services are similarly not open

S.A.I.

to redress; individuals can only use the more indirect control devices – complaints to MPs or councillors – to secure satisfaction. Very often, of course, refusal of services stems from scarcity: professionals ration services by using their discretion to determine priorities. But sometimes refusal stems from a view of what is in the client's best interests which differs from that perceived by the client.

Some writers on professions have stressed the professional ethic as a service ethic; in the words of Goode, 'the professional decision is not properly to be based on the self-interest of the professional, but on the need of the client' (Goode in Vollmer and Mills, 1961: 36). It is therefore necessary to turn from the discussion of barriers to access for clients, to look at ways in which professionalism at its best stimulates client access.

The stronger the professional involvement in the government of a service, the more possible it is for the goals and needs of that service to be set by professional ideals. For example, doctors are given a great deal of autonomy in prescribing medicines. While random checks are carried out to identify extravagant prescribers, and these remind doctors that they must not deviate markedly from the norm, there would be organized resistance if these checks led to significant controls. Doctors would argue that budgetary limits or rules preventing their prescribing particular kinds of drugs, limited their freedom to give that service to the public which they felt appropriate. These 'professional' powers of the doctors may be contrasted with the much lesser powers of the dentists whose activities are considerably hedged around in this way. Nevertheless, like the doctors, the dentists are, in various ways, provided with means of ensuring that their point of view is represented in high places in the relevant health service decision-making machinery.

In all the services considered here, professionals are active in pointing out to the government ways in which public needs are neglected. The cynic may argue that this implies merely advocacy of the expansion of their own professions; but even if this is all it is, the effect for the client is an advocacy of unrecognized, unconsidered and unmet needs. Moreover, many professionals are so dedicated to the service ethic that when client needs increase without a corresponding expansion in the size of the profession they accept longer hours of work without greater remuneration. There is of course a danger that some of the identified 'needs' are inventions of the professionals, as Ivan Illich suggests in his *Medical Nemesis*. But it is hard to accept his very extreme condemnation of the medical profession.

There are many examples of professionals playing significant parts in the development of new services for the public. In medicine, specialists in public health have had a reputation since the middle of the nineteenth century as pioneers in the exploration of ways to prevent disease. Some of the earliest statistical surveys were carried out by medical men eager to identify unrecognized or unmet needs. Public health specialists pressed the government to enable them to vaccinate and inoculate children. More recently local authority doctors have been strong advocates of preventative medicine, initiating screening techniques for early signs of illness and advertising campaigns to help the public to identify initial symptoms.

In education, many teachers have argued that good education requires parental participation. Most of the experiments in parental involvement described in McGeeney's book, requiring teachers to devote much of their otherwise free time to communicate with parents, came about as a result of teachers' initiatives rather than parental demand.

Within social work there is a strong ideological commitment to the identification of unmet needs and to assisting clients to articulate demands for services. Social work is a curious case in this respect, as was suggested on page 122, since clients have a very much lower level of awareness of what social work involves, and are very much less likely to make specific demands for social work services, than is the case with medicine or education. Clients come to social work agencies with a variety of problems and have few preconceptions of the social worker's role. In some cases, as Mayer and Timms have shown in their book *The Client Speaks*, they are surprised by the topics with which the social worker is concerned.

This aspect of social work has caused a great deal of controversy within the profession. There are two historical legacies here, the first of which is today disowned by most spokesmen for the profession, while the second is still of lingering importance. The first is the role expected of social workers by the Charity Organization Society at the end of the nineteenth century. People who approached charitable organizations because of their poverty were to be encouraged by social workers to reflect upon the causes of their poverty. True to the nineteenth-century self-help ideology, these causes were mostly seen to involve personal inadequacies. Thus social workers were engaged in the translation of requests for material assistance into needs for self-help and self-improvement, and saw themselves as the agents to help effect this transformation.

The other historical legacy comes from Freudian psychology. The idea that clients have unconscious needs may be, but is not necessarily, compatible with the Charity Organization Society's view that material needs were really personality needs. It is, however, to Freudian psychology that social workers largely owe their modern commitments to intensive case-work with clients. It is unfair to present the contemporary case-worker as a poor man's psychoanalyst, busy trying to penetrate to the unconscious. But it is argued in defence of case-work that (a) many individuals who come to an agency for help with an initial problem want social workers to move on to other more complex problems, (b) that these initial 'presenting problems' are often tied up with more complex problems, and (c) when people with problems come to an agency whose role is not clear to them, they may well not discover until they are in a case-work situation the many other ways in which they can be helped.

Intrusion into the lives of clients can be seen as interference with liberty and perhaps the playing of a social control role on behalf of the State (translating material demands into personality issues). Yet many social workers feel the need to risk overstepping the borderline into this form of intrusion in order to give a full and adequate service to their clients. The discovery of unarticulated needs is a crucial aspect of their task. This may as readily imply a radical role in society as a conservative one, since the deeper exploration of client needs may lead to new demands for benefits, services or social changes rather than to psychotherapeutic concern about personality change.

It is only too easy to be driven by the arguments about State-employed practitioners as agents of social control to perceiving a crude service/control dichotomy. One facet of social work (which is also in a slightly different sense a characteristic of education) which complicates this issue is the fact that there is often more than one person in the client part of the prac-titioner/client relationship. A role that may be regarded as a service one from a child's viewpoint, for example, may be a control one from the parents' point of view, and vice versa. Thus the professional may have an obligation to attend to needs that are, or are perceived to be, in opposition to those of some of his clients.

It may also be the case that where the State imposes duties on professionals primarily for reasons of social control, it places them in a position to attend to what would otherwise be un-articulated needs. In social work the probation officer may often be in this situation. In medicine one task which doctors strongly resent is the provision of medical certificates for patients who wish to claim sickness benefit. Cartwright, in her *Patients and their Doctors,* quotes some strong views on this, and the Fisher Committee on the *Abuse of Social Security Benefits* discussed official representations from the British Medical Association which was endeavouring, unsuccessfully, to have doctors relieved of this responsibility. Certainly certification intrudes into the doctor/patient relationship an element of authority which may not be in the best interests of therapy. Yet surely the requirement to go to a doctor for a certificate to allow absence from work for a comparatively minor ailment must sometimes contribute to early diagnosis of more serious illness. Hence the involve-ment of doctors in a control function on behalf of the sickness benefit scheme must play some part in securing patients' access to badly needed help.

Practitioners and clients in an established relationship

In the last section some references were made to communication difficulties. This is an important issue in all the service sectors considered here. In many cases a satisfactory service depends upon the breakdown of communication barriers. In the field of education Basil Bernstein and others have drawn particular attention to the extent to which children with limited linguistic skills, or linguistic 'codes' which differ from those of their teachers, are handicapped in the educational process. While most writers on education see the solution to these problems as lying in intensive language teaching early in the educational process, a minority, led by Brian Jackson, have stressed the need for teachers and the curriculum to be more sensitive to issues which are the concern of working-class people.

Social workers are beginning to recognize that these communications issues in education are relevant to their relationships with their clients. The linguistic codes and cultural behaviour patterns of their adult clients are already firmly established. The key issue, therefore, is how professionals should relate to individuals with very different backgrounds to their own. While attention is devoted to initial 'presenting problems' the issue is basically one of understanding, but once the social worker becomes engaged in a wider exploration of a client's problems, cultural differences can affect definitions of problems, or even agreement that there are problems.

Medical practitioners have probably been most insulated from these new discoveries, or developments of understanding, in psychology, sociology and linguistics. Of course, in some cases the doctor does not need to communicate very fully with the patient or understand his social background. Yet if realistic forms of domiciliary care are to be established this understanding will be important. Furthermore, for an adequate approach to psychiatric illness, as for the large volume of physical sicknesses with a psychiatric component, communication and understanding is of key significance. Bernstein has specifically argued that effective psychotherapy must rest upon the practitioner's capacity to relate to the linguistic code of his patient, but one can equally focus upon other aspects of this therapeutic relationship to suggest that, for example, an adequate understanding of the patient's socially-conditioned expectations of family life is essential too.

Earlier, Cartwright's evidence was quoted on patients' dissatisfaction about the lack of explanations from doctors. She stressed the need for doctors to be more 'approachable people'. Without in any way disagreeing with this conclusion, it is important not to forget that professionals face severe problems in deciding what they *should* tell their clients. Although in various parts of this book readers will detect implied criticisms of official secrecy and reticence, it is certainly not intended to be prescriptive here. Rather it must be acknowledged that this is one of the most delicate problems in the professional/client relationship. Obviously doctors face the most cruel dilemmas when they have information about a patient's chances of recovery or survival. At a less critical level teachers also have to bear in mind the fact that total frankness about a pupil's weaknesses may be as likely to inhibit progress as to stimulate it. They have to fashion comments and reports in such a way that they balance criticism with praise; this may inevitably involve an element of hypocrisy. The preparation of references for the pupil's future employers raises particularly difficult problems of this kind. Social workers face kindred difficulties, which are compounded by the necessarily incomplete and inexact nature of the pictures they acquire of situations and relationships. Many try to adopt a permissive and non-directive stance towards their clients that makes it quite imperative that they should often evade questions about their diagnoses of situations.

A kindred problem occurs in situations in which professionals differ from their clients in their conception of the latter's best interests. Teachers are probably most easily able to cope with this issue, either by taking the view that the immaturity of the pupils justifies a paternalistic stance, or by letting the pupil's view prevail because it is he alone who will suffer in the long run and he who must come to understand his error. The consequences of letting a client 'go his own way' may be more serious, however, in the other services, and particularly in medicine. Practitioners may therefore decide that it is appropriate to exert pressure to achieve adherence to their prescriptions, by securing interventions from family and other significant persons or by threatening the client or patient with the withdrawal of all help. In the mental health field, powers exist to compel patient compliance, but in these days informal pressures are more commonly used than the formal powers.

The powers to compel mental treatment and the institutionalization of the mentally ill involve not simply powers to prevent people harming themselves but also powers to prevent harm to other people. This leads naturally, therefore, to the next problem area in professional/client relationships: the many situations where the practitioner sees himself, or can be seen, to have obligations to persons other than a single client. This issue widens out, then, into the general topic of social control, to be considered in the next section.

There is a number of quite straightforward respects, to be distinguished from the general social control issue, in which the clients of State services are not people whose individual interests can be considered in isolation from anyone else.

First, many of the services are for children. Teachers, social workers with child care problems, and doctors with young patients are all likely to find themselves in situations in which, although their clients are children, the persons who represent the children's needs to them are their parents. So the practitioner may find himself taking a view of a child's best interest which is at variance with those of his parents. This sort of situation particularly arises, of course, for social workers who have child care responsibilities as a result of the inadequacies of parents. There will also be situations in which professionals take actions which are opposed by their child clients. Their justification may be that they are, or conceive themselves to be, *in loco parentis*. This latter situation is, naturally, common in the educational sphere. In both kinds of situation the law is far from clear. On the whole our society is evolving away from a position in which parents have a considerable degree of power over their children; children's rights and interests are increasingly emphasized.

To a considerable extent the social dilemmas on issues of this kind tend to be handled by giving professionals discretion to make crucial moral judgements, under the general supervision of the courts. These dilemmas are rarely susceptible to clear-cut judgements in the courts. The issues involve moral 'shades of grey' and not the clear 'black and white' which is needed if legal precedents are to be laid down. The consequence is a high level of insecurity for professional practitioners. Sometimes decisions have to be taken which time may prove to be incorrect. One of the most disturbing examples of this was provided by the Maria Colwell case. Here, a child was killed by her step-father after she had been returned from foster parents to her mother's care. A most sensitive exploration of the social worker's dilemmas is provided by Olive Stevenson's minority contribution to the committee of enquiry on this case.

Second, some professionals will, quite aside from any special responsibilities for children, see themselves in a relationship with a family rather than with an individual. Clearly, in most cases the child care issues described above involve *two* parents, who may have differing points of view. Equally, social workers find themselves assisting with marital problems where it is much more constructive to have a relationship with two parties, with real or alleged differing interests, rather than with just one. It is in social work that these complex relationships with families particularly occur. Other professionals are more able to retain their unitary practitioner/client model in their work. But sometimes they risk narrowing their effectiveness by so doing. In psychiatry, for example, it is argued that the 'presenting' client is not always the individual within the web of difficult family relationships who most needs treatment. It is increasingly beginning to be recognized that doctors, and particularly general practitioners, need to be involved with families rather than with individual clients. They may have to consider the impact of specific diseases and specific forms of treatment upon a whole family and adjust their actions accordingly.

Third, many professionals are involved in relating to their clients in a group rather than an individual context. Their treatment of specific individuals will be observed by a whole group, who may be expected to comment on it and to take it into account in their dealings with the professional. This is self-evidently the case in school teaching. Manifestly, in this case, dealing with the needs and interests of any single individual has to involve consideration of all other members of a class. Similar problems may arise for social workers engaged in group or community work. They are less common in medicine, except in therapeutic communities or where group therapy techniques are used in psychiatry. But even in physical medicine doctors, and more particularly nurses, often have to act in situations in which their treatment of some patients will be evident to others.

Fourth, the group discussed under the third heading can be widened out to comprise all the others who may be affected by individual decisions. For example, when doctors decide that a man is fit for work or when teachers award specific educational qualifications they set up expectations in other people. A lack of care in such decisions, over-readiness to allow a sick man eager to work to go back or over-generosity towards a weak pupil, have consequences for other people's confidence in the professional's subsequent decisions. However, while these arguments have been put in terms of the impact of decisions about one individual upon others, they lead inevitably to more general questions of the use of professionals as agents of the wider society or State and the possible relation their activities may have to social control over individuals.

Professional services and social control

Heraud has pointed out, with reference to social work, that the simple model of the professional/client relationship in which the former helps the latter to solve problems is inadequate because of the wider social interest. He argues:

The client must eventually . . . be identified as having a problem which is not just his but is the concern of the community and of society. Thus the 'appropriateness' or 'usefulness of ways of functioning imply certain social standards or norms. There will be some idea or model of 'social health' towards which clients . . . will be directed.

(Heraud, 1970: 189)

This argument is similar to that which has been developed – in different ways by Scheff, Laing and Esterson, and Szasz – about the treatment of the mentally ill. In regarding the client as in some senses mentally sick, reference must be made to a standard of normality. Diagnosis is a matter of identifying symptoms which distinguish the 'sick' person from those who are well. These symptoms will often be forms of behaviour which disrupt and disturb the lives of other people. Hence 'sickness' and 'deviance' may be almost synonomous. We may only know people are 'sick' because their behaviour deviates from the normal, and we are particularly aware of this when it is disturbing or threatening to other people. Likewise, it is often difficult to establish criteria for the identification of the cured; again, there is a danger that what will be seen as important is that deviant behaviour is modified.

Of course, all psychiatry cannot be portrayed in these 'social control' terms. Many patients do seek help voluntarily and suffer symptoms which are not disturbing to other people. However, the situations in which some kind of control is called for raise particularly difficult ethical problems for psychiatrists. Fear of the mentally ill, though perhaps not so widespread today, dominated approaches to this group in the formative years of our mental health services. Undoubtedly the fact that, despite the very rudimentary knowledge base of psychiatry even to this day, the 'mental health services' pre-dated most of the physical health services testifies to the dominance of the 'control' element in their history.

A related argument can be developed about the role played by educationalists in our society. It is only necessary to examine political arguments about education, from Lowe's concern in

1870 'to educate our masters' to Harold Wilson's emphasis in the 1960s on education for a technological society, to see that teachers are often seen as performing functions for *society* rather than for specific individuals. At the outset education plays a social control function as one of the key means of socializing individuals, of fitting them to their places in adult society. Then, as it gets more advanced, attention shifts to preparing and socializing people for specific roles.

Inasmuch as there is a concern to see that there is a good *fit* between the roles required and the individuals available, education is making a contribution to the stability of the existing social order. The education of the professional groups, with which we are concerned, is itself a good example of this. One of its concerns is to ensure that people who are given licences to exercise extensive discretion, and who are to have considerable responsibilities for our welfare, can be trusted in these roles. Educational institutions are expected to socialize them, inculcating values and standards of behaviour, and to reject those who seem unfitted to professional roles. Those who teach future professionals have, therefore, an onerous three-way responsibility: to those they teach, to the professional group which their students are to join, and to the public upon whom their charges are eventually to be 'let loose'.

Doctors practising physical medicine are very much more likely to be in relatively simple professional relationships with individual clients, yet clearly society has expectations of them. Mention has already been made of the use of doctors in relation to the sickness benefit scheme, but it is also the case that the State (and also private enterprise) makes much more specific use of some doctors for such tasks as checking the claims of individuals to be fit or unfit for particular jobs, and assessing claims for compensation for injuries incurred in war or other public service.

Can professionals in public employment resist demands that they play social control roles? Szasz suggests that psychiatrists should not agree to be used for social control ends. They should only see patients who come to them voluntarily. But what does 'voluntarily' really mean in this context? British psychiatrists could refuse to see the minority of patients who are compulsorily detained. What they cannot do is overcome the fact that people come to psychiatrists because of socially defined problems. These problems are today generally seen as illnesses, though this is a label which some progressive psychiatrists resist. Many of their patients seek treatment neither voluntarily nor entirely involuntarily. They come because of problems in holding down their jobs or maintaining their marriages. Many will have experienced pressures from family or employers to seek treatment. The narrowly legalistic distinction between the voluntary and involuntary patient is of little significance.

The essence of the above argument is that, logically, people like psychiatrists, social workers and teachers cannot escape social control roles. But there is a need to look at this issue at another level, to ask to what extent they can avoid playing the more extreme, or the more morally obnoxious, social control roles which may be asked of them. This is a question, then, about professional power, which was foreshadowed by the discussion at the beginning of the last chapter. Professional groups outside the public services depend upon State sanction to enable them to maintain their own control over individual practitioners, while by the same token professionals inside the public services depend upon the bargain they make with the State to guarantee their power. When the doctors in Saskatchewan refused to participate in a State health service the State could, in theory, have removed the public protection they possessed as private practitioners. In practice the indispensability of the doctors, and the public dangers of uncontrolled medical practice, prevented such an action. But the State wanted doctors in a health service and was accordingly forced to meet their terms. Hence professional autonomy could have come under attack either inside or outside the public service.

If, however, the same argument is applied to one of the weaker professions, say social work, it will be found that the possibility of opting out of State employment does not exist to any real extent, because no one but the State will normally *buy* social work services. However, this does not render the profession entirely powerless. The State would be severely embarrassed if it could not recruit social workers; but so, of course, would it be if it could not recruit people to do many tasks which entirely lack a professional content. For the weaker professions, therefore, the bargain with the State, inasmuch as it does not rest upon bargaining of a trade union type open to any occupational group, must rest upon State recognition that autonomy and power-sharing contribute to the achievement of an effective service.

Most professional groups, therefore, must expect to find that within State employment they have to accept a complex and often non-specific bargain which does not limit their power, as such, for it is a *consequence of* their *limited* power. This bargain will not leave them totally free in their relationships with their clients. A certain minimum freedom will be achieved because, as was suggested in the earlier discussion of discretion amongst non-professionals, (a) there are limits to the extent to which people's jobs can be 'policed', particularly where those jobs involve human relationships, and (b) high discretion contributes to effective job performance, particularly where highly skilled tasks are to be carried out. Beyond this minimum freedom such further autonomy and power as the 'weak' professions achieve will depend upon the readiness of those in dominant positions in the State to subscribe to liberal doctrines, such as the theory of academic freedom.

This book is concerned with the relationship between individuals and the agents of the State. Hence it is appropriate to interpose into this discussion an awkward question about State guarantees of professional autonomy and power. The assumption has been that this autonomy may enable professionals to limit the extent to which they are required to play social control roles, but may it not rather be the case that it limits the extent to which the laity can control the professionals? Academic freedom is normally presented as contributing to general freedom, but it may equally be seen as giving academics the right to do what they want with public money. The professional freedom of doctors may prevent the use of their skills for totalitarian ends but it may also contribute to a health service in which practitioners are very unresponsive to social needs, one in which, for example, the interests of scientific medicine are given more importance than the comfort and privacy of patients. What is involved here, then, is a delicate balancing of interests. Inasmuch as the State is not wholly in the control of an isolated élite but is also responsive to popular interests, then any part it plays in the checking of professional power may be in the general interest and not a totalitarian force. There is a danger of the creation of simple dichotomies in a discussion like this – the professions versus the people, or the State versus the professional groups that are a bulwark against absolute State power – when the realities are more complex.

Total institutions
Some of the professional services coming under the State are provided within institutions. In recent years social scientists have stressed ways in which institutions exercise a more complete control over their inmates than is characteristic of social control relationships in the world outside. They have also drawn attention to the impact of institutionalization upon the individual personality. To some extent the argument here is merely an extension of the social control argument. Schools socialize the child, and the more complete the child's involvement with the school – as for example is the case when he is a boarder – the more total that socialization process. Institutions that are able to compel the attendance of adults – prisons and mental hospitals – are seen as involved in a process of re-socialization. Even those institutions which cannot compel inmates to stay, ordinary hospitals for example, are seen as moulding the individual so that he fits more neatly into the system, facilitating a uniform pattern of institutional life in the interests of administrative efficiency.

The sociologist Goffman has laid particular stress on the way in which institutions mould individuals, starting with an elaborate initiation process and then gradually socializing the individual for a life totally under official control. He suggests that whereas outside institutions the individual is free to work, sleep and play in different places, with different people, in the total institution the barriers separating these different aspects of life are broken down. All aspects of life are conducted in the same place and under a single authority. Daily life is carried on in the company of a large group of residents who are treated alike and expected to do the same things at the same time. These activities are often tightly scheduled 'with one activity leading at a pre-arranged time to the next, the whole sequence of activities being imposed from above by a system of explicit formal rulings and a body of officials'. All these activities are embraced, Goffman argues, by a 'single rational plan purportedly designed to fulfil the official aims of the institution' (Goffman, 1970: 17).

Quite apart from concern with the extent to which this kind of institution intrudes into the personal freedom of its inmates, it has also been pointed out, for instance by the psychiatrist Russell Barton, that one consequence of long stays in institutions is that individuals come out unable to take their places in the outside world. Hence, far from it being the case that the mental hospital has cured its patient, it may be that it has turned him into someone who, while apparently quite normal in relation to the demands of the institution, is quite abnormal as a citizen in the outside world. This gives a new twist to Florence Nightingale's requirement that the hospital should do no harm to the patient, though her concern, of course, was with cross-infection.

The work of people like Goffman and Barton, together with that of psychiatrists like Bowlby who have stressed the damage done to children removed from family situations, has had an enormous impact. Attempts are now widely made (a) to prevent institutional admissions wherever possible, (b) to keep stays short, (c) to create small residential units either as separate entities or as part of a larger whole, and (d) to eliminate some of the pressures against individuality (regimentation, uniform clothing, etc.) which hitherto existed within institutions. These changes have had an impact upon the care of children, the treatment of mental illness and the organization of hospitals. Where little change has occurred has, of course, been in prisons, and accordingly professionals who work in association with prisons (psychiatrists, social workers and teachers for example) still feel a strong conflict between their desire to meet the needs of individual clients and the institutional pressures all around them.

It is important to acknowledge that institutions vary considerably in the demands they make upon individuals. There are great differences between them in the extent to which the services they give fall into a rigid framework of social control. The prison is at one extreme of this continuum, the short-stay hospital or the day school towards the other end. The impact of Goffman's theory was heightened by the extreme form in which it was stated, but few institutions are as 'total' as he seems to suggest. Yet some of Goffman's arguments are of relevance in almost any institutional context. The requirements of administration, the presence of a group of people all undergoing much the same process, and the existence of comparatively uniform institutional aims all impose some pressures which are hard to resist. In such contexts the fact, outlined earlier, that professionals often have to relate to groups, and to limit their responses to individual interests accordingly, is clearly very important.

Professionals and money

Finally, there are a number of situations in which professionals in the employ of the State have to deal with monetary issues in the course of providing services. This requires a short discussion because the position is rather different from that which exists when there is a direct cash nexus between the private practitioner and his client. Clearly, as was seen in the discussion of the evolution of the health service, it is the removal of that cash nexus which is one of the strongest points to be made in favour of State organization of professional services. Yet rarely is it the case that all monetary considerations are removed from the professional/client relationship.

The health service was made entirely free in 1948, but since then charges have been imposed for prescriptions, dental treatment, spectacles and some other ancillary benefits. On the whole, doctors have remained free of responsibilities for collecting money, except where (as in some rural areas) they are their own dispensers. The charges have, however, introduced some difficulties into the relationships between patients and dentists, pharmacists, or opticians. However, these practitioners have been relieved of the need to apply means tests themselves, though they do have some indirect responsibilities for identifying cases where payment will be difficult and where patients should go to the Supplementary Benefits Commission for help.

Although education is free, there is a number of benefits available to poor pupils – free school meals, uniform grants and maintenance grants. Like the medical practitioners, teachers have some responsibilities to identify cases of need, but are not required to take decisions or administer means tests themselves. Insensitive handling of these issues by teachers can cause distress and inhibit application for help.

Social workers have to handle monetary issues of a rather different kind. Not only may they have to help in the administration of means tests for persons in institutional care, but they may also have to give grants of money to help with payment of rents and other domestic bills. These latter powers are a comparatively recent addition to their responsibilities, stemming largely from the 1963 Children and Young Persons Act. Similarly, they may have to provide services, aids and domestic adaptations under the Chronically Sick and Disabled Persons Act 1970. In doing this they have to assess the charges that should be made to their clients. These responsibilities are a source of considerable anxiety to social workers since they raise the spectre that died in Britain with the Poor Law, but remains very much alive in the United States, of benefits becoming, or being believed to have become, available on condition of the acceptance of social work help or 'control'.

In each of the three professional groups discussed, therefore, it is not entirely possible to banish monetary considerations from the service relationship. In medicine and education they are of but minor importance, but in social work they assume growing significance. Social workers have extensive discretionary powers with regards to money, thereby adding another difficult dimension to a relationship with clients which is already quite the most delicate of those which have been considered in this chapter.

Conclusion

In this and the previous chapter it has been shown that in many cases where the individual seeks services from the State, he enters into a relationship with professionals or semi-professionals. While each of the professions has a commitment to an ideal of service to individuals, in practice the relationships involved are more complex. Professional occupational groups are not wholly disinterested bodies of people. They have a monopoly, or partial monopoly, position in society which they will zealously protect. This limits individual access to them to some extent, and imposes some barriers on communication between professionals and the public.

Professionals in the public service are often unable to relate simply to individual clients. In many of their professional relationships they have responsibilities to several people. They also have a relationship to the State, their employer, which inevitably constrains them in some ways, and sometimes places them in a relationship to their clients which is more a 'control' one than a 'service' one. At best they are giving services to all which, if they were not State-provided, would be *bought* by those able to afford them. At worst they intervene unwanted in people's lives because they, or those with power over them, consider that help or control are needed.

In this context, professional autonomy will be a bulwark of a free and democratic State so long as professionals are committed to ideals of service and are able to resist the demands of those who would manipulate them for purposes of social control. Yet resistance to unreasonable demands needs to be distinguished from an arrogant refusal to accept democratic leadership and from an authoritarian approach to powerless clients. There is a fine and difficult line to be drawn here, leaving considerable scope for argument as to whether our society achieves a satisfactory balance between professional power and individual freedom.

Chapter 7
The Redress of Grievances

Introduction
This chapter is concerned with the procedures available to citizens to secure the redress of individual grievances. It will deal with all the roles of the State outlined so far – as a controller of individuals, as a supplier of benefits, as a provider of services – but not with the planning issues discussed later in the book. Planning is excluded from consideration here because the key matters of controversy between citizens and the State are often of collective rather than individual importance. The consequence is that, even where there are specific individual grievances, the machinery available to deal with them is rather different. The conflicts entailed are often *between* citizens, while those discussed here are conflicts where the citizen normally sees himself as confronting the State, however much, at a more complex and abstract level, he may really be said to be advancing his claim against those of other people.

'Going up the hierarchy'
The most obvious course of action for anyone with a grievance is to try to 'go up the hierarchy', to find a more senior official who will review the action of his subordinate. Although superiors who countermand the action of their juniors are unpopular, and face the danger of undermining morale, in the public services they cannot be indifferent to the mistakes of their subordinates.

The distinction between the enforcement of rules and the review of discretion is important here, and will come up again and again in this chapter. It was with discretionary decision making in mind that I wrote what was perhaps the most angry passage in my article on the National Assistance Board:

> This emphasis on personal decision making meant, above all, avoiding having to seek the advice of the Manager on any problem, a situation very similar to that found by Blau in his study of a law enforcement agency, where he suggested that to consult one's superior was regarded as to reveal oneself as incompetent. In the light of this one can see why the response of the higher echelons of the NAB to complaints provoked so much resentment amongst the Executive Officers. It was not only a case of 'management' reversing sound decisions, but also unwarranted intervention from people one felt should be expected to protect one from criticism: intervention moreover from people who normally agreed with you – who even encouraged you in the kind of action for which they now seemed to be condemning you. One's superiors, it was felt, were too ready to give way to expediency rather than reason.
>
> *(Hill, 1969: 87)*

What rankled here was a feeling that, in the face of the ambiguities of discretion, management was giving way to those clients who were most effective at putting pressure upon the agency. Officials did not see this managerial involvement as necessary to prevent incorrect decisions. As a consequence junior staff tended to prevent clients discovering the true nature of the hierachy. Clients rarely knew who the Manager was, hence the not-infrequent demand from the counter to 'see the Manager' could produce from behind the scenes an individual who would defend the decision. This would generally be the person who made it and very rarely the Manager.

The exercise of hierarchical intervention where officials have considerable delegated discretionary powers obviously arouses resentments, and introduces uncertainty into decision making. Significantly, therefore, the more powerful professions have secured considerable freedom from such control for individual practitioners. With the introduction of the National Health Service one hospital role which was present in many of the local authority hospitals, that of 'medical superintendent', was phased out, leaving as the key medical figures a group of equals, the consultants. The general practitioners operate entirely outside the hierarchical framework.

A complaint against a general practitioner is then something that has to be handled by a quasi-judicial procedure, with a heavy onus of proof upon the complainant. This means that there is no opportunity for an aggrieved member of the public to raise his complaint in a more informal way, and no mechanism short of disciplinary action to enable a doctor to receive a warning that his actions are causing dissatisfaction.

The less powerful professions operate within a hierarchical structure but there are often informal understandings which govern the relations between headmasters and teachers or, within social work hierarchies, which limit the extent to which supervisory roles are played. When these understandings are broken, groups of colleagues may make it clear to their superior that they think he has gone too far in impinging upon their professional autonomy. There is often confusion and conflict however, about respective rights and obligations in situations of this kind. This creates a similar confusion for members of the public who may find that while sometimes their complaints are investigated, at other times they are told that the matter is within the area of professional discretion of the individual and should be taken up with him. Thus King says of education:

> The precise authority relationships existing between a head teacher and his local authority, his governors and the inspectorate, are not often well defined. It is often the case that the nature of the relationship only becomes clear when the head teacher's actions do not receive official approval.
>
> *(King, 1973: 429)*

Even where the pressures of professional or colleague solidarity do not inhibit hierarchical control, other factors may make superiors reluctant to interfere with the decisions of subordinates. Trade union strength and problems in replacing staff may limit the sanctions available to superiors. Even when superiors use their power to change a decision, this may not set a precedent for future decisions. It is important to recognize that many of the people who receive unfavourable treatment from an agency are regular customers of that organization. It is these people whom junior officials are likely to recognize, stigmatize, and set out to inconvenience. If they complain, this merely increases their unpopularity. In the social security field obvious examples are men who repeatedly fall out of work, or women whose matrimonial lives are very unstable. Where the behaviour of these 'regular customers' has at some time given cause for concern – they have become violent during an interview or have been caught defrauding the agency, for example – a 'vicious circle' may develop. Officials will be tempted, by their experience of such people, to give unsatisfactory treatment. Then, resulting complaints will tend to further escalate the conflict between officials and such 'unwelcome' customers.

Going to the top—MPs and councillors

Most Members of Parliament run 'surgeries' to enable constituents to come to them with their grievances. They also receive a steady stream of mail from people with difficulties in getting service from public agencies. These complaints cover both the national services for which Parliament is directly responsible and local services which are the primary responsibility of the local authority. Many constituents are not aware of the distinction. Members of Parliament often make their own contacts with local agencies rather than pass local grievances on to councillors. Indeed, MPs will also use their prestige to intervene with private agencies in some cases.

These personal problems take a considerable amount of Members' time. The electoral pay-off, in our highly organized party system, is often doubtful but most MPs express a sense of obligation to try to redress grievances. Most of the work they do on individual problems is entirely hidden from public view. When MPs use Question Time in the House of Commons to draw attention to specific problems, or when they seek Press publicity for cases, they will be dealing with the rare examples which come to their attention in which the problem at issue is not one which is most appropriately kept private, or which can be solved easily, and where the principle at stake is deserving of public debate.

Parliamentary questions have been widely studied and discussed. Senior civil servants devote a great deal of time to preparing answers to these questions. All the standard textbooks on the civil service describe the 'trouble' they cause. Written enquiries by MPs about individual cases are not generally given attention at quite so exalted a level, but their impact upon junior civil servants is comparably marked. When complaints are referred to local offices, cases will be investigated at managerial level in order to provide a speedy reply.

The machinery for the examination of grievances by way of a complaint to an MP has been reinforced since 1967 by the existence of the Parliamentary Commissioner, sometimes called the Ombudsman. This official can conduct an investigation into the affairs of a department on receipt of a complaint passed to him by an MP. He later reports his conclusions to that same MP (or another MP whom he thinks appropriate, if the original MP is no longer a member of the House). The Ombudsman cannot deal with areas of administration outside direct ministerial control, nor matters which concern 'Crown personnel' (civil servants and the armed services). His function is an extension of Parliamentary control inasmuch as he can send for the relevant files whereas MPs have to be satisfied with replies from departments.

The British Parliamentary Commissioner is nevertheless a pale reflection of the Scandinavian Ombudsman. Complaints to him from the general public must be filtered to him by MPs. Significantly, as many complaints reach the Parliamentary Commissioner direct from the general public, and thus have to be referred back, as reach him from MPs. Today his activities receive little publicity, and it may be surmised that most of the public do not know of his existence and that many of those that do are unaware of the procedure necessary to secure action from him.

Similar 'Ombudsmen' have now been appointed for local government (the Local Commissioners) and for the health service. Local government complaints normally have to be sent on to the Ombudsmen by councillors but may come direct from

the public where councillors have been unwilling to act as inter-
mediaries. The Commissioner for the health service, on the other
hand, does accept direct access. This anomalous development,
justified by the 'indirect' administration of the health service,
may perhaps lead in due course to the opening up of direct
access to the Parliamentary Commissioner.

The position of local councillors with regard to grievances is
rather different from that of MPs because of their much closer
relationship with the services for which they are responsible.
Although today a large majority of councils are organized on
party lines and committee chairmanships are often monopolized
by senior members of the majority party, in local government
there is not the clear-cut division which exists in Parliament
between members of the Government and the rest of the
MPs. Local services are the responsibility of committees. All
members of a council sit on one or more committees and therefore participate in the running of some of the council's activities.
Although chairmen become closely involved with chief officers
in decision making for the services responsible to their committee, they are not 'ministers' and are bound to bring important
matters to the full committee. Although, with the heavy responsibilities entailed in running public services today, and with the
elimination of small authorities under the 1974 local government re-organization, councillor involvement in the minutiae of
decision making on individual cases is declining, it is by no
means dead. In some small authorities, although the practice
was condemned by the Cullingworth Committee, allocation of
council houses by the housing committee still occurs, and even
in the larger ones it is not uncommon for special cases of
housing allocation or eviction to come to the committee.
Similarly, many social services committees deal with exceptional
decisions, for example about grants or the care of children.

Many councillors prefer being involved in this detailed
decision making to devoting themselves to large-scale policy
matters which require intensive study and a comprehension of
complex financial issues. Heclo, in an article on 'The Councillor's Job', quoted many remarks like these from councillors:

I sometimes feel like a glorified housing agent.

and

The thing I like best is dealing with the public interest. It sounds funny but the other day I got a low bathtub for a crippled veteran; that's the most satisfying thing I've done.

(Heclo, 1969: 201)

The implications of these aspects of the role played by councillors for their effectiveness as the representatives of aggrieved individuals are considerable. At first glance, councillors appear to be excellent representatives of individual interests, better at this job than at articulating wider political demands. But are people who are close to decisions good at questioning those decisions? Indeed, inasmuch as councillors make themselves responsible for discretionary decisions, they undermine the contribution they can make as either pursuers of grievances or as members of a 'court of appeal'. And if they adopt an appeal role they cannot, at the same time, also be satisfactory 'counsels' for the aggrieved. When councillors see themselves primarily as policy-makers concerned with the large decisions in the authority, their weakness is then that, as part-timers serving the community on a voluntary basis, they find they have little time to devote to individual cases. Moreover, in mastering policy issues, councillors have to work very closely with local officials, becoming, according to Lee, 'ministerialists' co-opted to the governing coalition of officials and councillors. While such closeness may facilitate the securing of decisions in individual cases it, too, will inhibit the adoption of an 'advocacy role'.

Appeals to tribunals
In some cases of State action or decision, there is provision for an appeal to an administrative tribunal. It is hard to provide a brief description of the character and scope of administrative tribunals which does not over-simplify, leave out some key examples and do less than full justice to their diversity.

Tribunals provide a simple procedure, avoiding the complex

legal system of the courts, to enable citizens to secure a judicial hearing of grievances against public departments. Typically a tribunal consists of three people who serve on a part-time basis like local magistrates. In a few cases, theirs is a full-time job. One of these members will be chairman, and in most cases he will have legal qualifications. Some of the more specialized tribunals have other professional members; valuers for example serve on some of the tribunals dealing with land and house values. Tribunal members are appointed either by the Lord Chancellor or by the Ministry with whose affairs they are concerned. The selection process is kept secret, but must depend heavily upon the existing network of people engaged in part-time public service together with the local contacts of government departments. Studies by Cavenagh and her associates provide some evidence on tribunal membership. They show, not surprisingly, that members 'tend to come predominantly from the "upper" socio-economic groups and social classes, with more qualifications and higher incomes than average, a low proportion of women, and a tendency to be in late middle age'. However, this generalization should be qualified in one respect: many of the tribunals concerned with social benefits have to include one member recommended by trade union organizations to 'represent the interests of work people'.

Bell *et al.* made some interesting comparisons of the characteristics of 'employers' representatives', 'employees' representatives' and appellants in respect of a sample of National Insurance Tribunals. The table opposite presents information on their social class.

Chairmen have not been shown on this table since all except one in Bell's sample were professional lawyers, and would thus be classified in social class I. Therefore, while the bias in these three-person tribunals is markedly middle-class, the inclusion of employees' representatives ensures that one member of the tribunal is likely to be a manual worker. However, appellants to these tribunals are very often of 'lower' social class, in terms of the Registrar General's classification, than any member of the tribunal.

Bell's study also showed that tribunal members were signifi-

Table 1

The social class (Registrar General's scale) of members of and appellants to National Insurance Local Tribunals 1970 (percentages)

Social class	Employers' representatives	Employees' representatives	Appellants
I	6	2	1
II	68	34	7
III non-manual	6	6	8
III manual	16	52	49
IV	3	2	20
V	0	4	14

(Bell *et al.*, 1974: 303)

cantly older than typical appellants. 70 per cent of the members studied were male, but so were 80 per cent of the appellants to National Insurance tribunals. (This was due to the fact that a high proportion of appeals concerned unemployment and industrial injury benefits).

Some tribunals were set up to deal with administrative issues in the middle of the nineteenth century, but typically they are twentieth-century developments. Wraith and Hutchesson suggest that the origins of the modern tribunal 'lay in the National Insurance Act of 1911'. Today the heaviest areas of tribunal activity are in connection with disputes over various social security benefits. The key institutions here are listed below, with the number of cases heard in 1971 given in brackets:

Supplementary Benefit Appeal Tribunals	(29,605)
National Insurance Local Tribunals	(33,096)
National Insurance Commissioner (a higher court of appeal for National Insurance cases)	(2,237)
Medical Appeal Tribunals (dealing with medical details of industrial injuries claims)	(17,614)
Pension Appeal Tribunals (dealing with war pensions)	(3,463)

There are also a number of important health service tribunals. Local 'service committees' operate as tribunals to hear complaints from patients about medical practitioners. These dealt with 826 cases in 1971. There is provision here for a further appeal to the Secretary of State and a national tribunal to deal with cases where the removal of a doctor from the list of practitioners is possible. There are also Mental Health Review Tribunals to monitor the powers of compulsory detention of the mentally ill. These dealt with 1021 cases.

An interesting new development in the use of tribunals has been the provision for 'adjudicators' to hear appeals against refusals of right of entry to the country by Commonwealth citizens and aliens. There is also the possibility of appeal from an 'adjudicator's' decision to the Immigration Appeal Tribunal. In 1971, 1944 cases were heard by the adjudicators and 118 went on to the appeal tribunal.

In the economic field various ministerial decisions can be reviewed by tribunals: for example decisions by the Minister of Agriculture about the registration of dairy farms, decisions about patents and trade marks, and about the licensing of passenger and goods vehicles. There are important provisions for tax appeals – to the General Commissioners, a lay body, and the Special Commissioners, experts employed by the civil service but independent of the Inland Revenue. The distinction between the over-lapping functions of these two bodies need not detain us here. In the taxation field a new tribunal to deal with Value Added Tax is likely to grow in importance.

The tribunals in the housing field are only partially the concern of this discussion since the key area of dispute is between landlord and tenant with the State only playing an adjudicatory role. The Rent Assessment Committees represent an in-between case in this respect, since they hear appeals from people dissatisfied with the decisions of rent officers. However, interestingly, rent officers do not have to defend their decisions at these tribunals; the 'conflict' is between landlord and tenant. Local Valuation Courts may be described as tribunals. They hear appeals against rating valuations and dealt with 24,515 cases in 1971.

Finally, there are some examples that are hard to categorize because of their similarity to ordinary courts. In Scotland, for example, Children's Hearings play a crucial role in the regulation of the social services, replacing the magistrates' courts which have this function in England and Wales. There have been a number of special courts set up in recent years – the Restrictive Practices Court, for example, and (until its abolition), the National Industrial Relations Court – playing crucial roles in relation to administrative activity and operating in an informal way similar to that of the tribunals.

This listing of tribunals has sought to identify the most important examples, excluding those whose main funtions are to deal with disputes between citizens. It is important to recognize that tribunals have developed in a patchy way and that there has been no attempt to provide comprehensive coverage of State services for the citizen. There is no appeal except to the minister from local education authority decisions, about allocation of children to schools for example; there is no appellate control over the activities of local housing authorities; and none over the various powers of social services committees to provide accommodation and other benefits. Wraith and Hutchesson argue with specific reference to these examples that it is impractical to establish tribunals when demand exceeds supply. It must be acknowledged that the key problem here is that any individual claim would have to be weighed against all competing claims, in order that a fair decision be reached.

The use of tribunals in these areas, though difficult, might nevertheless limit abuses such as allocation decisions without reference to any general principles and without a fair hearing for applicants. At the moment, where breach of the 'principles of natural justice' occurs in the procedures used by administrators which do not come under the scrutiny of tribunals, members of the public may seek redress in the High Court. This possibility will be discussed later and shown to be generally a less easy way to correct maladministration. More importantly, however, the Ombudsmen may deal with problems of this kind. At the time of writing it still has to be demonstrated that the new Local Commissioners can satisfactorily deal with issues like those cited above. However, one interesting consequence of their appointment is that individual local authorities are improving their own procedures for enquiries into grievances.

It is difficult to discuss criticisms of tribunals because the variations in rules and procedures are such that adverse comments that have been made about one system will not apply to another. The most criticized of the tribunal systems has been that provided to review supplementary benefits decisions – which is perhaps the least court-like of the systems. There are few procedural rules, there is no system of precedent and chairmen do not have to be lawyers. In the following discussion the main criticisms of supplementary benefit tribunals will be examined and the points that are made will be related to the characteristics of other important tribunals.

Supplementary benefits tribunal members are selected by the Secretary of State for Health and Social Security, whose department takes all the responsibilities for the organization of hearings and the provision of clerks. Clerks are in fact Department of Health and Social Security officers temporarily seconded to tribunal work. Criticism thus focuses upon the failure to provide for the unquestionable independence of the tribunals from official influence by means of independent organization under the Lord Chancellor's department or some new, independent, national tribunal organization.

With many of the other tribunals the Lord Chancellor is involved in the selection of members. Wherever chairmen have to be lawyers the Lord Chancellor either selects them or draws up a 'panel' of qualified people from which the Minister can select individuals. In several cases the Lord Chancellor appoints all members, sometimes independently, sometimes 'after consultation with the Minister' (as is the case with the Mental Health Review Tribunal).

When a department whose policies are under review plays a part in selection, initial screening by officials may well be expected to eliminate potential or actual critics of the department. Obviously we do not know how true this is today. Official records are available relating to the tribunals concerned with appeals against disallowance of unemployment benefit in the 1920s and '30s. These show that ministers and officials took considerable care to avoid selecting members likely to be out of sympathy with prevailing discretionary practices.

Some of the tribunals with regular extensive responsibilities have their own staff, the local valuation courts and the General Commissioners for Income Tax for example, and some are connected with bodies which are independent of the parties involved, notably the 'service committees' in the National Health Service. But many of the major tribunals, including all the local social security tribunals and the immigration 'adjudicators', are serviced by staff drawn from the department which may be said to have an 'interest' in appeal outcomes. Often staff are seconded to work on appeal duties for a limited time. Where these duties are light they may have to combine appeal work with other departmental work.

In the 1950s the Franks Committee carried out a thorough examination of the work of tribunals. They were particularly concerned about the issue of independence from the administration. As a result of the recommendations of that committee, the Council on Tribunals was set up to monitor the activities of tribunals, and to advise the Lord Chancellor. Franks had argued for more than an advisory role for this body, suggesting that it should have supervisory powers. The Council on Tribunals has helped to achieve greater independence for tribunals and has encouraged steps towards greater uniformity in the tribunal system. Nevertheless, there is scope for the development of a much more organized system, with an agency which is independent of individual departments to select members, provide clerks and generally supervise tribunal procedure. In a recent pamphlet, *Tribunals: a Social Court?*, Fulbrook, Brooke and Archer suggest the setting up of a social court, 'bringing tribunals more fully into the administration of justice'. This sort of proposal is designed to deal with the problems of the independence of members and staff together with other alleged abuses of the system to which we must now turn.

It has been argued that the informality of supplementary benefits tribunal procedure may lead to irregularities. Although in recent years the Council on Tribunals has been seeking to regularize tribunal procedure to prevent violations of 'natural justice', there is a relative absence of either legal expertise or extensive knowledge of procedural issues on the parts of chairmen or their clerks. Supplementary benefit tribunal chairmen do not have to be lawyers, and in fact rarely are. Studies of supplementary benefit appeals by Herman, Lister, Lewis and Fulbrook have cited such grounds for disquiet about procedure as clerks playing too active a part in proceedings, failure to pay regard to rules of evidence so that appellants were unsure when to explain their cases or were interrupted while making statements, preferential treatment for official 'presenting officers', and the presence of Department of Health and Social Security 'observers' when tribunals were making decisions. Evidence of this kind has strengthened the argument for the evolution of these tribunals towards more court-like procedures and the introduction of legally qualified chairmen. It has also been suggested that legal representation should be facilitated by the provision of legal aid for the appellants. The present position is that appellants can bring a friend to help them present their case. This individual may, of course, be a lawyer, but without legal aid such representation will be rare except where a 'law centre' agrees to help.

Given the diversity of tribunals, it is not surprising that supplementary benefit tribunals are at one end of a continuum of tribunal 'judicialization', at the other end of which are tribunals like the Lands Tribunal (with various responsibilities in regard to valuation and planning) which function more or less as courts. While many tribunals have lawyer chairmen, and legal representation of appellants is quite common outside the social security group of tribunals, legal aid can only be obtained for the hearing of the Lands Tribunal and the ephemeral and unimportant Commons Commissioners. At the time of writing the Lord Chancellor's Advisory Committee has just recommended that legal aid should be extended to all tribunals which are supervised by the Council on Tribunals.

The arguments for limited procedural rules are that informality helps to put ill-educated lay appellants at ease, and that 'adversary procedures' characteristic of the courts are not appropriate to tribunals in which the appellant's interest and the department's interest cannot be said to be opposed.

Fulbrook, Brooke and Archer, lawyers themselves, recognize that there is some substance to the view that lawyer involvement is a threat to tribunal informality, but argue that their profession is capable of adapting to less formal contexts. Certainly, I have observed rent tribunals where formal adversary procedures, presided over by legally qualified persons and with solicitors representing landlords, have been conducted with an air of informality which has enabled unrepresented tenants to feel at ease in presenting their cases. Yet is it the case that a fair procedure can only be achieved by bringing tribunals under the control of fully trained lawyers? Could not a central, quasi-independent tribunal organization develop procedural codes for those tribunals where decisions are not so much concerned with legal technicalities as with the impartial review of discretion? In this way weaknesses of the existing system might be corrected without transforming tribunals into courts which citizens will wisely avoid unless they are legally represented.

The development of a large corps of welfare rights lawyers ready to work for the poor in opposing the more niggardly or repressive decisions of departments of State is a fine ideal — but is it a practical possibility? Might it not be better to try to improve the more informal tribunal system so that citizens can be their own advocates, and avoid having to call on representatives of what is still, by and large, a conservative and exclusive profession? Bell's study of national insurance tribunals showed that legal representation was rare at these hearings. The most common kind of representatives were from trade unions. This group of representatives had marked success rates and the authors of the study suggested that, while many members and appellants thought legal representation useful, the ideal representative seemed to be 'an accessible person with knowledge, experience and skill, but not someone who, in acting for the appellant, takes over the case completely and assigns him to a purely passive role' (Bell, 1975: 21). Bell and her associates sought to find out the kind of 'tribunal model' appellants had in their minds when commenting on their experiences. They report:

A court model did not emerge. Rather, it was a body with a competent legal chairman balanced by active lay members. Indeed, the significance attached to lay members is one of the important findings of the research.

(Bell, 1975: 21)

They found that a substantial number of appellants criticized the lay members for being too passive, thought the tribunal should be reinforced by additional lay members, and 'wanted to increase the representation of working people who understand conditions in factories and mines' (ibid).

If those who argue that tribunal decision making involves essentially an 'adversary' process are correct then the case for involving lawyers is so much the stronger. It is they who, as advocates, are expert in manipulating such a process, and as judges are experienced in presiding over it. There is a need to consider whether it is an adversary process or, at least, whether this is what it will inevitably tend to become regardless of legal involvement. If it is not inevitably an adversary process, will the best decisions be reached if this development is resisted or if it is encouraged?

Richard White, in his *Social Needs and Legal Action*, argues of supplementary benefits tribunals that 'many claimants and their advisers now see the system as one of contending parties with no atmosphere of service. It is notable that employees of the Commission see it as a hostile act to appeal against a determination' (White, 1973: 27). However, Ruth Lister's interviews with tribunal members suggested that many deny that this is the case and resist the adversary interpretation of typical proceedings. Clearly, the behaviour of the parties on each 'side' is crucial here. It may be argued that the increasing involvement of advocates in tribunal hearings must push the proceedings in an adversary direction; in this sense welfare rights activists secure the procedure they expect. However, both actual advocacy at tribunal hearings and an adversary approach to hearings seem increasingly inevitable as 'welfare rights' orientations develop, and it is unlikely that efforts of tribunal members could turn back the clock in this respect. We must also accept the evidence of many tribunal observers that supplementary benefits 'presenting officers' see themselves as the 'defenders' of decisions. Certainly, back in the days when I was in the National Assistance Board, when welfare rights advocates were almost unknown, there was nevertheless a tendency to see the appeal as a challenge to the department. Indeed one advantageous consequence of this, as Coleman has shown in his *Supplementary Benefits and the Administrative Review of Administrative Action,* is that cases are thoroughly examined beforehand. This is done to ensure that the department has a sound position to defend at the tribunal. The consequence is that many appellants' grievances are met before the hearing.

Yet it may be argued that this adversary attitude within the ranks of the supplementary benefits staff should be discouraged and not simply heightened by emphasizing it in the appeal tribunal. If departmental representatives are to be regularly confronted by lawyers at tribunals, will they not want to have lawyers on their 'side' too? Has the time come for some reduction of the level of conflict? While appellants rightly want to present their cases as effectively as possible, cannot the presenting officers be seen more as witnesses than as defendants? A shift in approach here would have to come from the Supplementary Benefits Commission, with encouragement from the tribunal members. The question which is difficult to answer is, is it possible? Is it inevitable that civil servants will see appeal tribunals as places where their decisions are on trial?

Finally, if reducing the extent of conflict in tribunal hearings *is* possible, is it desirable? It is important to be clear about what is at issue here. Typically, tribunals are not concerned with maladministration; administrative review before hearings weeds out most of the 'bad cases', in the formal legal sense. Rather, they are concerned with discretionary powers and with decisions taken in interpreting the Acts. In her pamphlet about supplementary benefits tribunals Ruth Lister attacked the view of members that they were engaged in 'an exercise in human relations, not in the law' on the grounds that this implied a general ideology of helping the 'deserving'. Of course, this seems to have little to do with 'rights'. I have similarly reacted angrily to a rent tribunal chairman who presented his role as distinguishing 'good' and 'bad' landlords and tenants. Yet what else can discretionary power, or the review of discretionary decisions, involve? Ruth Lister's argument is part of the case against discretion itself. Surely the adversary procedure, or for that matter most judicial decison making, is concerned with black and white, good and evil, the deserving and the undeserving? The law is not very skilful at dealing with shades of grey!

The 'adversary' conception of the tribunal hearing is entirely compatible with the British legal tradition. Some European systems of administrative law provide for an 'inquisitorial process' in which bodies similar to British tribunals have responsibilities to interrogate witnesses in order to arrive at decisions. Some of the tribunal members interviewed by Ruth Lister seemed to be suggesting that theirs was a system of this kind. Yet to ensure the development of an effective 'inquisitorial' rather than an 'adversary' system the official view of the appeal process would have to change markedly, and the tribunals would have to become very much more aware of the implications of such a system. There would still be scope for unease about the impartiality of the clerk, since unbiased expert advice would be required to help the tribunal pursue their 'investigations'.

It may well be that the distinction between legal formalism and informality is made in such a way as regards supplementary benefits tribunals that claimants are insufficiently protected by the procedure. A recent Child Poverty Action Group pamphlet by Fulbrook cites some disturbing findings on the extent to which hearsay evidence, stereotyping and innuendo are allowed to pass unchecked in the presentations of officials to these tribunals. The implication is that tribunal chairmen and members, because of their ignorance of legal procedure and their lack of awareness of the adversary nature of their hearings, are letting their desire for informality trap them into providing insufficient protection for appellants. Tribunal proceedings can very easily get out of hand when one 'party' is in a familiar situation and able to use the hearing very effectively, while the other is very unsure how to proceed and what evidence to present. The chairman is then presented with a dilemma. Should he question the less experienced person to help him bring out his case, or does this involve 'leading' him in ways incompatible with impartial chairmanship? Lawyers can perhaps best cope with this dilemma, but in any case there is a need to clear up some of the uncertainties about the extent to which hearings should be based upon the 'adversary' model.

The last of the major criticisms of the supplementary benefits appeal system concerns the absence of a body of 'case law'. A contrast is often made between that system and the national insurance one, since with the latter there is a two-tier arrangement which provides for the review of local decisions by a central National Insurance Commissioner, who publishes his leading decisions and thereby introduces an element of 'precedent' into the system. Thus, two possible improvements to the supplementary benefits system – a second court of appeal and the development of rules of precedent – could, it is argued, be introduced.

Many tribunal arrangements provide a two-tier system of some kind (from the 'adjudicator' to the Immigration Appeal Tribunal, or from the Local Valuation Court to the Lands Tribunal, for example) but there are other one-tier examples, the Mental Health Review Tribunals and the Rent Assessment Committees being two such. In the case of all tribunals whether one- or two-tier there is the possibility of appeal to the High Court on 'a point of law'. Appeals from tribunals to the High Court are rare.

When a two-tier tribunal system exists a body of case-law is likely to be developed. Without a system of case-law a two-tier system cannot be very effective, since the responses of the top-tier body will be unpredictable. Hence the implication of the introduction of a top-tier tribunal for supplementary benefits would be the establishment of greater consistency within tribunals by means of 'precedent' or judge-made law. Like the courts, the upper-tier body might in some cases refuse to review decisions where discretion had been exercised quite legitimately within the framework of the Acts, but in other situations it might attempt to define precedents to guide future decisions. It would probably do a little of each, varying according to the availability of rule-making criteria. The two-tier system for national insurance operates in this way. Many matters brought before the National Insurance Commissioners involve the exercise of discretionary judgement, for example about conflicting accounts of the circumstances in which people were sacked which affect entitlement to unemployment benefit. Other matters, however, can be regulated by the laying down of precedents by the Commissioner. The National Insurance Commissioner regularly publishes key decisions for the benefit of local tribunals.

The implication of this is that, inasmuch as tribunals are concerned with 'pure' discretion, there is no case for a second body. But inasmuch as there is scope for innovation by means of rule-interpretation and the dictation of precedents, it is important to recognize that this is really a form of legislative activity. A top-tier tribunal for supplementary benefits would be operating quite independently of the Commission, the Minister or Parliament in filling in all the gaps in the statutes. The analogy with national insurance is not entirely satisfactory because this is a more complete system of rules, and in fact even in this area there are 'Ministers' Questions' with which the Commissioner cannot deal. Admittedly, existing divergences of practice between supplementary benefits tribunals, which owe nothing to local circumstances or unique conditions, give cause for concern. But is the right approach to the eradication of these a top-tier tribunal to 'legislate' by laying down case-law? Or is it further Parliamentary legislation to eliminate unnecessary discretion? Not surprisingly, most of the other one-tier systems similarly occur where wide discretionary powers exist. Perhaps the one curious example amongst the tribunals is the two-tier system for immigration appeals, since this is also a high-discretion area in which it is hard to imagine elaborate case-law developing. A study of this new system would throw interesting light on the argument advanced here.

It has already been stressed that appeals on points of law are rare. Though primarily this is because of the absence of disputable *legal* points, the prohibitive costs of such appeals for unaided benefit claimants must have further reduced their occurrence. However, the position is changing a little and more such appeals may occur if legal aid becomes available. The Child Poverty Action Group has already begun to take an interest in appeals of this kind, and has won one interesting victory in a situation where the Supplementary Benefits Commission had developed a rule in place of a statutory requirement to exercise discretion (Cusack, J. R., v Birmingham Tribunal *ex parte* Simper 1973 2 W.L.R. 709). Yet this case is significant in a negative sense since the judicial finding was that officials and the tribunal should have used *discretion*, whereas the most important concern about supplementary benefits procedure is that there is too little predictability – too much discretion. Wade stresses that the courts are committed to a wide concept of discretion:

> A tribunal which *has to exercise discretion* must . . . be careful not to treat itself as bound by its own previous decisions. Unlike a court of law, it must not 'pursue consistency at the expense of the merits of individual cases'.
>
> *(Wade, 1967: 69; my italics)*

The courts

While tribunals have been given fairly extensive coverage in this chapter, very much less will be said about the ordinary courts of law as agencies where individuals can secure the redress of grievances. This should not be taken to imply, however, that Britain lacks an extensive system of administrative law. On the contrary, what is being avoided is the presentation of a great deal of detailed legal information which is rarely of any relevance to the individual citizen with a grievance. While it is the case that administrative agencies have to be aware of the legal framework within which they operate, and cases exist which serve as due warning of the consequences of maladministration, just about the last thing that would occur to an isolated aggrieved citizen is to try to take his case to the High Court. Litigation is an extremely expensive process, and legal aid is (as was shown in Chapter 5) only available when it is deemed that the civil case which the litigant wants to pursue is of a kind which a 'reasonable' man with resources would pursue. Hence, expenditures running into perhaps thousands of pounds are not normally contemplated to secure, for example, a small increase in a social security benefit or to combat a local education authority's refusal to admit a child to a preferred primary school. Traditionally, therefore, the development of administrative case-law has depended upon the pursuit of grievances against public authorities by private enterprises, together with resistance to public innovation by wealthy individuals. Except in the area of damages for serious wrongs, for example medical negligence, individual litigation has been rare. But today welfare rights organizations are becoming interested in pursuing individual cases for collective ends. While it is natural that their main concern has been with tribunals, we may expect to see developments in the courts raising issues which have so far been given little attention.

At the same time legal aid and advice centres extend the possibilities for legal action by ordinary people, and particularly by poor people. Faced as they are with an infinite range of possibilities in relation to their resources, many of these agencies have decided to concentrate on 'class actions', cases where a victory will establish a precedent for many others to go forward and claim rights without difficulty.

Control over administration by the courts is concerned with situations in which authorities act unlawfully, carelessly or unreasonably. These must be defined in relation to the statutes that give them power. In this sense the *ultra vires* principle is important in preventing actions which have not been given statutory authority. The courts have been very concerned to adopt a narrow interpretation of those statutes which give administrative authorities – be they Ministers, officials, or local government – discretionary powers. This has been seen as a curb on extension of State, or administrative, power beyond the intentions of Parliament. Yet it has equally prevented innovative uses of discretion. Judges have been ready to regard as 'unreasonable' some discretionary decisions which appear to be permitted by statute. Perhaps the most famous of such judicial rulings was the decision in 1920 that Poplar Borough Council's statutory right to pay its servants 'such salaries and wages as [they] may think fit' did not extend to giving them the power to pay wages the House of Lords considered 'excessive'. Moreover, this case cannot be dismissed as dated for, in 1955, Birmingham City Council found that its power to impose such fares for its transport as it thought fit did not extend to the provision of free travel for pensioners, and St Pancras Borough Coucil discovered that its discretionary powers to pay subsidies to prevent rent increases for the tenants of derequisitioned houses were similarly limited.

More elusive aspects of judicial control of administration are those situations in which actions have been deemed to be in violation of natural justice. Critical principles here have been the rule against bias, 'that no man should be a judge in his own cause', and the rule which gives a right to a hearing. Clearly these rules provide scope for litigation by aggrieved citizens, but it is important to recognize that it is a procedural and not a substantive right which is at stake. Nevertheless, as paternalism in administration is increasingly resisted we may expect to hear more talk of natural justice.

Readers will need to go elsewhere for a detailed account of administrative law (see the 'Guide to Further Reading' p. 235). The mechanisms for securing the redress of grievances are complex. They have emerged slowly and in a curious form because legislatures have been slow to discard that principle of absolute monarchy which protected the State from legal action, that 'the king can do no wrong'.

Welfare rights

In Chapter 2 emphasis was laid upon the role of the State as the controller of the activities of individuals. It was shown that, as the role of the State increased in importance, much of the emphasis in political debate was upon the extent to which the State ought to restrain individuals from the pursuit of self-interest. The individuals who were being restrained were, in the main, entrepreneurs or, in Marxian terms, the bourgeoisie. Much of the case for restraint emerged simply out of the fact that unlimited self-interest had consequences which, far from advancing the capitalist State to higher and higher levels of achievement, in fact undermined the pursuit of progress. Disregard of considerations of health and safety, and a failure to recognize the need to attend to the welfare of workers, even merely as a 'factor' of production, required the intervention of the State to protect capitalism from itself. This case for the development of State power, and ultimately for the evolution of a welfare state, was reinforced by a recognition that political responses were required to cope with unrest amongst working people. The drive to do this was supported by humanitarian considerations. What, however, rarely entered into political debate was any concern to develop a welfare state on the grounds that fundamental rights were at stake.

The Establishment approach to the development of State services was then a combination of political opportunism and paternalism. The response by British working-class people to this was largely deferential, even when it took apparently socialistic forms. The emphasis was upon *earning* a right to consideration, upon gradualism, and upon self-help. It is significant that insurance came to play a large part in the social security system, and that the emphasis in educational advances was upon equality of opportunity and the right to compete for scarce resources, and not upon absolute equality. Even in the period of mass unemployment between the wars, the distinction between the deserving and the undeserving poor was kept alive to become an obsession in all discussions of the characteristics of the unemployed. Then, with the greater security and prosperity provided by a combination of favourable economic conditions and State protection for a broad section of the working class, people were only too ready again to regard those incompletely protected in this way as an undeserving group, who should be grateful for what little help they received.

The emergence of a 'welfare rights' movement in Britain has therefore entailed a reaction against paternalism and deference, a recognition that many of the political gains of the past came primarily not – as school history books so often taught –

because of the humanitarianism of the élite but through a fear of the consequences of disregarding a working class who were growing in political importance. It has gradually been recognized that underprivileged groups have to take steps to assert their rights.

Yet, even here, to emphasize a changing class consciousness is only to tell one part of the story. The other part has its roots in a middle-class intellectual movement more characteristic of traditional approaches to social problems in Britain. In the late fifties young intellectuals in Britain, many of them trained in the social sciences, began to react against the complacency of the age. They reacted against what they saw as a society in which capitalist institutions were propped up by links with America, requiring uncritical support of the 'Cold War', and a Welfare State which had involved the buying off of industrial unrest rather than the eradication of poverty. They attacked nuclear weapons, the American alliance, and the neglect of the Third World. Those who were interested in domestic social issues began to show that there were still many gaps in the Welfare State.

Out of the experience of direct political action, particularly within the Campaign for Nuclear Disarmament, and the awareness of the condition of the poor provided by social research, arose commitments to create new pressures to demonstrate social needs. This entailed engagement with the poor, recognizing that they needed to make their own claims and overcome their own apathy to secure really firm gains. Yet even here a dilemma emerged, a continuing point of difficulty for the 'welfare rights movement'. Individuals among the poor fail to get many benefits to which, even under the present system, they are entitled. They also confront discretion, which, as we have seen, can be exercised in varying ways to provide varying amounts of benefit or service. Should welfare rights movements, therefore, concentrate on helping individuals to gain all they can from the existing system, or develop group political action to improve or change the system? And if the emphasis is upon the latter, to what extent is the system susceptible to piecemeal reform? Should concentration be upon exploring the detailed weaknesses of welfare measures or should some more wholesale attack be launched upon the political and economic system which determines the main characteristics of the 'Welfare State'?

The wider political dilemma outlined here will be examined further in the last chapter. Here, concern is with the narrower issues, the resolution of the potential conflict between individual and group action. This tactical dilemma is particularly a problem for those who, not in need themselves, commit themselves to working with the poor. Individual poor people will obviously make their own choices on whether to go for personal immediate gains or for more long-term change; often they don't need to choose, but can do both. But outsiders committed to the welfare rights movement have to recognize that because the underprivileged are apathetic and ignorant any role they play will have an educational component. The poor themselves are the frontline troops in the battle for better benefits, but which battle are they going to be encouraged to join? Any struggle for rights may have a politicizing impact if the individuals learn directly how the system has operated to their disadvantage in the course of securing attention for their personal grievances. But where gains are made 'for' people rather than 'by' people, through middle-class advisers who are skilful at 'working the system', wider perspectives may not be acquired by the experience. Yet it is natural that any middle-class 'welfare rights activist' who perceives poor people with problems will tend to seek to eradicate those problems by the most efficient means.

Middle-class welfare rights activists find that they can build relationships with decision-makers which enable them to solve many individual problems smoothly and efficiently, without recourse to appeals or to any forms of direct action. They may recognize that more militant tactics may alienate officials and delay their work of eliminating individual grievances. Even such a militant movement as the London squatters' campaign has been able to move from confrontation with local authorities to peaceful accommodation in some areas. For example, the Lewisham Family Squatters' Association secured an agreement with the local borough council in which 'half-life' houses are maintained and occupied by an organization which applies principles of management acceptable to the authorities.

Radicals grow uneasy at the development of working relationships between welfare rights groups and official bodies. They see depoliticization occurring, and some degree of 'co-option' of activists by the authorities. Thus, Hilary Rose has suggested, when middle-class advocates appear at tribunals:

> There is a tendency for a form of middle-class co-option to emerge, whereby the educated and the expert enter into a compassionate complicity, where the chairman and the well-briefed middle-class representative retreat into an expert's world, leaving the appellant no longer an actor in his own destiny but merely the object of the case at issue.
>
> *(Rose, 1973: 411)*

It is, of course, easy to argue that middle-class involvement in working-class radical movements should be avoided, but this is a hard ideal to achieve. Even where movements come close to it, the process of role-differentiation, as Michels showed in his classic study of socialist movements (*Political Parties*), tends to create an élite group who develop life styles and social roles which differentiate them from their rank-and-file followers.

Associations of claimants for State benefits, 'Claimants' Unions', face severe organizational dilemmas. Jordan, in his book *Paupers*, has shown how unstable their membership can be because bodies of people in need of benefits, but below pension age, are inherently changing groups. Claimants' Unions have rightly recognized that they cannot expect to form elaborate organizations while avoiding domination by a non-claimant group. The rise and fall of individual 'unions' is inevitable.

Hilary Rose, in her article 'Up against the Welfare State', has identified what she calls 'the tyranny of structurelessness'. Publicity about Claimants' Unions is, without any clear role definitions, dominated by a small number of self-appointed spokesmen. Furthermore, she argues:

> The rhetoric of the movement denies that leadership as such does exist, yet the reality is that it is concealed in the friendship

networks which serve to link the disparate unions both geographically and over time. While the unions were right to reject the situation whereby office holding becomes the privatized property of the office holders, they have moved to the other extreme where instead of an at least visible tyranny of office holders, they have created the invisible tyranny of the network.

(Rose, 1974: 200)

Claimants' Unions have to some extent modelled themselves on the informal radical factions which operate inside trade unions. They aspire to link up with these manifestations of the working-class movement, and in a few situations where benefits for strikers has been a key 'rights' issue they have forged such links temporarily. However, their difficulty in developing a comparable approach to trade unions is that they are organizations of consumers not producers. As such they lack weapons to use in pursuit of their demands. In order to avoid either the conventional middle-class pressure group model, or the pattern of individual conflict discussed above, they have to develop direct action weapons. Yet the only such weapon they possess, the disruption of the work of State agencies, offers little threat to the system. Indeed, in many ways the only major sufferers from such disruptions are the claimants themselves. The disruptive tactic is therefore a difficult one to sustain. While Hilary Rose sees the Claimants' Unions as making a contribution 'to the working-class movement in revealing the nature of the Welfare State and in resisting its oppression', it is obvious from her article that they are a very fragile development, desperately needing allies from elsewhere.

Not surprisingly, therefore, apart from the squatters, the welfare rights movements that have attracted most attention are linked with two organizations which lie much closer to the middle-class type of radical political movement. These are the Child Poverty Action Group and Shelter. Both organizations have faced dilemmas about their roles. The Child Poverty Action Group started as a pressure group in the classic mould, committed to increasing political awareness of the facts about the inadequacies of the social security system. Then gradually it moved into a welfare advice role. Later, as this role developed, it enabled experience in dealing with claimants' problems to be used to support arguments, in its journal *Poverty* and in pamphlets, about the weaknesses of the system. More recently, work with claimants has led to the development of another strategy, the use of appeals and high court cases to try to force removal of abuses in the system. CPAG has today developed from a purely London-based pressure group into a national organization with a number of active, partly autonomous local groups. At the local level some links have been forged with claimants' organizations, but these tend to be suspicious of an organization which is dominated by the middle class, many of them academics working in the social administration field.

CPAG has had a less stormy history than the other leading welfare rights group, Shelter. That organization has faced continual role definition problems. Originally set up to raise funds to secure accommodation for the homeless and ill-housed, it gradually became engaged not only in trying to convince the public of the problems in this field but also in demonstrating the inadequacies of government policies. Its local branches and some of the local projects it set up have found a need to concern themselves with details of housing law and local authority policies in two ways: first, to back up the general assault on failures to provide sufficient housing with detailed evidence about the existing status of poor tenants and the lack of rights of the homeless; second, to supplement the inevitably puny contribution of its housing association activities to the housing stock with advice to the many who approach it for help.

The overall scarcity of housing has tended to undermine the relevance of some of the practical activities. Trying to help tenants and to reform landlord and tenant law has had to occur in a context in which the weak position of the tenant in the market limits the usefulness of legal approaches to these issues. Attacking local authorities' allocation policies, similarly, is an important activity, yet much of the arbitrariness in this field of administration can be attributed as much to scarcity of resources as to disregard of rights. Hence, while Shelter's main dilemma has been whether to concentrate on housing associations or on pressure-group activities (see Seyd), a secondary issue for local groups has been whether they should carry out work on individual housing problems too. In some cases groups have succeeded in getting local authorities, often backed by urban aid funds from central government, to take on the housing aid and advice functions, either directly or (more satisfactorily since this work often entails pressure on the local authorities as landlords) by backing semi-autonomous agencies.

There are many other local groups which have engaged in activities in the welfare rights field. These groups have often grown up as part of community activities with wider aims, about which more will be said in the last chapter. One rapidly growing branch of social work, community work, though centrally concerned with the kinds of collective activities which are to be discussed later, has nevertheless found welfare rights activities of some importance in any programme of work designed to meet needs in deprived communities and encourage community mobilization.

Community workers, however, are not the only group of social workers to give attention to welfare rights. Those engaged in work with individuals are increasingly concerned with identification of unclaimed benefits, intervention with other agencies on behalf of clients, advocacy at appeal tribunals, and the encouragement of welfare rights demands. These are activities which some social workers regard as undesirable extensions of social work activity, either because their other responsibilities are considered to leave little room for such tasks or because they are suspicious of the political implications of an active role which may bring them into conflict with public agencies, including perhaps the other departments of their own authority. Of course, as this discussion has already made clear, there are a variety of possible roles in relation to welfare rights. It is hard to see how objection can be raised to activities merely aimed at ensuring that clients acquire hitherto unclaimed benefits. The problems arise at the level where the 'rights' are a matter of dispute or where tactics involve the harassment of agencies.

Social workers also worry about the extent to which the

advocacy of the client viewpoint by means of informal contacts with benefit-giving agencies leaves them open to 'co-option'. They may develop a reciprocal relationship with another agency in which, in return for favours for some clients, who are regarded as more deserving, they may be expected to 'cool out' others, regarded as less worthy. Their agencies are also alternative sources of benefits which are the statutory responsibility of the Supplementary Benefits Commission. This is a state of affairs that many want to avoid but, since 1963, when grant-giving powers were provided for social workers, some awkward and anomalous overlaps between them and supplementary benefits have arisen. Hence social workers may not only have to sort out the strategy issues outlined above – to what extent they should intervene *for* people with the social security department and what methods they should use – but also to decide whether they should insist on a struggle to get the national relief agency to pay to meet some clients' special needs or use their own agency's resources. Their own agency may have granted them discretionary power to decide on payments, or it may require them to make a case (and perhaps fight) for resources in the control of their superiors. All this may be very confusing to their clients, who in any case may see both social security and social services as different branches of 'them'. The whole situation may add up to one in which clients see obtaining help as depending upon securing the right people to speak for them ('my social worker will sort things out for me') and certainly not as a matter of 'obtaining rights'. Inasmuch as social workers may play crucial roles in intervening with other agencies on behalf of clients, the view of some social workers that they are essentially outside the 'system' and alongside their clients in battles with 'them' can involve a measure of self-deception, and unexpected ambiguities in their relations with clients.

This problem for social workers is one that is likely to face any State-supported agency which tries to develop a 'welfare rights' role. Community Relations Officers have found that they sometimes face opposition from the local authorities, who provide some of their funds, when they intervene on behalf of immigrants with grievances against local government departments. The staff of the similarly hybrid Community Development Projects, jointly backed by central and local government, have also run into similar difficulties. Those who have the opportunity to try to finance welfare rights activities with public funds have always to risk this sort of opposition when they embarrass public agencies, despite the fact that those agencies proclaim an ideal of impartial service and a commitment to a comprehensive programme to meet needs. The dilemma for would-be welfare rights activists is that, since people in need of help naturally cannot pay for it, and private charity to support such activity is rare, State agencies are the most likely source of funds.

It must be stressed, to be fair, that both central government (by means of efforts like Community Development Projects) and some local authorities (by financing centres to provide legal or housing aid and advice, for example) have recently taken some quite promising steps towards the financing of what may broadly be termed welfare rights activities. But these steps cannot themselves be expected to lead to dramatic changes, if only because any government that was prepared to finance welfare rights activities on a wide scale would doubtless also be prepared to reform the social security system in such a way as to make much welfare rights advocacy unnecessary. It has been shown that most welfare rights activity has emerged from the work of pressure groups. Most welfare rights activists will acknowledge that what they really want is not a claimants' advocate in every social security office but the elimination of those selective benefits which provide the public with such ill-defined rights.

Chapter 8
Planning: Its Impact upon People

Introduction

Clearly a discussion of the State, administration and the individual needs to look at the activities of the State which are designed to affect the lives of large groups of individuals, up to the level of a nation as a whole. Yet to do this issues have to be introduced that are difficult to confine within the framework of this book. Logically a book about the State, administration and the individual should be about every field of public policy. Defence or foreign policy has an impact upon the individual, while the management of the economy has enormous significance for the individual citizen. Yet it would be foolish to try to deal with all these fields of activity in this short book. Instead, the focus is upon those aspects of public administration in which individuals and State officials are brought frequently into contact with each other.

This chapter, therefore, will concentrate upon those aspects of planning for collective needs which most tangibly involve the individual. Land use, or town and country planning, will receive the most attention. At the end of the chapter some consideration will be given to issues in the planning of services and the use of resources which are increasingly bound up with more 'physical' land use planning. These are also, of course, connected with what is probably the most important kind of planning of all, that concerned with the economy. So this must not go unmentioned. However, economic planning raises so many other political and administrative issues, requiring a very different and more detailed treatment in a separate book, that it cannot be adequately discussed here. It needs to be noted as an area where the relationship between the individual and the State is at its most tenuous, despite the fact that the decisions made often have a more fundamental impact upon individual welfare than any other decision by the State.

The development of town and country planning

'Town and country planning' is perhaps the most neutral name to give to the kind of planning to be discussed. Often it is called just 'planning', a shortened title which it is convenient to give it here. Yet it is important neither to imply that it is the only real kind of planning, nor, as Eversley does in his book *The Planner in Society*, to suggest that it readily embraces all other forms of planning. Alternative names for this kind of planning are 'land use planning' or 'physical planning' but these names tend to be resented by contemporary town and country planners who are trying to get away from such relatively narrow conceptions of their work.

However, to provide an accurate account of the impact of town and country planning upon individual citizens it is important not to lose sight of the extent to which it has been, and largely remains, a concern to limit damage to the physical environment which motivates many of the activities described as 'planning'. Books on planning often quote an exalted line of founding fathers from Thomas More (of the original Utopia), through Robert Owen and the nineteenth-century builders of model communities, to Ebenezer Howard and the Garden Cities movement in the present century. These theories, schemes and visions have contributed to an ideal of comprehensive planning, cherished by many professional planners. Yet the planning legislation, and the practical activities which are involved in translating plans into action, have tended to bring planning down to a much more mundane level. At this level the crucial heritage of contemporary planning is the Victorian concern to control 'nuisances', as they discovered the negative effects of uncontrolled urbanization and industrialization. Primarily, this concern was with the control of disease, as it was discovered that infections spread in the unplanned and overcrowded new cities. But there was also an influential group of writers on planning who saw urban renewal as a crucial means of attacking immorality and crime, seeing squalid and unplanned cities as particular sources of vice.

Concern to limit the worst abuses of the industrial revolution was reinforced by a concern to protect the country from the town in a society in which a landed ruling class has been of much importance. The successful industrialists sought to emulate the landed gentry by securing country retreats for themselves. This aspiration to escape the town began, by the end of the nineteenth century, to be shared by the middle classes and even the more prosperous of the working class. Improvements in transportation facilitated moves from urban centres to growing suburbs. In the inter-war period new overspill estates and ribbon developments of cheap owner-occupied housing intensified this movement. Finally, in more recent times widespread car ownership has made escape from the cities more feasible, at least for weekends or holidays, for a large proportion of the population.

The first significant step towards land use planning in Britain was the Town Planning Act of 1909, which Allison portrays as 'something in that it was an attempt on a national scale to use the control of land use for the solution of a major social problem, the condition of the urban proletariat' (Allison, 1975: 3). This, then, is firmly in the Victorian tradition of limiting 'the worst abuses of the industrial revolution'. It was a weak and permissive first step, however, towards a more comprehensive approach. Significantly, therefore, the pressure to improve on it, and widen it to play a part in protecting 'the country from the town', developed in the inter-war period. The Town and Country Planning Act of 1947, therefore, was very much more concerned to embrace both of these objectives. The philosophy of the 1947 Act is still dominant in British planning.

The implementation of the main objectives of planning, described above, has brought planners up against new issues requiring more positive approaches than the controlling functions implied by limiting industrial abuses and protecting the countryside. As the alternative to city growth has been overspill and the development of satellite areas much planning controversy has centred upon issues connected with this process. Battles have been fought over the areas in which overspill should occur, and about the kinds of overspill which are welcome. Early beneficiaries from the development of suburban England and from the emergence of 'commuter villages' have become, not unnaturally, fierce protectors of their environments from later would-be beneficiaries. The connection between the political battles over issues like this and the 'utopian' theories of the town and country planners is often a tenuous one, more apparent in the rhetoric of the planners than in the reality of planning enquiries.

More recently, attention has increasingly been given to the need to revitalize the inner-cities. Here at last, it might be believed, was an opportunity for planners disappointed by the extent to which the 'garden cities' ideal for overspill had degenerated into sordid class-conscious political battles. Here was a chance to undo the damage done to the urban environment by the Victorians. Yet here, once again, truly comprehensive attempts to undertake planning have been undermined by more immediate and practical political considerations. A critical problem, one that has tended continually to make it difficult to achieve planning goals, is the fact that in Britain planning operates within a mixed economy. Indeed, planning is seen as a crucial facet of the mixed economy. The consequence of this is that urban redevelopment has been a partnership between public and private enterprise. Many local authorities, eager to share the burden of risk, have involved private developers at an early stage. Those that have operated on their own have nevertheless had to take into account the ultimate needs of private firms as tenants of shops, offices and factories. Many have had their hands forced by private developers eager to build in advance of any comprehensive planning by the local authority. Where planning in the 'fifties had not moved beyond a general 'zoning' stage, local authorities were powerless to influence anything more than the most general map of their town, together with matters of a physical nature such as densities and road spaces.

Planning and the public

Such development as has occurred in planning, from a negative concept, restricting activity to the curbing of 'nuisances', to a positive one, has been within a political context in which the development of comprehensive approaches has been very difficult. Yet town and country planners have been popularly regarded as 'utopians' pushing around an unwilling populace to conform with their visions. Why should this be? Perhaps it is because, as planners have tried to justify their activities with a rhetoric, with a view of themselves as the builders of the 'new Jerusalem', they have tended to convince the public that they are more powerful than they really are. It is important to bear in mind that where planning has had a considerable impact upon the shape of our society, it has often not been the impact the planners had in mind. Planning activities have unleashed forces that planners themselves have found hard to control. Planners have often been 'powerful' in terms of the success in disrupting people's lives, without at the same time being 'powerful' in attaining their own goals.

A more concrete exploration of the relation between myth and reality in the characterization of planners must involve looking at their impact upon various kinds of people. We have to consider three different kinds of situations in relation to planning processes: those in which the citizen is seeking permission for development, those in which he is directly affected by a development, and those in which he is indirectly affected.

One general difficulty about relating planning to public interests is that when critical planning decisions are made, they are often not perceived as having any clear relation to specific individual interests. At the core of British planning legislation are requirements for local authorities to draw up plans for the areas they govern. Hence one of the crucial innovations in the 1947 Town and Country Planning Act was that

planning was to be no longer merely a regulative function. Development plans were to be prepared for every area in the country. These were to outline the way in which each area was to be developed, or, where desirable, preserved.

(*Cullingworth, 1974: 32-3*)

Similarly, the most important contemporary statute, the 1968 Town and Country Planning Act, builds upon the principles of 1947 and requires the drawing up of 'structure', 'action area' and 'local' plans. The central problem with comprehensive planning along these lines is the gap, both in time and in the extent of conceptualization, between planning and the implementation of plans. The initial process of drawing up plans is a long and complex one, punctuated by consultations between the various authorities involved, including central government. Whereas under the old legislation members of the public often found it difficult to secure any right to consultation about these plans, the new Act makes provision for public participation (this will be discussed more fully in the last chapter).

The problem for individuals is that the planning process is an abstract one in which specific future developments are set out in a relatively vague, even hypothetical form. Furthermore, some of the projected developments, or measures taken to maintain existing use, may be of little direct interest to people when plans are drawn up. Maps consisting of zones in which particular kinds of development will or will not be allowed mean little to individuals when specific changes in the environment are not being immediately considered. At a much later stage people discover that they have a more specific interest at stake, but that much of the decision making which they want to influence has already been completed. Their own freedom to develop, or their capacity to resist development, is already limited by global policy decisions which occurred at a stage when they did not have, or did not recognize, a specific interest.

In the past, this problem has been seen as being exacerbated by the extent to which planning decisions are taken in secret, with a minimum of public participation. The 1968 Act and the Skeffington Report on Public Participation in Planning made some attempt to rectify this. There are some intractable problems however. While very firm commitments on future land use are undesirable because of the rigidity they give to development patterns, looser commitments create expectations which are not necessarily fulfilled. Two issues which cause particular problems are the impact of planning decisions on land values and 'planners' blight'. There seems little doubt that some of the secrecy surrounding planning and the vagueness of long-term plans reflects the planners' desire to evade these problems, though the actual effect of secretive behaviour may be to complicate rather than decrease them.

Planning decisions have a crucial impact upon land values. If a piece of agricultural land is within an area where development is to be allowed, its value to its owner is naturally enhanced. Conversely, a zoning scheme which decrees that such land is to remain in a 'green belt' denies any similar opportunity for profit. There are many other more complicated ways in which property values are affected when projected roads, housing estates or industrial areas are drawn upon planners' maps.

The phenomenon of 'planners' blight' occurs when there is uncertainty about the outcome of planning decisions. This is particularly the case where an inner-city area is scheduled for redevelopment. Then house owners find they cannot sell properties on the open market, and home improvement tends to involve a pointless expenditure of money or effort. Accordingly, a run-down area, appearing on a plan as needing redevelopment at some unspecified time in the future, rapidly declines so that specific action becomes increasingly necessary. The 1968 Act tries to avoid this by replacing the designation of relatively small redevelopment areas by the specification of 'action areas'. These are areas, typically larger than those hitherto designated for urban renewal, where redevelopment is possible, but where equally 'rehabilitation' may occur as an alternative. While this may prevent planners' blight in as intense a form as in the past, an atmosphere of uncertainty must still hang over an 'action area'. These two issues of land values and planners' blight illustrate difficulties in relating the long run to the short run in planning.

When citizens are seeking planning permission they naturally tend to perceive the negative aspects of planning. For the individual who is concerned with a small development – an extension to his house, for example – the relationship between his interest and planning policy is often particularly obscure. He has to cope with the local authority both as planning authority and as agency responsible for enforcement of the building regulations, and he may well not distinguish these functions. Equally confusing will be the relationship between officials and councillors in determining the outcome of his application. The 1968 Act enables councillors to delegate to their officers responsibility for giving approval to planning applications, but all cases of refusal or conditional approval still have to be considered by a council committee.

Any local authority has to deal with a large number of 'small' planning applications. Cullingworth argues that the pressing volume of work of this kind increases the danger of decisions which do not accord with planning objectives, and makes good relations with planning applicants (particularly unsuccessful ones) difficult to obtain. He suggests that the terms in which planning refusals are commonly worded tend to confirm applicants' suspicions that their cases have been inadequately considered:

> Phrases such as 'detrimental to amenity' or 'not in accordance with the development plan' . . . mean little to the individual applicant. He suspects that his case has been considered in general terms rather than in the particular detail which he naturally thinks important in his case.
>
> *(Cullingworth, 1974: 296)*

A former colleague of the author's joined the planning committee on being elected to a local authority, hoping to be involved in *planning* in the full sense. He left the committee after a year, disillusioned since he had had to give up an enormous amount of time – the planning committee met more often than any other – to sessions that consisted of no more than the presentation, at two-minute intervals, of minor planning applications that the committee members had neither the time, nor inclination, nor expertise to consider properly.

An unsuccessful planning applicant can appeal to the Secretary of State for the Department of the Environment. There are several thousand such appeals each year, and about a third of them are likely to succeed. Although the Secretary of State may order a local enquiry, the procedure for most minor matters is more informal, no more than a site visit and correspondence. Under recent legislation many minor matters can be dealt with by semi-autonomous inspectors, appointed by the Department of the Environment, and need not go to the Secretary of State. This both simplifies and shortens the procedure, and eliminates the possibility, which otherwise exists in connection with this curious semi-judicial procedure, of an inspector's recommendation being overturned by the Secretary of State.

It is necessary to explain why this has been called a semi-judicial procedure. All the way through the planning procedure the authorities involved are required to operate in conformity with the rules of natural justice. Their decision-making procedures are required to be fair, and their decisions to be in conformity with existing policy. Yet the very fact that both the local authorities and the Department of the Environment are *policy-making* bodies means that they are to some extent 'judges in their own causes', ensuring that developments are in conformity with *their own* policies. Furthermore, as Jowell has pointed out, the policies which are being interpreted may relate to standards rather than involve specific rules:

> Where the standard specifically incorporates the question of individual taste, the difficulty of standard application is sharply illustrated. Thus a judge was not able to enforce a covenant restricting the erection of 'any new building of unseemly description'. Planning for aesthetically pleasing architectural standards poses similar problems.
>
> *(Jowell, 1973: 204)*

In this area of administrative discretion, as in the areas of discretion involving matters of individual welfare, there is a reluctance to formulate rules or to allow decisions to be treated as precedents. Mandelkar has described the prevailing Departmental attitude, as follows:

Conditions vary so fundamentally from case to case and from one part of the country to another that it would be impossible, if not wrong, to draft rules that would hold good uniformly. The basic problem is that a variety of factors operate in a planning case; the art of making a decision lies in the striking of the proper balance.

(Mandelkar, 1962)

Therefore, the Department of the Environment's guidelines to planning authorities consist of little more than the listing of crucial factors to be considered, together with certain 'rules of thumb which will help select those which should preponderate' (ibid).

Although the appeal procedure is simple and informal, the individual small applicant for planning permission is, in many cases, likely to be deterred by the further bother, delay and cost in mounting an appeal. Without expensive expert help he will find it difficult to contest the local authority's reasons for its decision. The large-scale developer, on the other hand, will have used considerable professional assistance in the preparation of an application. At all stages the procedure adopted by a large developer will probably have been different. He will have engaged in discussions with the planning staff of the local authority from an early stage, and will have formed a fairly clear idea of what would and what would not secure approval. His role will be very much that of a *negotiator* with the authority rather than simply an *applicant* for planning permission. Elkin in his *Politics and Land Use Planning* provides a clear account of just such a negotiating process over the development of Centrepoint in London. In such a situation, indeed, a developer may be in the strong position of knowing what he wants while the planner is in the weaker position of knowing only what he cannot allow. As one of the planners interviewed by Elkin said:

Developers have enormous influence because planners don't have the answers. When a developer knows what he wants it is difficult to stop him. Often the planner doesn't know his own mind.

(Elkin, 1974: 158)

Planning, however limited and irrational a process it may be, has an enormous impact upon the capacity of one individual to make a profit which is unavailable to other individuals. It therefore raises some very difficult questions of equity, in which the State's activities may alter the balance of gains and losses as between individuals in ways which are seldom intended by the planning exercise in itself. Hence governments, particularly Labour ones, have attempted to prevent large profits from accruing to developers. Their actions have been motivated not merely by desires to prevent large windfall gains, but by concern about the disturbance of the market for land which comes about as a consequence of planning.

Once there are planning policies, a mechanism is set in motion which grants gains to some people while denying them to others. If there are two farmers each owning fields on the fringe of a large town, in a free market they may compete to attract developers and the resulting competition will affect sale prices. If, however, a planning decision that his area should be in a 'green belt' prevents one of these farmers from offering land to developers, the other farmer will make a gain that the first is unable to make. Furthermore, the element of competition will have been removed. An artificial scarcity will have been created which will inflate the price paid for the development land. One farmer will have been prevented from making a gain, the other will have made an enhanced gain, and the purchaser (almost certainly the ultimate purchasers of buildings put on the land) will have had to pay an increased cost. The reaction of the State, or planning authority, may be to say 'so be it'. But it may equally decide that equity requires the compensation of the farmer who cannot sell, or the taxation of the one who can sell, or the subsidization of those who pay the inflated land costs. Directly or indirectly, governments have at various times attempted to achieve all three things. Yet as soon as they intervene in this way, the consequence is some further distortion of the market. They are still struggling to resolve this problem, one to which there is no ideal consensual solution. Hence the ideological content of the debate about the control or taxation of land values, where views differ as to who is to benefit and who is to be penalized.

The 1947 Town and Country Planning Act sought to tackle this issue by imposing a 100 per cent tax on profits arising out of 'development value'. At the same time a compensation scheme was devised effectively to buy out all development rights in land, so that while those able to develop were compensated, so too were those prevented by planning decisions from developing. The implementation of this scheme ran into difficulties. The tax was intended to prevent land prices rising over existing use values but instead it was passed on in increased prices. The calculation of the compensation scheme also posed problems. Hence in 1954 these parts of the 1947 Act were repealed.

The intense land development activity in the late 1950s and early 1960s, occurring after the ending of building controls, pushed prices up very considerably in a market where planning limited the land available. Hence, in 1967 the new Labour government introduced the 'betterment levy' to tax development profits. This was set at just 40 per cent of the gain. It was planned to raise the levy later to 45 per cent and then to 50 per cent. Once more the success of the scheme as an attempt to limit the rise in land prices, and to cope with the equity issue raised above, was undermined by the tendency for the tax to be 'passed on' to the final owners or occupiers of the land.

Now the Community Land Act offers a form of public ownership of future development land. This raises again problems about compensation of those who lose development opportunities. Throughout the post-war period the other alternative policy, the subsidization of those who pay the inflated land costs, has taken various forms. Between 1947 and 1959, where compulsory purchase occurred it was at 'existing use' values and not 'market prices'. This meant that public developments benefited but private ones did not. Government attempts to help council house building by subsidies, and to aid owner occupiers by abolishing Schedule A income tax, granting tax relief for mortgages and subsidizing building societies, are also measures which may be regarded as attempts to compensate those who are affected by the inflated cost of land.

The autonomy of planners?

Reference has already been made to the importance of utopian visions of a more ordered society in the creation of town planning ideology. When looking at the more positive aspects of planning upon individuals, at planning *for* people rather than planning as the restriction of private development, it is necessary to look more closely at this ideology. Two recent books have exposed the characteristics of town planning ideology, and have examined its implications for individual citizens. Jon Gower Davies, in his book *The Evangelistic Bureaucrat*, has seen the planner as an arrogant individual with a vision of the ideal society, and a belief that the 'new Jerusalem' can be created if only the ignorant public can be prevented from obstructing his work. He argues:

> Planning has its mythology, its personified precepts, in which the profession's heroes are shown defeating the profession's foes, in which the great triumphs are shown being accomplished in the face of malevolent or factious opposition, and in which the ultimate righteousness of the cause is shown as defeating the mean and ignoble band of persecutors.
>
> *(Gower Davies, 1974: 94)*

Gower Davies goes on to argue that planners have grown to 'expect' this kind of opposition. This expectation provides the planner with a 'device to enable him to deny the rationality of the criticism, for what is *inevitable is also irrelevant*'. Armed with such a crusading vision of his activities, the planner goes on to stress the need to see planning issues as wholes, and to create environments which are aesthetically satisfying in total. These are criteria for his activities which render criticism particularly difficult. Opponents who attack aspects of plans can be accused of not perceiving the total situation, while, as has been argued, judgements on standards are peculiarly difficult to dispute. When faced by such opposition planners will tend to present themselves as outside politics, with the interests of the whole community at heart. Gower Davies cites two statements by planners which particularly emphasize this sort of claim:

As planners we realize, whatever political opinions we have outside our job, that somehow something or other has to be done to
safeguard the fundamental interests of the community . . .

Chartered town planners belong to one of the very few professions which are wholly devoted to increasing human welfare.

(Gower Davies, 1974: 96)

James Simmie, in his discussion of the ideology of town planning, argues that planners' ideologies are quite different in
character, determined not so much by utopian visions as by
class interests:

First, they spring from an ideological view of the nature of society
which, in British terms, is associated with those who extol the
virtues of the market place. Second, they serve the particular
interest of the better-off classes and town planners themselves
rather than, for example, those of disadvantaged groups.

(Simmie, 1974: 193)

Can these two apparently opposing views be reconciled? To
some extent it is true that Gower Davies overemphasizes the
'evangelistic' character of planning ideology, as opposed to
Simmie, who sees that planning is rooted very firmly within
bourgeois politics. The trite, but readily forgotten, point must
be made that planners, like other professionals, are a mixed
group of people with varying orientations to their work. However, there are two ways in which the views of Gower Davies and
Simmie can be seen to be quite compatible with each other.
First, because there is a gap between planning rhetoric and
planning reality, which is recognized in Gower Davies's book,
and which is brought out even more strongly in the work of his
colleague Norman Dennis. Second, because there is a distinction
to be made in our society between those who tend to be *planned
for*, and thus experience planners at their most 'evangelistic', and
those who may be said to be *planned with*, and thus enmesh planners willingly or unwillingly in a middle-class political process.
These two related points must be examined more clearly.

The earlier discussion of the impact of planning upon individuals stressed that there are many problems about relating
planning output to objectives. Successive Town and Country

Planning Acts and successive generations of planners have been trying to make their activities more comprehensive. Let us beg the question a little and look at the hypothetical career experiences of a planner whose ideals match up to Gower Davies's portrait of the 'evangelistic bureaucrat'. He will have discovered early in his career that Parliament has not given him all the powers he wants and that his own local councillors are eager to restrain him further. His response to these constraints is to argue both nationally through the Town Planning Institute and locally with his committee, that he needs more powers. To make a case to obtain those powers he has to claim to be able to cope with the total situation.

In claiming such omniscience the planner will expose himself to attack in a number of ways. First, historically speaking, the planning profession, under the strong influence of architecture, found it easier to give their 'total' visions a physical dimension rather than a social one. They readily came under attack, therefore, for insensitivity to the needs of the people whose lives they were transforming. The criticism by Michael Young and Peter Willmott of the way in which the people of Bethnal Green were mindlessly decanted into the overspill estates of Essex became the example for any number of attacks upon redevelopment, new housing estates and New Towns. The fact that there were obviously many things wrong with new communities, despite the trouble that had been taken to design the physical environment, gave force to these criticisms.

The response of the evangelistic bureaucrat was to take on board these criticisms and to become a social planner too. It was just a matter of building 'social needs' into his model. There are, however, no easy prescriptions for doing this. The work of Young and Willmott, supplemented by a few other small studies, does not provide a basis for building assumptions about social needs into plans. The real message of Young and Willmott's book was that efforts need to be made to find out what people want. This is a slow, cumbersome and difficult business. Furthermore, it tends to reveal that people differ in what they want. Hence, doing this will tend to complicate enormously the planning process. Our evangelistic bureacrat's decision-making problems are difficult enough without this. So, where he does not – as Simmie alleges – just retreat to physical planning, he tends to hide behind the argument that what people *need* is not necessarily what people *want*.

Even the process of finding out what people need is complex enough. Increasingly these days planners are committed to surveys of the population in areas where redevelopment is planned. However, Norman Dennis has shown in his two studies of Sunderland, *People and Planning* and *Public Participation and Planners' Blight*, how crude and perfunctory information-gathering by planners may in fact be. In Sunderland planners presumed to make statements about community needs on the basis of the most inadequate survey data. Hence the evangelistic bureaucrat, committed to a large vision of the future and forced to persuade, not the people affected by his plans, but his political masters, that he has a command of the total situation, may well be tempted to prefer assumptions to facts. In all kinds of planning today, economic and resource planning as much as land use planning, those who claim comprehensive approaches develop models of the 'system' in which many of the variables are assumptions filled in, because of the need for a total approach, wherever facts are absent. The claim to rationality in planning often seems to rest upon the possession of sophisticated models, not of adequate facts.

The suggestion that planners need to know more about what people want has been emphasized in contemporary discussions of participation. What is particularly threatening to the evangelistic bureaucrat is that participation introduces more politics to a process he is already inclined to regard as over-politicized. Trying to find out what people want is likely to involve activating a hitherto passive element in the planning process. After all, those who are already participating in politics are making clear what *they* want without being asked.

It is the redevelopment of decaying residential areas which has given planners the most scope for comprehensive action. By contrast, the redevelopment of commercial areas, the planning of roads, and the siting of new developments in rural or suburban areas has tended to involve much more difficult 'political' activities for planners. The successful planners in these areas are likely to have been those who shared the values described by Simmie.

The residents of those parts of our towns which are 'ripe for renewal' are in a particularly vulnerable position when faced by those who want to sweep away their homes and replace them by modern developments. The sentimental attachment of Young and Willmott to traditional Bethnal Green should not blind us to the fact that when, first in the nineteen-thirties and then again in the late fifties, attention in housing policy turned to slum clearance there were large numbers of people in irredeemable slum dwellings. Today Norman Dennis's work in Sunderland, and the Government's own gradual acceptance that urban renewal need not always involve the sweeping away of houses, has led to a suspicion of wholesale redevelopment. Vast council estates on the edges of our cities full of social problems, and tower blocks of flats which no one wants to live in, have led to criticism of the radical programmes of slum clearance which created them. In the process it is only too easy to forget the deplorable slums which were pulled down. At the time many were grateful for the evangelistic bureaucrats who worked so hard and so fast to destroy the slums. They were in a weak position to demand that consultation and participation which might have prevented some of the worst mistakes.

Most of the people involved in these large-scale redevelopment schemes were tenants. Their houses often belonged to small property owners who had acquired their interests long ago. These landlords had found that their own low resources, together with rent restriction, prevented efforts to improve their property. Neither landlords nor tenants were in a position to argue effectively with authorities committed to sweeping their houses away. Today the position in the remaining 'down-town' areas of our cities is rather different. Very many of the occupants of small elderly houses are owner occupiers. If they have bought their houses as a first step up the ladder towards good class suburban housing, they want to be adequately compensated before they move out. If they have acquired inner-city houses through choice, as middle-class people who want to avoid commuting, they will be committed to the 'gentrification' of their house and their area. If, like many newcomers to our cities, they have bought old inner-city dwellings because that is all they can afford, they will equally be committed to making the most of their acquisitions. While inner-city areas will still contain houses that are irredeemable, and tenants who are only too eager to move out, they also contain people who are not ready to be pushed around. Hence in contemporary Rye Hill, Newcastle (see Gower Davies), and Sunderland (see Dennis), and St Annes, Nottingham (see Coates and Silburn), the evangelistic bureaucrat meets a challenge in the one area in which he has hitherto been able to operate relatively unconstrained by politics.

Jon Gower Davies provides a good account of the aspirations of planners and of the approach they have been able to adopt in areas where those they plan *for* are weak. Simmie's portrait of the planner is perhaps more accurate for the many situations in which planning is forced to be a thorough-going political process. As American studies, like Meyerson and Banfield's *Politics, Planning and the Public Interest*, have shown, once planners are forced to confront what people *want*, they must become political animals or go under. The evangelistic bureaucrat who is insensitive to middle-class interests in the planning process will become a very unsuccessful planner, unless he can find an area in which to operate where people will be grateful for what they are given.

However, there is a need to avoid an undue polarization between, on the one hand, conceptualization of planning as pursued by evangelistic bureaucrats, deaf to all expressions of public opinion and, on the other, presentation of it as hedged around by the interests of those with property in such a way as to eliminate all vestiges of comprehensive rationality. American observers of British planning have argued that, to a much greater extent than is the case in the United States, planners have been able to pursue their goals with surprisingly little inter-ference from recognizable propertied interests.

Elkin describes the case of town and country planning in the United States as follows:

. . . in general, land use politics in American cities involves a number of actors with influence whose co-operation must be assured before anything important can be done, although the poor and unorganized have tended to play a limited part here. Concomitant to the mutiplicity of actors is the widespread use of local government as a kind of holding company or arbitrator, not as an initiator of policy.

(Elkin, 1974: 187)

He suggests that, while a more participative system of government in London at the time he studied decisions there would have more readily exposed the weaknesses of the planners' decisions, it would 'very likely have vitiated the planning system as a result'. Elkin's contrasting case studies are instructive. In one case there was a comparatively high level of bargaining with interested groups. The outcome was a large office block, Centrepoint, which remained unlet for several years. Many might agree that *that* development should have been prevented. But in the other case the outcome was more public housing in Chelsea. Elkin was surprised to find that in this case such controversy as occurred was all about densities, and was almost entirely a private dispute between the London County Council and the Borough Council. No effective local amenity groups emerged to try to stop development. In an American context this latter development might well have lapsed in face of opposition, while the commercial interest in the Centrepoint scheme might well have ensured its survival. For better or for worse, large-scale public housing is perhaps the major achievement of British local government and the biggest source of social contrast between cities on either side of the Atlantic. It is this contrast that leads Elkin to speculate about factors that enable local authorities to build in middle-class areas with comparatively little opposition. His explanation rests partly upon pointing out the lack of strong class conflict over public housing. This consensus tends to reduce the amount of conflict over the siting of council estates. He quotes one councillor as saying:

As to local people, yes, they object but it depends on the area . . . People in Wimbledon say council housing will depreciate the area.

> They do object on the whole, that is owner occupiers do. Also
> they usually get overruled. It doesn't matter what the complexion
> of the Council is . . . All told though there was a fair agreement
> to build council houses among the parties.
>
> *(Elkin, 1974: 88-89)*

This part of Elkin's argument does not sound altogether con-
vincing in the context of a political situation in which class
cleavages are so salient. Perhaps more important in explaining
the passivity of citizens who might object to planning of this
kind is Elkin's emphasis upon the lack of participatory political
culture in Britain. He quotes some of Almond and Verba's data
from their book *The Civic Culture* to suggest that British people
are less inclined to expect participation or to question authority.
The difficulty with this data is, of course, that the lower pro-
pensity to participate is not particularly a characteristic of those
in the middle classes most likely to object to planning decisions.

However, the most important point made by Elkin is that
those councillors he interviewed, who might have intervened in
a class-based way on planning matters, felt very strongly that
decisions should be based upon 'rational' considerations for the
good of the community and not upon bargaining. He quotes a
councillor as saying:

> In order to help the general pattern one has to put the community
> first – In town planning . . . you don't get bargains and com-
> promises. It depends on the integrity of the council doesn't it.
> There are great dangers in town planning and you need great
> integrity. You don't get the sort of thing in which neighbour-
> hoods bargain.
>
> *(Elkin, 1974: 122)*

Of course this statement need not be taken as the whole truth,
but it expresses an ethos. If such an ethos is widely held, it will
tend to inhibit protest groups.

Finally, Elkin stressed the extent of delegation to planners
and the extent to which these officials saw themselves as having
wide responsibilities of a kind which may be called political,
though not party political. Planners he interviewed expressed
views, like those quoted above from Gower Davies's work, about

a commitment to the community interest overriding more partisan political allegiances. One said, for example:

> , . . the planner is the custodian of the community. He can speak as the guardian of the public interest because he is a detached and disinterested party. His choices are not motivated out of self-interest.
>
> *(Elkin, 1974: 33)*

The implication of this for a body like the Greater London Council, organized on strong party political lines, would be that politicians faced planners who would not be inhibited in arguments which involve questions of interests or values. Indeed, as Darlow pointed out in a symposium on the relations between politicians and administrators, British local government officers may react strongly to politicians who fail to pay attention to their 'professional' advice. Elkin's study is a sound reminder that we should not adopt uncritically American models of the urban political process, in which politics is so much more concerned with explicit community conflict unchecked by professional values. However, the weakness of his approach is, as Dearlove has argued, that his study was set in the 'pluralist tradition of American political science concentrating on the *process* and *personnel* of government to the detriment of any sustained concern with the substance of the public policy' (Dearlove, 1975: 93). Dearlove goes on to argue that Elkin gives us a picture of the planning process similar to that given by planners themselves. He provides evidence of such overt bargaining as occurs and shows that, in the Chelsea case, this did not substantially involve outside interests. What he cannot so easily consider is the extent to which there were covert bargains with interests and the extent to which respect for interests is implicit in planners' activity.

Third party status in planning
Elkin's study shows the absence of clear provision in British planning for formal representation of people not directly affected by decisions. Planning law underlines this formal weakness.

People with an indirect interest in a planning matter, for example objectors to public housing projects without property which is to be purchased, are described as having 'third party status'. Cullingworth describes the position of 'third parties' as having no statutory right to make representations to a planning committee. If a planning enquiry is held 'third parties have an "administrative" privilege' to appear, but they have 'generally no similar privilege in relation to a planning application!' (Cullingworth, 1974: 304).

This narrow interpretation of the 'interests' involved in a planning matter has led Allison to suggest that orthodox planning ideology is Benthamite in character, concerned to reach correct decisions by weighting, according to some 'felicific calculus', the real direct interests involved. But Allison's analysis gives insufficient attention to the roles played by planners and administrators as paternalistic 'representatives' of the wider public interest. Cullingworth points out that 'it is the job of the local planning authority to assess the public advantage or disadvantage of a development, and of the Secretary of State to review it', and he says that third parties 'cannot usurp these Government functions' (ibid.). A former Permanent Secretary of the Ministry of Housing and Local Government (the Department of the Environment's predecessor), Lady Sharp, has put this more bluntly:

> Third party status is pretty low unless they can prove some real and direct interest. It is very rare that they will produce any decent suggestions. Their objections are generally discounted.
>
> *(Sharp, 1969: 37)*

Clearly, third party interests range from those very directly affected by neighbouring developments to a large number of citizens who are in some small degree concerned. Quite distant industrial or residential developments may affect the values of our properties or the amenities of our districts. Furthermore, if we are quite regular visitors to a recreational area (a National Park or seaside area, for example) may we not have an 'interest' in the limitation of development? If we are regular travellers on a particular route, may we not have an 'interest' in road development? The siting of schools, public buildings, libraries, swimming pools and football grounds, for example, will concern a wide range of people. There are manifestly problems for the planning process of assessing the relative importance in connection with, for example, the siting of a football ground of, on the one hand, those football supporters who want that ground to be accessible, and, on the other, residents of an area who will suffer from noise, vandalism and parking problems if it is in their neighbourhood.

The issues raised in connection with 'third party status' may be met by the argument that it is one of the functions of 'representative democracy' to achieve a balance between interests like those outlined above. This appeal to political theory may, however, not provide a very satisfactory answer to those who feel that they want a more direct opportunity to put their point of view to the planners. The complexity of the interests involved may moreover further encourage planning authorities to hide behind paternalistic interpretations of their roles. Lady Sharp's statement represents a rather old fashioned view, but, as will be seen in the next chapter, progress towards a much more open approach to planning has been slow.

Yet it is important to recognize the extent to which a very much more open approach to planning must come into conflict with the conception of the role of government which is widely accepted in this country. It has already been pointed out that local planning authorities are not just expected to adjudicate on planning matters, but are also policy-making agencies. As Cullingworth says: '. . . the local planning authority is not an impartial body: it is an agency of government attempting to secure what it believes to be the best development for its area' (Cullingworth, 1974: 305).

At the same time Dearlove's criticisms of Elkin's and Simmie's books remind us that paternalism, and the narrow view of legitimate participation, may conceal commitments to specific interests which planners are unwilling to make explicit. Indeed they may not even be aware of some of their assumptions which have the effect of protecting specific interests. We are confronted here by the debate about the character of power between those social scientists who confine their attention to identifiable interventions in the policy-making process (the 'pluralists' identified by Dearlove in the quotation above) and those who argue that policy-outcomes are often determined by value biases and assumptions about interests, without any direct intervention by those who have most to gain. British planning is particularly deserving of study by those who wish to evaluate this debate.

Conclusions

The shift of attention in this part of the chapter to situations in which citizens are indirectly rather than directly affected by the activities of planners, leads logically enough to the brief discussion of other types of planning promised at the beginning of this chapter.

In a recent book, *The Planner in Society*, David Eversley sets out a view of the role of the planner today in which he is seen as very much more than just a land use planner. Eversley argues that he is an 'allocator of scarce resources'. This means, he says, abandoning the distinction between:

> . . . the 'physical' planner who is concerned merely with the allocation of land uses and the control of building elevations . . . the 'economic' planner who allocates the capital for housing, infrastructure, or industrial purposes, and the 'social' planner who allocates land, capital, employment opportunities, educational and other social services, revenues and manpower . . .
>
> *(Eversley, 1973: 5)*

That kind of planning which is concerned with questions of land use in a relatively small discrete area can be related to the concerns of citizens very much more easily than resource allocation planning, attempting to take into account a wide range of factors and seeking to implement specific redistributive goals. When these are his aim, Gower Davies's 'evangelistic bureaucrat' is operating at a level at which interaction with members of the public likely to be affected by his activities is very improbable if not impossible. Eversley's book illustrates very clearly the peculiar inconsistencies that arise where planners claim a comprehensive brief and a role as agents of social change, and yet express a commitment to consultation of, and mediation between, community interests. A role as 'allocator of scarce resources' does not preclude sensitivity to social pressures, but it does imply an ultimate detachment in which choices are made between groups. The more factors to be taken into account in such choices, the less real can be the involvement with the people to be affected by those choices. This point will be discussed more fully in the next chapter.

Although central and local governments present themselves as committed to this more comprehensive kind of planning these days, their actual plans tend to be highly generalized documents which are difficult to relate to public needs and interests. As Townsend argues of social planning:

> Most social planning in Britain is narrowly departmental; it is conceived within administrative and not functional boundaries. Rarely is the risk taken to spell out its logic to the general public, on grounds either that this might reveal administrative ignorance and ineptitude or encourage criticism of central thinking and action. Planning is also gravely subservient to traditional interpretations of what is good for the economy.
>
> *(Townsend, 1975: 56)*

Townsend quotes as examples the various plans for local authority social services and the national Hospital Plan of 1962, together with the National Plan of 1965 which he suggested was formulated with little attention being given to actual social service needs. Furthermore, as he points out elsewhere, all such planning exercises of recent years have had to give way 'to restrictive Treasury control over public expenditure' (Townsend in Townsend and Bosanquet (eds.), 1972: 296).

The title of Heclo and Wildavsky's book on the control of the expenditure process within British central government, *The Private Government of Public Money*, perhaps most adequately emphasizes the way resource-allocation decisions are distanced from the public. Heclo and Wildavsky see Britain as a country where the privacy of this decision-making area is particularly well preserved. Their observations on this are comparable to those of Elkin on British land-use planning. In both central and local government in Britain in recent years, such attention as has been given to the development of rational resource planning techniques has been facilitated by the 'privacy' of British government. Administrators have been the key actors in these developments. At all levels of government public servants have been concerned to develop professional management skills. Political representatives are involved in these activities largely as what J. M. Lee has called 'ministerialists', individuals who can be consulted because of their own abilities and their capacities to understand what is going on, and not particularly as 'representatives of the people'. Pressure groups are largely kept at arm's length, except inasmuch as their leaders can be co-opted into the decision-making processes, again largely as individuals and not representatives. Of course some pressure groups are strong enough to make a larger impact. Then, surely, their roles have been as disrupters of planning processes, forcing resource-allocation decisions which set up countermanding demands from other powerful groups. In other words, despite the extensive rhetoric of participation in recent years, the evolution of planning has depended on the privacy of government. The advocates of planning, far from being eager to be in touch with community demands, have been involved in trying to protect what they see as rational government from public pressures. Most of their activity has been removed from that public scrutiny which might have exposed its claims to rationality.

Chapter 9
Participation

Introduction
There is a number of ways in which representative democracy, and more specifically that version of representative democracy existing in Britain, has come under fire in recent years. The tenuous nature of the link between the electorate and politicians, the oligarchies within the political parties and the weakness of Parliament in relation to the executive, have all featured in discussions of the inadequacies of our political system. The weaknesses in the formal political apparatus are all indirectly relevant to the concern of this book, the relationship between the citizen and the administration. In Chapter 2 it was made very clear that British government developed as government *of* the people, as far as all but a privileged minority were concerned, rather than as government *by* the people. This élite tradition of government lives on. Therefore, there is in some respects no need to look to developments in contemporary politics or administration to explain the citizen's difficulties in exercising control over government activities which affect his life. However, the twentieth century has seen efforts to establish a more democratic form of government. If nothing else, wide sections of the public have acquired aspirations to 'self-government'. Yet during this period we have acquired very much 'more government', and therefore administrative activities have developed which affect most aspects of our lives. Movement towards self-government tends to have been thwarted by the growth in the range and complexity of government activity.

To those who still want to increase the extent of self-government two groups of possibilities exist: to try to remedy the weaknesses that are perceived in the system of representative government, or to try to forge new ways of achieving direct control over the activities of government. The concern of this chapter is with the second group of possibilities, yet it will be seen that many proposals to increase 'direct' involvement in government or administration must, in practice, tend to imply the elaboration of new approaches to 'representative' government.

Perhaps the most commonly-used slogan in contemporary debates about control over administration by the people is 'participation'. Participation is open to a range of interpretations. As Dilys Hill points out, there is a need to distinguish between an empty slogan and a very real preoccupation about power:

> We must realize that 'participation' and 'involvement' may become catch-phrases rather than real solutions. These words have become fashionable in the current debate about the quality of modern society, because we fear that many people do not share in making decisions and there is a large and potentially dangerous gap between the governors and the governed.
>
> *(Hill, 1970: 18-19)*

Hence, there are grounds for suspicion about participation when it becomes a catch-phrase popular with government. This suspicion was most effectively portrayed in a French student poster produced in 1968:

je participe
tu participes
il participe
nous participons
vous participez
ils profitent

An important theme in this chapter will be the argument that participation without an effective shift in power is likely to be a sham. This argument is very much more complex than it appears. In political analysis both 'participation' and 'power' are extremely slippery and ambiguous concepts. It is necessary there-

fore to go very thoroughly into the various kinds of participation
which are suggested.

Participation in planning: the impact of
the Skeffington Report

The most clearly focused discussions on this subject have been
concerned with participation in town and country planning. The
Government set up the Skeffington Committee to make specific
proposals for involving people in the planning process. This
Committee reported in 1969, Its recommendations relate to
some of the provisions of the 1968 Town and Country Planning
Act. This Act provides that in drawing up the overall 'structure
plan' for its area a local authority must give adequate publicity
to their survey report and to the policies on which the plan is to
be based. They must also publicize their subsequent proposals,
enable representations to be made by the public, and take into
account those representations in drawing up the eventual plan.
They must then publicize the plan itself and inform the public
of the timetable for 'objections' to go to the Secretary of State.
Finally, when submitting their plan to the Secretary of State they
must provide an account of the provisions they made for all the
above representations. Local plans require similar treatment, but
they do not have to be submitted to the Secretary of State.

The Skeffington Report amplifies these provisions by suggesting ways in which local authorities can publicize plans, make
provisions for discussion and educate the public about the nature
of the planning process. It also suggests that the public should
be involved very early in the planning process, in making surveys and discussing local environmental issues. It suggests, for
example, that local authorities should consider setting up
'community forums' to

> provide local organizations with the opportunity to discuss
> collectively planning and other issues of importance to the area.
> Community forums might also have administrative functions such
> as receiving and distributing information on planning matters
> and promoting the formation of neighbourhood groups.
>
> *(Skeffington, 1969: 51)*

The Skeffington Committee gave some attention to the problems that arise because only a relatively small, and unrepresentative, section of the public is organized into associations or groups. In these circumstances a participation exercise might give undue influence to this minority. Their proposals to overcome this problem was, as follows:

> Community development officers should be appointed to secure the involvement of those people who do not join organizations. Their job would be to work with people to stimulate discussions, to inform people in the neighbourhood, and to give people's views to the authority.
>
> *(ibid.)*

It is rather easy to show how the proposals in the Skeffington Report can lead to empty forms of participation. The main difficulty in judging the report 'in action' is that the Government did not enforce the implementation of its more positive proposals. A Department of the Environment circular in 1970 said that 'neither community forums nor the appointment of community development officers will prove to be necessary in the specific context of development plans'.

Coventry Community Workshop became engaged in the consideration of the Structure Plan for their city in 1972. They produced a leaflet arguing that Coventry Council had chosen to fulfil only its minimum statutory responsibility to ensure participation. The council had called some public meetings, secured articles in the evening paper, used an exhibition bus and circulated questionnaires. Less than 500 people attended the meetings and under 700 questionnaires were returned. The Community Workshop complained that many of the meetings were sited in inappropriate places, that the meetings were organized as question and answer sessions rather than as open debates, and that much of the information given to the public was couched in the 'language of the planners'. They felt that the public were left with the impression that 'policies had already been decided and the Council was simply trying to explain its decisions'.

This example from Coventry is cited to show the kind and

level of participation achieved under the influence of the Skeffington Report. It is not intended to suggest that Coventry Council's behaviour was exceptionally unsatisfactory; indeed, its approach was better than that of many other authorities, and was quoted as a model in Cullingworth's book on planning. The Coventry Community Workshop made a number of suggestions for increasing the scope of participation: that community groups should be involved in planning the form that participation would take, that local authority fieldworkers (housing assistants and social workers for example) should be asked to communicate policy proposals to those affected by them, that members of the public in prominent positions (their examples are shopkeepers, publicans, works managers and shop stewards) should be given information about proposals and should be asked to feed back people's comments, and that councillors should engage in open debate about their preferences and the factors that influenced their decisions.

However, all these efforts to raise levels of participation may still be comparatively fruitless if careful attention is not given to the identification of points for decision. What is so difficult in a planning exercise is to recognize some overall planning goals, and to identify the relationship between specific proposals and these goals. Often planning goals can become the subject of public debate only when they are set out in the most general terms, and when extreme positions can be adopted: for or against the building of a motorway, and so on. In the implementation of these goals, public involvement again tends to become feasible only when the focus is upon relatively small details. Having settled that there should be a motorway, various 'lines' are considered. The public become engaged in debate about those lines. This debate is largely about the effects of the lines upon specific interests and amenities, however it may be wrapped up in more general considerations. Victories for participation are claimed when people secure the rejection of the line affecting their village, or an adjustment of a line moving the road a mile or two further away from them. It is hard to conceive an open public debate about motorway routes that is set out in terms of maximizing the 'general good' except by reference to squabbles about individual 'goods'. Furthermore, it is generally logically impossible to translate this form of participation into that ultimate participative instrument, the referendum, in any way that would be perceived as satisfactory. Could people vote on the preferred motorway line? If so, who would be entitled to vote, how could you define the affected locality? How would such a mechanism cope with the fact that, for example, people voting for route B might really prefer route A if it were marginally adjusted? How would you cope with the problem of equating the optimum route, in amenity terms, with the optimum route in technical – and therefore probably cost – terms?

Redevelopment involving people's homes raises particularly crucial problems. Should the participating community be confined to those directly involved in these cases? If so, what about those who benefit or suffer from living on the margin of the development, those who may use the new roads or shops created, and those who may be affected in various long-run ways by a transformation of part of their town? Then, within the affected community, are all 'votes' equal, or is not the impact of redevelopment different in intensity and character for different people? Again, as with the motorway route problem, minor changes in the detail of the development plan may be of crucial significance for some individuals.

These rather detailed arguments have been set out, not to denigrate participation as a false god, but because so much of the clamour for more participation, and criticism of participation exercises, pays no attention to the definition of 'optimum participation'. If participation in decision making is desired, what measure of 'opening up' of this process will be deemed adequate? How can a participatory exercise be designed in such a way that maximum involvement of the people concerned is achieved at one and the same time? Discussions of participation do not seem to come to terms with these problems. In the paragraph above some fairly difficult examples were used, relating complex planning issues to a participative device, the referendum, which requires the posing of simple and straightforward questions. Yet the exponents of increased participation seem sometimes to be suggesting that they will only be satisfied by the adoption of levels of public involvement close to the referendum ideal. So long as exaggerated demands are made, or the advocates of more open government are unable to specify their objectives, it must be expected that what will be granted will tend to be sham participation.

Participation as pressure group activity

Perhaps a common and relatively low level of achievement at which the advocate of increased participation may be aiming is the extension of pressure group activity. British political scientists were slow to recognize the importance of pressure groups in British political life. One of the reasons for this was the dominance of an ideology of government in which participation, except through the electoral process, was regarded as illegitimate. The contemporary fashion for urging that there should be more participation is in some cases merely an attempt to legitimize and extend pressure group activity.

Participation in pressure groups, like participation in representative politics, is essentially a minority activity. To urge, therefore, that politicians and administrators should pay more attention to pressure groups is to seek to give more power to these minorities. Outside the trade unions, pressure group membership is predominantly middle class. Pressure group leaders are generally 'higher' in social class than their rank and file members. Successful pressure groups in the planning process have been essentially middle class.

It is, of course, the unrepresentative nature of many organized groups which enables the planner to present himself as the protector of individuals against these groups. Organized interest groups may be dismissed because they represent a narrow sectional interest, or because they are oligarchical, or because they only represent a minority of the group they claim to speak for. So the official can claim a wider mandate, an interest in the welfare of the whole community. Ironically, therefore, officials who are in direct touch with none of the individuals affected by their policies will claim to represent *all*, in the face of pressure groups who manifestly represent only a biased sample.

The radical advocates of increased participation are well aware of the middle-class dominance of existing pressure groups. Their concern is with the development of new pressure groups to advocate hitherto unrepresented points of view.

Community action and direct action

The stimulation of new pressure groups has been seen as one of the aims of 'community workers' and of programmes of community action. Community action groups aim, according to Lapping:

> to get people involved in decisions affecting their lives, partly through exerting group pressure on the decision makers; partly by getting people in the community to throw up the issues through participation rather than the representative democratic procedures they have grown to distrust.
>
> *(Lapping, 1970: 2)*

Similarly Bryant has stressed that community action involves an approach to the organizing of local groups in which:

> the political impotence or powerlessness of these groups is defined as a central problem and strategies are employed which seek to mobilize them for the representation and promotion of their collective interests.
>
> *(Bryant, 1972: 206)*

There are several difficulties which the advocates of these community action strategies face. They are operating against the existing bias of the social structure. By definition, the wealthier a group the more resources it has to apply to pressure group activity. One of the consequences of pressure group activity by hitherto passive groups may be *even more* activity from the existing active groups. Furthermore, wherever pressure group activity is concerned with complex matters, like planning, where technical expertise is necessary, it tends to be costly, unless experts will work for the group without requiring fees. Clearly middle-class groups are much better placed, both to raise money and to secure the free contributions of middle-class experts, than are organizations of the poor. Committed community workers of many kinds are engaged today in trying to overcome this particular bias; for example, young radical lawyers and planners are engaged in working with underprivileged community groups.

However, these middle-class 'community work' professionals face some of the dilemmas discussed earlier in the section on welfare rights work. The quotations of 'community action' philosophy made clear the commitment to community self-help as a route out of apathy and political weakness. Trying to take that route whilst critically dependent upon professional advisers, who are probably therefore assuming leadership roles, may be rather self-defeating. Clearly many 'professional' community activists are sensitive to this problem, and many are eager to avoid playing leadership roles.

Perhaps a greater problem for community action strategies is that, by comparison with those pressure groups which aim to prevent government action so that the *status quo* may be preserved, the pressure groups for the poor often seek positive action to redistribute resources in society. It is a much harder task for a pressure group to get something done than to prevent something happening. Significantly, the major successes of the great American community action advocate, Saul Alinsky, have been in preventing action that would harm the poor. One of his most widely quoted triumphs was in preventing the acquisition of property by the University of Chicago which would have led to evictions and demolition in a poor neighbourhood. Similarly, those amongst the local community groups, studied by Dennis in Sunderland and Coates and Silburn in Nottingham, who had the most clear cases to make were the owner occupiers of sound houses who wanted to prevent redevelopment by the local authority. The tenants of sub-standard houses who desired redevelopment were in much weaker positions to make their views heard.

The participation of more groups in conflict over public policy decision making must complicate the process. Indeed Allison argues that the planning process is already so lengthy and complicated that anything that makes it more so threatens to undermine it. Hence he argues that 'too real a sense of participation might make planning unworkable' (Allison, 1975: 105).

It must be likely that more participants in an involved multi-dimensional conflict are likely to increase the extent of dissensus. Then, all any one group may hope to achieve is a measure of veto power, since it will be very hard to bring together a coalition for any single perspective. Again, *less* rather than *more* government may be the consequence. Administrators and professionals who are committed to positive action may feel free to proceed, disregarding 'public opinion' as too fragmented to guide their actions. In this sort of situation, the effort required to build up pressure group activities, particularly amongst the hitherto unorganized, may seem hardly worthwhile. However, it may be tactically advantageous to bring new social forces into the pressure group arena, to demonstrate that those who are otherwise most vocal do not speak for the public as a whole. To show that anti-redevelopment groups or groups committed to saving Grammar Schools, for example, do not alone speak for the public may be sufficient in some cases to ensure desired actions, when administrators are looking for reasons to disregard negative pressures.

Clearly public dissensus on complex policy issues poses some very difficult problems for those who wish to see 'democratic' decision-making processes. There is a great danger that issues will be simplified to enable conflict to be polarized and thus resolved. Those who invest considerable time and resources in pressure group activity may have to recognize that the balance of power at the end of all their efforts is much as it was in the beginning. Individuals who have been persuaded to engage in unfamiliar political activity may well find that it is ultimately a disillusioning rather than a politicizing experience. The apathy of the poor and politically weak is, after all, a source of protection against being hurt in an unequal struggle. Perhaps they really know, better than the idealists who seek to politicize them, how difficult it is to achieve change. If the resolution of community conflict is not simply to rest upon a head counting exercise, then it may well depend upon the power of the groups engaged in the conflict. Having many members, or having the resources to mount an attention-seeking campaign may help to win. So, too, may having the right contacts, the ears of the right decision-makers. But if all these things are relatively balanced, the real source of power may be more concrete. Some groups may be able to bargain with the decision-makers because their co-operation is essential.

Bryant outlines two strategies for 'community action': 'bargaining strategies' and 'confrontation strategies'. He argues that the choice between these two strategies will be determined by the extent to which the holders of power are willing to accede to negotiation. But both strategies are forms of 'bargaining' so long as the ultimate aim is to secure concessions from local authorities and not either to overthrow those authorities or simply (as is often suggested as one of the aims of community action) to raise political consciousness. Logically, so long as there is a concrete short-run aim in mind the object of direct action or confrontation must be to bring an unwilling authority to the point at which it is prepared to bargain.

However, Bryant's distinction between 'bargaining strategies' and 'confrontation strategies' is an interesting one because the problem which new pressure groups, in the 'community action' mould, face is that they possess few power resources. Characteristically middle-class pressure groups are strong because their members are drawn from a similar social group to the decision-makers. Indeed, some of their members may in fact *be* the decision-makers. It is natural, therefore, that they secure attention when they make demands. The decision-makers may want their agreement and support in so many related ways. Patterns of residence and social life will militate against the development of conflict. Even if few interlocking relationships do exist, the middle-class pressure groups will have the power to delay and complicate the activities of the decision-makers. They will be able to prolong and elaborate processes of negotiation in many ways, including using the always enormously time-consuming process of litigation. The co-operation of related professional and business groups may be essential for other government activity. The possession of widespread property interests also implies a considerable potential for the obstruction of government activity.

Working-class groups, without extensive property and with few social links with decision-makers, possess only one really significant weapon, the power to withdraw labour. Even this weapon has been forged in long and bitter conflict, and the legitimacy of its use for ends other than the furtherance of industrial conflict, so-called 'political ends', is widely challenged. Furthermore, when working-class groups are engaged in conflict over public policy or administration the strike weapon is not usually available. The parties to the conflict are not generally the parties to work contracts. The residents of areas threatened by demolition, the tenants of council houses facing rent rises, the underprivileged groups demanding new educational or recreational facilities for their area, are not generally homogeneous groups of employees who could withdraw their labour to secure attention to their demands.

Hence, groups of this kind may adopt other tactics to *force* attention to their demands. Just as we have seen during the past two centuries a debate about the legality and legitimacy of the use of the withdrawal of labour as a weapon in industrial conflict, so now similar arguments are developing about the use of other direct action or 'confrontation strategies'. The argument against such tactics is that there are 'proper channels' for pressure group activity, and that the process of government is one in which 'moderate' and 'reasonable' representations are sufficient. The argument for confrontation tactics is that it is only by the use of demonstrations, squatting, rent strikes and 'sit-ins' that groups who are weak and outside the ranks of the Establishment will secure attention to their demands. The losses and the embarrassments resulting from direct action will give underprivileged groups the leverage to counterbalance their inherent weaknesses when using 'conventional' tactics. As Dearlove has argued:

Democratic rhetoric encourages the public to believe that reasonableness and consensus are possible, but in reality a 'low-keyed' strategy is just not available to bring success to groups of 'newcomers' . . .

(Dearlove, 1974: 29)

The success of the less violent of these techniques depends crucially, however, upon the political culture. If ruling groups are genuinely concerned to meet the grievances of the under-privileged, success will be quite easily achieved. But in such situations, in any case, protest outside the regular political channels will have been largely unnecessary. Where decision-makers are less responsive, but nevertheless care about their capacity to maintain an orderly society, a society in which the 'established channels' are used and respected, they will be acutely embarrassed by tactics that demonstrate that, for others, reality is rather different. However, if they are strongly committed to maintaining their dominance and to resisting direct action, they may repress confrontation tactics ruthlessly. Then it may be that the only way in which deprived groups can continue to force attention to be given to their views is a violent one.

Accordingly a debate similar to that outlined above about non-violent action tactics has developed about 'violence'. To those concerned with the maintenance of order any use of violence, except by agents of the State, is illegitimate. Against this view it is argued that a repressive State uses violence to repress dissent, and *this* use of violence is a provocation to retaliatory violence.

We see here how conflict may be escalated. There are various interpretations of situations of this kind, which govern the way antagonists behave. A revolutionary view is that a shift in power can only be achieved by violently overthrowing the existing order, that real concessions cannot be secured by a 'little' direct action or a 'little' violence. The struggle must be escalated to breaking point. This view is matched by an authoritarian conservative argument that making concessions in a conflict of this kind only pushes up the demands that are made, and that therefore a firm stand against 'illegitimate' tactics is necessary. Between these extremes is a view that people only resort to such tough tactics when they are desperate. Therefore it is argued, a new order can be negotiated when reasonable demands are met. Responses in conflicts of this kind are clearly dictated by both the ideologies of the protagonists, and by their assessments of each other's ideologies.

The underlying issue is the character of the society within which this conflict occurs. It is instructive here to refer back to White's three models of society, outlined on pages 58 to 60, the 'consensus', 'conflict' and 'open' models. Birrell and Murie have contrasted social policy in Britain with the superficially similar policies existing in Northern Ireland. They have suggested that while, in White's terms, the 'open model' of resolvable conflict occurs over policy in Britain, in Northern Ireland there is 'no accepted area of debate or system of bargaining within which conflict and interests can be continually reviewed and compromise reached' (Birrell and Murie, 1975: 255-6). Disagreements over education and housing policy have not been resolved in Northern Ireland since neither Catholics nor Protestants have been prepared to sink differences in the interests of what would be seen in Britain as common 'welfare' goals. Protestants, dominating State agencies, have been prepared to use housing policy to influence the composition of electoral districts, to consider reducing family allowances for large families, and to operate powers to make deductions from social security allowances for rent in order to break rent strikes. Catholics have seen in this uncompromising use of State power the justification for the escalation of conflict to a violent level. Of course, as Boyle, Hadden and Hillyard have shown, of particular significance in this escalation process has been Protestant domination of the machinery of justice and the police.

The position in conflicts in Britain between direct action groups and State agencies is complicated by the fact that it is often unclear who first turns to the use of violence. The squatting campaign described by Ron Bailey in *The Squatters* provides some excellent examples of situations in which the discipline of the squatters enabled them to gain the maximum from the

British non-violent tradition and win public sympathy, by showing how bailiffs used unnecessary force against a purely passive group. But he also gives examples of situations which were not so well controlled, in which squatting groups lost this legal and psychological advantage. One difficulty that radical action groups face is that they tend to have within their ranks individuals with very varied perspectives on the use of violence. A revolutionary Marxist, who is irreconcilably opposed to the existing order and prepared to use any means to overthrow it, may not be willing to use the law effectively, and may thereby exploit cultural attitudes to law and order to maximize tactical gains. The exponents of 'direct action' range from people like this on the far left to individuals, at the other extreme, who merely want to add certain non-violent direct action tactics to the traditional pressure group armoury.

Participation and pressure group activity in social policy making

This discussion of participation has been concerned so far very largely with examples of policies in the fields of planning and housing. To what extent, it may be asked, can participation in the formulation and implementation of policies be extended in the areas of policy other than planning?

As far as the provision of material benefits is concerned, it is very often the most socially isolated and most demoralized who have major grievances about policies. These will tend to be seen as individual problems – 'how can I get a grant?', 'how can I get back the allowance that has been stopped because of alleged cohabitation?', and so on – and not as matters that can be the subject of collective action. Individuals with such grievances rarely meet each other. Or they meet in contexts, such as the offices of the Supplementary Benefits Commission, where many are inhibited by a sense of shame and degradation from comparing notes with each other. Specific grievances, moreover, are passing problems. Individuals confront decisions they feel are unfair, fight against them in their own way, win or lose, and then pass on to the next phase in their struggle for a livelihood.

However, there are a number of examples of the formation of pressure groups for recipients of State benefits. These, it follows from the arguments above, are at their strongest when there are substantial groups of active and healthy people with common grievances. Perhaps the most famous example of such a group was the National Unemployed Workers' Movement. This was founded by Wal Hannington in 1921 and was conceived as a Marxist movement against the capitalist system. However, it became involved in pressure group activities against government relief policies for the unemployed. Perhaps its highest point came in 1935 when it led large scale protests against the harsh benefit scales adopted for the new Unemployment Assistance Board. The extent of the protests at this time had some influence upon the Government, which decided to delay the implementation of the new scales. In 1936, also, the NUWM staged a massive hunger march against the means test.

The mantle of the NUWM has been taken up today by the Claimants' unions. However, the absence of *mass* grievances surely helps to explain the weakness of these organizations. Jordan has shown how the membership of a Claimants' Union changes as the individuals with grievances change. The absence of a large number of young, able-bodied men who are continuously unemployed robs these groups of the crucial, dynamic element which was present in the NUWM. But the Claimants' Unions have other problems, too, in securing a coherent organizational form, as Hilary Rose has shown. As compared with the Communist-led NUWM, the Claimants' Unions have been concerned, in line with the more libertarian socialist ideology more prevalent today, to avoid creating a coherent leadership group. They have also refused to organize themselves nationally, except in a very loose and unstable federal structure. Finally, they have not altogether resolved the conflict between attention to individual problems and attacks on collective wrongs which was referred to in the chapter on individual grievance procedures. All these factors have tended to make the impact of Claimants' Unions rather minimal.

Pensioners are clearly a group of State beneficiaries who exist in large numbers and may relatively easily get in touch with each other. Pensioners' organizations seem to have some impact as pressure groups from time to time. They stage quite large demonstrations and seem to be well placed to draw public sympathy. It is hard, however, to assess the true effectiveness of pensioners' movements.

All these movements of State beneficiaries suffer from a common problem, a lack of sanctions. Only when their numbers are sufficiently large, or they are sufficiently concentrated to affect elections can they have a significant impact. Thus pensioners' movements secure attention because of the large number of elderly in the electorate. Similarly, as Hampson has shown for Sheffield, groups of council house tenants with a common grievance against a rent rise, may intervene successfully in a local election.

Where there are difficulties with any attempts to use electoral tactics, however, there are few alternatives available. It is all very well for the Claimants' Unions to argue that they are modelled on trade unions, but they lack the crucial weapon in the trade union armoury, the strike. A 'sit-in' at a social security office may cause some embarrassment, it may play upon feelings of 'order' of the kind described above. But it is likely to be a rather obscure and isolated event of short duration, and its main achievements may be delaying service to other social security applicants and increasing the hostility of office staff.

One group which has discovered a usable tactic for seeking more positive State action on their behalf are the homeless. The squatters' movement has demonstrated that its direct action can move authorities to response. By contrast with people who occupy social security offices the squatters secure, whilst taking action, what they most immediately need, temporary homes. They can make their point about the inadequacies of policies and help themselves at the same time, without these ends being in conflict, except inasmuch as some negotiations may require tactical withdrawals.

Some of the problems of absence of tactical ploys to overcome powerlessness also affect pressure groups concerned to influence policies about the provisions of services. As was shown in the chapter on services, professionalism tends in various degrees to protect practitioners from public control. Inasmuch as very real expertise is involved, it is manifestly hard to *force* experts to give their best services. However, there is much pressure group activity concerned with State-provided services. The patterns of pressure group activity affecting the three services, health, education and social services, are markedly different.

There has grown up in recent years a variety of national and local pressure groups concerned about education policy. The controversy over secondary school reorganization has provided an impetus for this growth, but some of the groups which are particularly concerned about this issue have other objectives too (this is the case, for example, with the Confederation for the Advancement of State Education). There are groups concerned about specific issues other than the comprehensive issue, such as the extension of nursery education and the educational problems of handicapped or gifted children. A particular feature of the educational pressure groups seems to be the extent to which the teachers are themselves very actively involved. They tend, therefore, to be alliances of consumers and politically conscious professionals. Hence, they are very largely middle-class 'respectable' pressure groups with tenuous links with the large majority of parents. At the 'grass roots' level, however, parental involvement in education has been enhanced by the promotion of parents' associations, or parent-teacher associations of various forms. Clearly, at the school level there is a potentiality for community involvement of some importance, if it is that level which is the critical decision-making locus for consumers of education.

The relatively high levels of local controversy about fairly detailed questions of education policy is in marked contrast to the lack of pressure group activity in connection with the health service. There are patients' organizations, and occasionally such issues as parents' rights when their children are in hospitals or the arrangements made for childbirth attract controversy. But the general level of activity is very low, and active local groups comparable to those that exist in the education field are largely absent.

Several factors may account for this. Our involvement with the health services is sporadic and often unpredictable. By contrast, parents remain continuously involved with the school system for at least eleven years. Visits to hospital are rare, and not often events we care to anticipate. Our most continuous relationships with the health service are with individual practitioners – doctors and dentists – and not with institutions. Hence issues which might be the subject of public controversy such as the organization of hospital services do not readily come to our attention.

It has already been noted that the practitioners in the health service are more successful than other groups in preserving their autonomy, and ensuring a role for themselves in the government of their service. This helps to remove health service policies from popular control. It may be suggested to those who see a potential for increased participation in our society by way of greater industrial democracy, or 'guild socialist' control of enterprises and services by their employees, that this may well increase the difficulties of ensuring greater consumer participation.

Partly as a result of professional suspicion of popular control, the government of the health service takes a form which is singularly removed from the normal machinery of representative government, as was shown on pages 111-114. The public confront a structure of regional and area health authorities which contain lay members. But these members are ministerial nominees with no special obligation to keep in touch with consumers. Community health councils have been set up to try to provide a link with consumers. It remains to be seen how 'representative' of the general public these bodies will be. What is clear, however, is that they have no executive powers. They can merely make representations as 'officially sponsored pressure group(s)' (Brown, 1975: 262).

Pressure group activity concerned with the social services and social work is at a very low level. There are a variety of national organizations concerned with the welfare of different groups amongst the disabled. Many of these developed as charitable ventures to provide services where public provision was largely absent. Some of these organizations have operated as pressure groups to try to secure government help. As the extent of such help has widened, there has been an increasing tendency for them to operate in this way to try to secure further extension of State aid. However, their 'charitable' background has inhibited political activity and has meant that they have rarely been movements of groups of the disabled themselves. This situation is, nevertheless, changing today with disadvantaged groups gradually beginning to make their own claims for State help towards fuller 'citizenship'.

Groups of the latter kind face the problem described for groups seeking improvements in State benefits: they lack the means to secure attention to their demands. They are generally small in numbers; since society has traditionally disregarded their needs there is no reason why it should stop doing so; sometimes their disadvantages are seen as stigmatizing; and they have to compete in making their claims for more help with many other groups who may be seen to have a comparably strong claim. In many cases everyone is in favour of doing more for them, but politicians and administrators are under no practical pressure to do anything. Year after year, for example, the disabled drivers have secured government sympathy for their campaign to increase the mobility of the disabled and to secure the replacement of the officially supplied three-wheeler 'trike'. Yet their demands have been met with the argument that 'we would like to help but it is all a question of priorities'. There is no way to push their claim up the list of priorities except through moral pressure unsupported by any sanctions.

Where minorities in receipt of special services argue for more involvement in their running, they have to face the difficulty that much of the crucial decision making which affects their welfare involves weighing their claims for more resources with the claims of other groups. It is the overall pattern of the deployment of resources which is crucial for their welfare and not, generally, the mechanics of the day-to-day running of the service. Social service pressure groups, therefore, are rendered particularly-weak by minority status.

Beyond pressure groups?

It may be objected that much of the discussion in this chapter has been concerned with a comparatively ineffective form of participation, through pressure group activity. Arnstein has suggested that forms of citizen participation may be seen as rungs in a ladder. At the bottom are two forms of 'non-participation': 'manipulation' and 'therapy'. Next are three rungs which she describes as 'tokenism', 'informing' and 'consultation', involving various degrees of rights to be heard but not necessarily to be 'heeded'. Then comes 'placation', where 'the ground rules allow have-nots to advise, but retain for the powerholders the continued right to decide'. It is only above this that there is true citizen power, she argues, with 'partnership' enabling negotiation and 'trade-offs with traditional powerholders', and then the two 'topmost rungs': 'delegated power' and 'citizen control' (Arnstein, 1969: 216-17).

Arnstein is quite right to emphasize the crucial importance of 'power' in relation to participation. Yet clearly she would tend to reject the pressure group forms of participation as inadequate. Therefore, what kinds of 'total power sharing' are possible? It need not be denied that our existing form of representative government implies government by an oligarchy. It can easily be shown that Members of Parliament, local councillors, senior civil servants, top local government officers, and the members of nominated advisory boards or management committees are, in varying degrees, drawn from narrow, unrepresentative sections of the population. There are a number of books which chart this quite clearly (Guttsman, Bottomore, Stanworth, Urry and Wakeford). What is not so clear is how governmental institutions can be developed which eliminate oligarchical rule, as opposed to measures which change the character of our ruling élites.

A great deal of attention has been given to ways of increasing industrial democracy, giving producers more control over the organizations in which they work. But industrial democracy is not the solution to the powerlessness of welfare beneficiaries, patients or parents. On the contrary, as was suggested above, such a reform may further reduce the power of consumers. In the last section of this chapter some of the possibilities for extending consumer control over public enterprises and services will be examined, to explore what is entailed and what is difficult about increasing participation in this way.

Even the most radical advocates of the rights of benefit claimants would admit that, in the final analysis, benefits are *transfer* payments from taxpayers (in one form or another) to the needy. It may be the case that the existing administrative structure gives very much more power to the representatives of payers of taxes than to the representatives of recipients of benefits. It has earlier been shown, for example, that appeal tribunal members are, in various respects, unlike appellants. Equally, except perhaps in the case of war pensioners, the various advisory committees which have been tried to help administer social security benefits are, or were, unlikely to include many with much direct experience of seeking such aid. There is no mechanism, apart from the isolated survey carrying little weight, to enable benefit recipients to influence the way local offices are run, forms are designed, or rules to fetter discretion are formulated. However, the transfer element inherent in social security benefits would in any case limit the extent to which customers of such agencies could be involved in decision making. Transfer benefits are social exchange relations in which we are all involved either as givers or receivers or, more likely in the course of our lives, as a combination of both. It is therefore entirely appropriate that the governmental relationship designed for these services should embrace us all. In this area, therefore, the radical critique of the distribution of power can surely go no further than to point out how unrepresented the recipients of benefits are in the overall power structure, and how unconcerned the authorities are to consult them on matters of detailed administration which have an intimate impact upon them.

Much the same argument may be advanced about the tenants of local authority houses. There is a great deal of scope for the increased involvement of such people in the day to day management of their estates. But the critical decisions affecting their welfare are concerned with rent levels and with the selection or eviction of tenants. It surely must be argued that all rate- and tax-payers must have a view about rent levels to be considered alongside those of the tenants, even though it may be argued that in particular authorities at present (or at least before the Housing Finance Act) one or other of the parties in this relationship has undue influence. Similarly, selection or eviction raises general questions of social justice; for example, fairness to all who might become local authority tenants or to those, in effect, subsidizing unpaid rents. It would be unfair to seek only the opinions of those directly involved.

A similar point may be made about hospital patients, inasmuch as their claims for increased resources are claims on the general pool. However, further problems arise about the involvement of a group like this in decision making. Manifestly there is a great deal more that can be done to find out how patients feel about the services they receive. Surveys indicate that patients can often make suggestions about the improvement of services which are practical and not costly. Nevertheless, it would be ludicrous to suggest, except in the special cases of very long-stay hospitals for the physically or mentally disabled, that such ephemeral members of the hospital community as the patients should have formal positions in the government of the institution.

Notice, however, how the last sentence needed to be qualified with the reservation about long-stay patients. There is room for considerable debate about the extent to which a particular group's involvement with an institution should be regarded as 'ephemeral'. This is an important point of dispute as far as educational institutions are concerned. To what extent should current students be involved in decisions which have an impact upon future students? How does one cope with the problem that, by the time a student knows enough about his institution to play an effective part in its government he will soon be leaving it? Too much can be made of this point. Staff often turn over rapidly too, but their claims to involvement in decision making are not denied on this ground.

More fundamental in motivating opposition to student participation is a view about the authority of knowledge. This seems to the author to be a rather unconvincing argument since it is not self-evident that student participation in the government of an institution will undermine the value of the education given. A rather stronger argument against some forms of student participation concerns the obligations of teachers to the wider society. This issue was explored a little in the chapter on personal services. The threat here is that this kind of consumer involvement might affect the awarding of qualifications, and thus undermine the institution's role as a setter of standards which are respected outside.

In the case of education, however, just as much as with the other services discussed, one critical area where consumer participation in government is likely to be limited is resource allocation. There are considerable possibilities for the development of schools run by the communities they serve. In the United States conflict over white dominance in educational administration has led in some areas to the seizure of control over schools by Negroes. But to control a school in this way does not secure the resources which are needed to run it. Indeed, underprivileged communities are weak and vulnerable precisely because the control of money lies outside them. If such communities are to finance their own schools, or any other major social institutions for that matter, enormous strain will be placed upon very limited resources.

This brings up, therefore, some most critical problems of level and scale, and of the independence of local or community institutions, which confront those who want to extend participation. The arguments for institutions operating at a level at which there can be broad participation are similar to the arguments for local government. The trend away from local government in Britain has been heavily influenced by central concern about the efficiency of local services and the unevenness which develops because of local autonomy. Much of the case against local government, and for the enlargement of the areas of local government to such an extent that they can no longer be considered 'local' (as has been the case with the recent local government re-organization), rests upon considerations of efficiency rather than democracy. However, there are two important arguments which can be said to derive from a concern about democracy. One is the argument about territorial justice, while the other is concerned with the identification of the essential 'locus' of control.

Students of variations in local services, like Bleddyn Davies, have shown that inequalities may emerge that cannot readily be tolerated in a small and homogeneous country. Thus, they argue that it may be incompatible to seek to achieve both 'territorial justice' and 'local democracy'. It is not surprising that central government, concerned to raise standards of education, to put the subsidization of council houses on an equitable basis, or to ensure that innovations in the social services are really effective, has wanted to intervene to reduce local government autonomy. Reports like those of Skeffington, on participation in planning, and Cullingworth, on council house allocation, have been derided for recommending courses of action on local authorities without central government intervention to force that action. In practice, governments continuously come under pressure to increase the inroads into local autonomy.

It is perhaps inevitable that those local issues which excite most controversy, and on which therefore different local councils are most likely to adopt policies with a characteristic local stamp, are those on which central government has been most prone to intervene. The two topics on which local parties have tended to be most divided are housing and education. When the 1964-70 Labour Government was faced by Tory councils opposed to comprehensive education it moved, gradually, towards compelling the introduction of comprehensive schemes. The 1970-74 Conservative Government similarly, with the Housing Finance Act, introduced a measure of central control over rents policy which hit at policies adopted by the more 'committed' Labour council groups. When Clay Cross Urban District sought to fight this policy it placed the central Labour Party in a dilemma since it could hardly pretend to be an unequivocal defender of local government autonomy. Rather, it anticipated that a principled stand might weaken its position when it returned to coerce Conservative councils over education policies.

The other drawback to local control of services is one that

community workers have increasingly come to recognize recently. This, as Dennis has argued, is that the 'form and content of those activities which remain in the residential locality . . . are progressively less locality-determined' (Dennis in Pahl, 1968: 80). This is a theme taken up by Richard Silburn in an article, 'The Potentials and Limitations of Community Action', where he argues that action to deal with the grievances of a deprived population, while important for the development of self-respect and social understanding, is 'not a sufficient remedy for its problems, which need overall solutions such as can only be canvassed by nationally structured political and social organizations' (Silburn, 1971: 143).

It is recognition of the extent to which the key determinants of local situations are often well outside these localities, at national or even international level, that has frustrated many workers involved in the government and local authority sponsored Community Development Projects. These projects were conceived to focus upon small multi-problems areas and to engage in monitored community work to revitalize them. John Bennington has effectively set out the weaknesses of the original approach to these projects. He argues that many problems in a 'CDP' area are

> not inherent in or specific to that neighbourhood, but are manifestations of wider processes in society. To isolate a small geographical area for study or action can isolate that population from the wider class structure within which 'deprivation' has to be examined.
>
> *(Bennington, 1974: 275)*

Hence political concern with territorial justice within a relatively homogeneous society has effectively undermined the autonomy of the existing local government system; and sociological study of the characteristics of local communities in a complex society has suggested that a narrow focus of attention upon social problems is likely to be unproductive.

Autonomous institutions, or services which are community controlled, offer many gains in terms of control of day-to-day administration, freedom from paternalistic control, and experience in 'self-government'. But to expect them to achieve freedom from major financial controls, in a society where the central political problems are the distribution of resources between competing claims and the management of the overall economy, is quite unrealistic. At best they can become sufficiently autonomous to be effective pressure centres for their own clients, but they must always face the fact that they are tied to a central machine with which they need to bargain. They cannot expect to achieve total independence whilst remaining heavily subsidized.

The complexity of the decision-making process, the interlocking nature of the issues at stake, and the weaknesses of attempts to provide autonomy for small-scale institutions, means that the forms of so called 'popular control' which are attainable inevitably involve new kinds of representative institutions. It is perfectly feasible to envisage school government in the hands of committees of parents, lay hospital boards, and even the consultation of clients in connection with social security decisions. But such innovations would involve the electing of representatives, and the formation of executive committees, and would not be simply government by mass meetings of all eligible to be involved. Indeed, even if the pattern of government adopted did involve mass meetings there would still be a form of selection – self-selection, inasmuch as only a minority would attend and an even smaller proportion would play active roles.

It is very difficult to envisage systems of popular democracy operating in relation to institutions whose activities affect large numbers of people, without some representational system developing. With such representational systems would come the potential for the development of oligarchy, outlined by Michels in his classic study of leadership patterns in avowedly democratic political parties and trade unions. The representatives would become involved in the details of decision making, and would be drawn close to the full-time officials, in such a way that problems of alienation from the rank and file, whom they represented, could arise. Again, therefore, when our system of representative government is attacked, or when the character of the existing distribution of power is considered, it would be helpful if critics would make clearer the probable character of the alternatives they envisage. 'Participation' and 'popular democracy' can too easily be fine but empty slogans which do not contribute to an effective attack on contemporary reality, because they relate it to an ideal which cannot be translated into a concrete form.

The modern activities of the State which are the concern of this book depend crucially upon very complex structures of government and administration. One of the prices we have to pay for the 'Welfare State' is a structure which is hard to control and to which individual consumers find it difficult to relate. Perhaps the best-known observation made by Michels is 'who says organization says oligarchy'. But equally his book makes perfectly clear that without organizations we can achieve very little. A critical problem for those who wish to achieve greater control over the activities of the State by ordinary people is that systems have to be developed which are open to real influence but which do not sacrifice the advantages of large-scale government activity.

If it is true that Britain is beginning to become ungovernable, one important reason for this is that as government becomes more complex, more and more people clamour for consultation. There is a need to explore the limits of the possible, to work out where consultation or participation is possible and feasible, and to explain to people when critical government processes would be undermined by open government. It may sometimes be necessary, too, to acknowledge that the real problem is 'too much government'. Sometimes there are good reasons for not making government too complex, for not trying to involve us all in administration when we would just as soon go about our business and delegate such difficult and time-consuming responsibilities. It is important to determine when this is the case, and to set out the reasons why more participation is thought undesirable. The present tendency to pay lip service to increasing participation, while in practice a largely private system of government is maintained, is a recipe for disaster.

Guide to further Reading

(For details of publisher, date and place of publication, see 'Works cited in the text', pp. 241-9).

General

In the introductory chapter it was stressed that only the field of administrative law had attempted to cover the subject of the book as a whole, and that lawyers' concern was with remedies for malpractice and maladministration. Hence, while there are various textbooks in administrative law, their contribution is primarily on the topics covered in Chapters 7 and 8, and their value for the matters considered elsewhere in the book is rather limited. H. W. R. Wade's *Administrative Law* is a very sound and widely used textbook in this field. Professor Griffith is another administrative law expert who has been involved in debates about the control of government in recent years; a new textbook by T. C. Hartley and J. A. G. Griffith, *Government and Law*, is therefore a useful addition to the subject. W. Friedman's *Law in a Changing Society*, though a wide-ranging and comparative discussion of the role of law, was of use to the author in sorting out ideas for this book.

It was suggested that, after administrative law, social administration is the academic subject which has been most concerned with relations between administration and the citizen. Richard Titmuss's two books of essays, *Essays on the Welfare State* and *Commitment to Welfare*, are both deeply concerned with ways in which needs are met, or fail to be met, by the social services. Much the same can be said of the work of Peter Townsend. His important contributions can also be found in two books of essays, *The Social Minority* and *Sociology and Social Policy*.

Throughout the book use is made of social history to provide accounts of the ways in which relations between citizens and the State have developed in Britain. Those who wish to go more deeply into this subject will find D. Fraser's *The Evolution of the British Welfare State* invaluable. Of interest to those who want to explore how social policy has evolved in the twentieth century is H. H. Heclo's *Modern Social Policy*, a comparative exploration of the factors in the development of aid to the unemployed and the elderly in Britain and Sweden.

Researchers may also want a more comprehensive account than this book supplies of the current state of social policies. The key textbook for generations of social policy students has been Penelope Hall's *Social Services of Modern England*. There have been several editions of this book. Recently it has been completely revised by a group of writers, under the editorship of A. Forder. Readers should ensure they obtain the most up-to-date edition. For the services which come under the control or supervision of the Department of Health and Social Security R. G. S. Brown's book in this series, *The Management of Welfare*, is an important source.

Chapter 2

The key text for the historical discussion in this chapter has already been cited: Fraser's *The Evolution of the British Welfare State*. In addition, important explorations of the evolution of more positive State action during the Victorian era are O. MacDonagh's *A Pattern of Government Growth*, D. Roberts's *Victorian Origins of the British Welfare State*, and I. Paulus's *The Search for Pure Food*. More adventurous readers may enjoy A. V. Dicey's influential attack on the collectivist state, published in 1905, *Lectures on the Relation between Law and Public Opinion in England*.

An influential American work which argues that social security is a form of social control is F. F. Piven and R. A. Cloward's *Regulating the Poor*. A more polemical British work of the same kind is J. C. Kincaid's *Poverty and Equality in*

Britain. Both books owe a great deal to the historical research carried out by B. B. Gilbert and reported in *British Social Policy 1914-1939.*

A twentieth-century attempt to both update and attack Dicey was provided in a book of essays edited by M. Ginsberg, *Law and Opinion in England in the Twentieth Century.*

Chapter 3

Many essays in the books by Titmuss and Townsend, cited above, are concerned with the topics discussed in this chapter. Particularly important is Townsend's 'The Scope and Limitations of Means-Tested Social Services in Britain' which has been reprinted in *Sociology and Social Policy.* Olive Stevenson's study of the work of the Supplementary Benefit Commission, *Claimant or Client?,* also examines many relevant issues in more detail. Denis Marsden's *Mothers Alone* is important for the relations of mothers to social security agencies. In drafting the chapter much use was made of the publications of the Child Poverty Action Group, including their journal *Poverty.* In a rapidly changing field these are a great help for those who want to keep up to date. A review of the many studies which have been done on the under-claiming of benefits, Ruth Lister's *Take-up of Means-Tested Benefits,* is one of the most useful of the pamphlets from this source.

Wider theoretical discussions of the issues raised in this chapter are provided in R. Pinker's *Social Theory and Social Policy,* R. White's article 'Lawyers and the Enforcement of Rights' and G. Sjoberg, R. A. Brymer and B. Farris's 'Bureaucracy and the Lower Class'.

Chapter 4

Much of the argument in this chapter is either based upon, or developed from, my *Sociology of Public Administration.* There are many works on organization theory. Perhaps the most useful recent contribution to this literature is a short and provocative book by Charles Perrow, *Complex Organizations: A Critical Essay*. Studies of British public organizations are few. Readers particularly interested in social services departments will find the study by the Brunel Social Services Organization Research Unit of interest. An important recent book has explored the roles played by receptionists in social services departments: Anthony Hall's *The Point of Entry*. R. G. S. Brown's book listed under the General section above, provides a good account of many of the relevant British organizations.

K. C. Davis's *Discretionary Justice* is a very influential American discussion of administrative discretion. In Britain perhaps the most important contributions to the discussion of this topic are Jeffrey Jowell's 'The Legal Control of Administrative Discretion' and Richard Titmuss's 'Welfare Rights, Law and Discretion'. Police discretion in Britain is examined in J. R. Lambert's *Crime, Police and Race Relations*. A valuable American contribution on this subject is J. Q. Wilson's *Varieties of Police Behaviour*. The literature on discretion in law enforcement is well summarized in A. K. Bottomley's *Decisions in the Penal Process*.

Chapters 5 and 6

Good theoretical discussions of professionalism are provided in T. J. Johnson's *Professions and Power*, P. Elliott's *The Sociology of the Professions*, and a reader edited by H. M. Vollmer and D. L. Mills, *Professionalization*. A. Etzioni has edited a useful American discussion of such partially professionalized groups as teachers and nurses, *The Semi-Professions and their Organization*.

Two books by Ann Cartwright, *Human Relations and Hospital Care* and *Patients and their Doctors* provide good accounts of service relationships in the medical sphere. B. Jackson and D. Marsden's *Education and the Working Class*, though rather old, has still to be bettered for insight into the impact of educational institutions upon individuals. There is a lack of good books on relations between social workers and their clients. J. E. Mayer and N. Timms's *The Client Speaks* is the most influential work of this kind, but it is concerned with social work practised by an atypical voluntary agency. The rudimentary state of legal services is presented in B. Abel-Smith, M. Zander and R. Brooke's *Legal Problems and the Citizen.* At the time of writing some important research on this topic is in progress. Its first findings are set out in P. Morris, J. Cooper and A. Byles's 'Public Attitudes to Problem Definition and Problem Solving' and P. Morris's 'A Sociological Approach to Research in Legal Services'.

B. Heraud's *Sociology and Social Work* discusses the issues set out at the end of Chapter 6. In this field the importance of E. Goffman's *Asylums* is self-evident. R. D. Laing and A. Esterson's *Sanity, Madness and the Family,* and I. Illich's two books *Medical Nemesis* and *Deschooling Society* are all influential polemics setting out jaundiced views of the helping professions. There is a lack of similar books setting out more orthodox views in defence of the professions, but such views are implicit in most other writing on the medical, educational and social services.

Chapter 7

The importance of writings in administrative law for this chapter has already been set out. On the Ombudsman, the articles by Gregory and Alexander have now been supplemented by a book *The Parliamentary Ombudsman* by R. G. Gregory and P. G. Hutchesson.

R. E. Wraith and P. G. Hutchesson's *Administrative Tribunals* is an unrivalled source on its subject. This can be supplemented by the two articles by K. Bell and her associates, 'National Insurance Local Tribunals', and an article by W. E. Cavenagh and D. Newton, 'The Membership of Two Administrative Tribunals'. Those who want to follow up the debate about supplementary benefits tribunals should look at M. Herman's booklet *Administrative Justice and Supplementary Benefits,* N. Lewis's article 'Supplementary Benefit Appeal Tribunals', R.

Lister's pamphlet *Justice for the Claimant*, and the author's article 'Some Implications of Legal Approaches to Welfare Rights'.

Bill Jordan's *Paupers*, Hilary Rose's 'Up against the Welfare State' and Ron Bailey's *The Squatters* provide accounts of welfare rights activities, each from an ideological position which they make quite clear. Patrick Seyd is engaged on research on 'the poverty lobby'; at the time of writing his only publication on this is an article on Shelter but interested readers may want to watch out for further publications.

Chapter 8

The standard textbook on planning policies is J. B. Cullingworth's *Town and Country Planning in Britain*. This has been through several editions as policies have changed, so readers should try to obtain an up-to-date version. There is a growing literature on the impact of planning on people. The most important examples of this genre are two books by Norman Dennis, *People and Planning* and *Public Participation and Planners' Blight*, and J. Gower Davies's *The Evangelistic Bureaucrat*. For two contrasting discussions of planning in Britain James Simmie's *Citizens in Conflict* and Stephen Elkin's *Politics and Land Use Planning* are recommended. David Eversley provides an entertaining and contentious discussion of the role of the planner in his *The Planner in Society*.

Chapter 9

Two books by Dilys Hill *Participating in Local Affairs* and *Democratic Theory and Local Government* explore aspects of participation. Readers who wish to explore some of the underlying problems in democratic theory might consult J. Lively's *Democracy* and C. Pateman's *Participation and Democratic Theory*. Some of the issues in the definition of legitimate political action are explored in R. Benewick and T. Smith (eds.) *Direct Action and Democratic Politics*. There is a growing literature on community action. Important collections of essays exploring this field are D. Jones and M. Mayo's *Community Work: One* and *Two*, Ann Lapping's Fabian Tract *Community Action*, and R. Bryant's article 'Community Action'. The article by Arnstein is widely quoted, but readers may find it difficult to obtain the original, published in a fairly obscure American journal.

The rate at which the literature on participation is growing suggests that the recommendations in this section will become out of date rather fast. We may expect to see in the near future a number of accounts of attempts to secure and stimulate forms of participation.

Works cited in the text

Abel-Smith, B. and Townsend, P., *The Poor and the Poorest*, London, Bell, 1965.

Abel-Smith, B., Zander, M. and Brooke, R., *Legal Problems and the Citizen*, London, Heinemann, 1973.

Allison, L., *Environmental Planning*, London, Allen and Unwin, 1975.

Almond, G. and Verba, S., *The Civic Culture*, Princeton, Princeton University Press, 1963.

Arnstein, S. R., 'A Ladder of Citizen Participation', in *AIP Journal*, July 1969, pp. 216-24.

Atkinson, A. B., *Poverty in Britain and the Reform of Social Security*, London, Cambridge University Press, 1969.

Bailey, R., *The Squatters*, Harmondsworth, Penguin Books, 1973.

Baker, A. J., 'On the other side of the counter', in *Poverty*, 8, 1968.

Bakke, E. W., *The Unemployed Man*, London, Nisbett, 1933.

Barton, R. W. A. G., *Institutional Neurosis*, Bristol, 1959.

Bell, K., Collison, P. and Webber, S., 'National Insurance Local Tribunals', *Journal of Social Policy*, 3 (4) and 4 (1), 1974 and 1975.

Benewick, R. and Smith, T. (eds.), *Direct Action and Democratic Politics*, London, Allen and Unwin, 1972.

Bennington, J., 'Strategies for change at the local level: some reflections', in D. Jones and M. Mayo (eds.), *Community Work: One*, London, Routledge, 1974.

Bernstein, B., 'Social Class Speech Systems and Psycho-Therapy', *British Journal of Sociology* XV(1) 1964, pp. 54-64.

Beveridge Report, *Social Insurance and Allied Services*, London, HMSO, Cmd. 6404, 1942.

Birrell, D. and Murie, A., 'Ideology, Conflict and Social Policy', in *Journal of Social Policy*, Vol. 4(3), July 1975, pp. 243-58.

Blau, P. M., *The Dynamics of Bureacracy*, Chicago, University of Chicago Press, 1955.

Bottomley, A. K., *Decisions in the Penal Process*, London, Martin Robertson, 1973

Bottomore, T., *Elites and Society*, London, C. A. Watts, 1964.

Bowlby, J., *Child Care and the Growth of Love*, Harmondsworth, Penguin Books, 1953.

Boyle, K., Hadden, T. and Hillyard, P., *Law and State: the Case of Northern Ireland*, London, Martin Robertson, 1975.

Brooke, R., 'Social Administration and Human Rights', in P. Townsend and N. Bosanquet (eds.), *Labour and Inequality*, London, Fabian Society, 1972.

Brown, R. G. S., *The Management of Welfare*, London, Fontana Books, 1975.

Brunel Social Services Organization Research Unit, *Social Services Departments*, London, Heinemann, 1974.

Bryant, R., 'Community Action', in *British Journal of Social Work*, 2 (2), Summer 1972.

Bull, D. G., 'Out-of-form Post Offices', in *Poverty* 12/13, 1969.

Burgess, T., *Guide to English Schools*, Harmondsworth, Penguin Books, 1969.

Burney, E., *Housing on Trial*, London, Oxford University Press, 1967.

Burns, T. and Stalker, G. M., *The Management of Innovation*, London, Tavistock, 1961.

Carson, W. G., 'White Collar Crime and the Enforcement of Factory Legislation', *British Journal of Criminology*, Vol. 10, 1970.

Cartwright, A., *Human Relations and Hospital Care*, London, Routledge, 1964.

Patients and their Doctors, London, Routledge, 1967.

Cavenagh, W. E. and Newton, D., 'The Membership of Two Administrative Tribunals', in *Public Administration*, 48, Winter 1970, pp. 449-68.

Coates, K. and Silburn R., *Poverty: The Forgotten Englishman*, Harmondsworth, Penguin Books, 1970.

Cole, D. Wedderburn and Utting, J., *The Economic Circumstances of Old People*, Welwyn, Codicote Press, 1962.

Coleman, R. J., *Supplementary Benefits and the Administrative Review of Administrative Action*, London, Poverty pamphlet 7, n.d.

Colwell Inquiry, *Report of the Committee of Inquiry into the Care and Supervision Provided in Relation to Maria Colwell,* London, HMSO, 1974.

Coventry Community Workshop, leaflet entitled *Public Participation in Structure Planning in Coventry,* 1972.

Cullingworth, J. B., *Town and Country Planning in Britain,* London, Allen and Unwin, fifth edition, 1974.

Cullingworth Committee, *Council Housing Purposes, Procedures and Priorities* (Ninth report of the Housing Management Sub-Committee of the Central Housing Advisory Committee), London, HMSO, 1969.

Darlow, G. F., contribution to Royal Institute of Public Administration symposium 'Who are the Policy Makers?', in *Public Administration,* 43, 1965.

Davies, B., *Social Needs and Resources in Local Services,* London, Michael Joseph, 1968.

Davies, J. Gower, *The Evangelistic Bureaucrat,* London, Tavistock, 1974.

Davis, K. C., *Discretionary Justice,* Louisiana, Louisiana State University Press, 1969.

Dearlove, J. 'The Control of Change and the Regulation of Community Action', in D. Jones and M. Mayo (eds.), *Community Work: One,* London, Routledge, 1974.
review of S. L. Elkin's *Politics and Land Use Planning,* in *Public Administration,* Vol. 53, Spring 1975, pp. 92-3.

Dennis, N., *People and Planning,* London, Faber, 1970.
Public Participation and Planners' Blight, London, Faber, 1972.

Deutscher, I., 'The Gatekeeper in Public Housing', in I. Deutscher and E. J. Thompson (eds.), *Among the People: Encounters with the Poor,* New York, Basic Books, 1968.

Dicey, A. V., *Lectures on the Relation between Law and Public Opinion in England,* London, Macmillan, 1905.

Elkin, S. L., *Politics and Land Use Planning,* London, Cambridge University Press, 1974.

Elliott, P., *The Sociology of the Professions,* London, Macmillan, 1972.

Etzioni, A. (ed.), *The Semi-Professions and their Organization,* New York, Free Press, 1969.

Eversley, D., *The Planner in Society,* London, Faber, 1973.

Fisher Committee, *Report of the Committee on Abuse of Social Security Benefits,* London, HMSO, Cmnd. 5228, 1963.

Forder, A. (ed.), *Penelope Hall's Social Services of England and Wales,* London, Routledge, 1971 (Eighth edition).

Fox, A., *Beyond Contract: Work, Power and Trust Relations*, London, Faber, 1974.

Francis, R. G. and Stone, R. C., *Service and Procedure in Bureaucracy*, Minneapolis, University of Minnesota Press, 1956.

Fraser, D., *The Evolution of the British Welfare State*, London, Macmillan, 1973.

Friedman, W., *Law in a Changing Society* (Second Edition), London, Stevens, 1972.

Friedson, E., *Patients' Views of Medical Practice*, New York, Russell Sage Foundation, 1961.

Fulbrook, J., *The Appellant and his Case*, London, Poverty research series 5, 1975.

Fulbrook, J., Brooke, R. and Archer, P., *Tribunals: a Social Court*, London, Fabian Society, 1973.

Gilbert, B. B., *British Social Policy 1914-1939*, London, Batsford, 1970.

Ginsberg, M. (ed.), *Law and Opinion in England in the Twentieth Century*, London, Stevens, 1959.

Glastonbury, B., Burdett, M. and Austin, R., 'Community Perceptions and the Personal Social Services', in *Policy and Politics*, Vol. 1 (3) March 1973, pp. 191-212.

Goffman, E., *Asylums*, Harmondsworth, Penguin Books, 1970.

Greenwood, E., 'Attributes of a Profession', *Social Work*, 2, 1957, pp. 45-55.

Gregory, R. and Alexander, A. 'Our Parliamentary Ombudsman', in *Public Administration*, 50, Autumn 1972, pp. 313-331 and 51, Spring 1973, pp. 41-60.

Gregory, R. G. and Hutchesson, P. G., *The Parliamentary Ombudsman*, London, Allen and Unwin, 1975.

Gunningham, N., *Pollution, Social Interest and the Law*, London, Martin Robertson, 1974.

Guttsman, W. L., *The British Political Elite*, London, MacGibbon and Kee, 1963.

Hall, A. S., *The Point of Entry*, London, Allen and Unwin, 1974.

Hampson, W., *Democracy and Community*, London, Oxford University Press, 1970.

Hartley, T. C. and Griffith, J. A. G., *Government and Law*, London, Weidenfeld and Nicolson, 1975.

Heclo, H. H., 'The Councillor's Job', in *Public Administration*, 47, 1969, pp. 185-202.

Modern Social Policy, New Haven, Yale University Press, 1974.

Heclo, H. H. and Wildavsky, A., *The Private Government of Public Money*, London, Macmillan, 1974.

Heraud, B. J., *Sociology and Social Work,* Oxford, Pergamon, 1970.

Herman, M., *Administrative Justice and Supplementary Benefits,* London, Bell, 1972.

Herron, F., *Labour Markets in Crisis,* London, Macmillan, 1974.

Hill, D. M., *Participating in Local Affairs,* Harmondsworth, Penguin Books, 1970.

Hill, D. M., *Democratic Theory and Local Government,* London, Allen and Unwin, 1974.

Hill, M. J., 'The Exercise of Discretion in the National Assistance Board', in *Public Administration,* 47, 1969, pp. 75-90.

The Sociology of Public Administration, London, Weidenfeld and Nicolson, 1972.

Harrison, R. M., Sargeant, A. and Talbot, V., *Men Out of Work,* London, Cambridge University Press, 1973.

'Some Implications of Legal Approaches to Welfare Rights', in *British Journal of Social Work,* Vol. 4, 1974. .

Hughes, D., 'The Spivs', in Sissons M. and French P. (eds.), *Age of Austerity,* London, Hodder and Stoughton, 1963.

Illich, I., *Deschooling Society,* Harmondsworth, Penguin Books, 1974.

Medical Nemesis, London, Calder and Boyars, 1975.

Jackson, B. and Marsden, D., *Education and the Working Class,* London, Routledge, 1962.

Jacques, E., *Equitable Payment,* Harmondsworth, Penguin Books, 1967.

Jahoda, M., et al., *Marienthal: The Sociography of an Unemployed Community,* London, Tavistock, 1972.

Johnson, T. J., *Professions and Power,* London, Macmillan, 1972.

Jones, D. and Mayo, M. (eds.), *Community Work: One,* London, Routledge, 1974.

Community Work: Two, London, Routledge, 1975.

Jordan, W., *Paupers,* London, Routledge and Kegan Paul, 1973.

Jowell, J., 'The Legal Control of Administrative Discretion', in *Public Law,* Autumn 1973, pp. 178-220.

Kahn-Freund, O., 'Labour Law', in M. Ginsberg (ed.), *Law and Opinion in the Twentieth Century,* London, Stevens, 1959.

Kaufman, H., *The Forest Ranger,* Baltimore, Johns Hopkins Press, 1960.

Kincaid, J. C., *Poverty and Equality in Britain,* Harmondsworth, Penguin Books, 1973.

King, R., 'The Head Teacher and his Authority', in G. Fowler,

V. Morris and J. Ozga, *Decision Making in British Education,* London, Heinemann, 1973.

Klein, R., 'The Doctors' Dilemma for Accountability', paper given to Joint University Council for Social and Public Administration, Public Administration Committee Conference, York, 1974.

Laing, R. D. and Esterson, A., *Sanity, Madness and the Family,* Harmondsworth, Penguin Books, 1970.

Lambert, J. R., *Crime, Police and Race Relations,* London, Oxford University Press, 1970.

Lapping, A., *Community Action,* London, Fabian Tract 400, 1970.

Lee, J. M., *Social Leaders and Public Persons,* London, Oxford University Press, 1963.

Lewis, N., 'Supplementary Benefit Appeal Tribunals', *Public Law,* Winter 1973, pp. 257-84.

Lister, R., *Take-up of Means-Tested Benefits,* London, poverty pamphlet 18, 1974.

Justice for the Claimant, London, Poverty Research Series 4, 1974.

Lively, J. F., *Democracy,* London, Oxford University Press, 1974.

MacDonagh, O., *A Pattern of Government Growth,* London, MacGibbon and Kee, 1961.

Mandelkar, D., *Green Belts and Urban Growth: English Town and Country Planning in Action,* Madison, 1962.

March, J. G. and Simon, H. A., *Organizations,* New York, Wiley, 1958.

Marsden, D., *Mothers Alone* (Revised edition), Harmondsworth, Penguin Books, 1973.

Mayer, J. E. and Timms, N., *The Client Speaks,* London, Routledge, 1970.

McGeeney, P., *Parents are Welcome,* London, Longmans, 1969.

Merton, R. K., 'Bureaucratic Structure and Personality', in *Social Theory and Social Structure,* Glencoe, Illinois, Free Press, 1952.

Meyerson, M. and Banfield, E. C., *Politics, Planning and the Public Interest,* Glencoe, Illinois, Free Press, 1955.

Michels, R., *Political Parties* (trans. E. and C. Paul), London, Constable, 1915.

Mills, C. W., *Power, Politics and People* (ed. I. L. Horowitz), New York, Oxford University Press, 1963.

Ministry of Pensions and National Insurance, *Financial and Other Circumstances of Retirement Pensioners,* London, HMSO, 1966.

Ministry of Social Security, *Circumstances of Families,* London, HMSO, 1967.

Morris, P., 'A Sociological Approach to Research in Legal Services', in P. Morris, R. White and P. Lewis, *Social Needs and Legal Action*, London, Martin Robertson, 1973.

Morris, P., Cooper, J. and Byles, A., 'Public Attitudes to Problem Definition and Problem Solving: a pilot study', in *British Journal of Social Work*, Vol. 3 (3), pp. 301-20.

Mosca, G., *The Ruling Class* (trans. A. Livingstone) New York, McGraw Hill, 1939.

National Health Service Reorganization: England, London, HMSO, 1972, Cmnd. 5055.

Neumann, F., *Behemoth*, New York, Oxford University Press, 1944.

Pahl, R. E., *Readings in Urban Sociology*, Oxford, Pergamon, 1968.

Parris, H., *Government and the Railways*, London, Routledge, 1965.
Constitutional Bureaucracy, London, Allen and Unwin, 1969.

Pateman, C., *Participation and Democratic Theory*, London, Cambridge University Press, 1970.

Paulus, I., *The Search for Pure Food*, London, Martin Robertson, 1974.

Perrow, C., *Complex Organizations: A Critical Essay*, Glenview, Illinois, Scott Foresman, 1972.

Pinker, R., *Social Theory and Social Policy*, London, Heinemann, 1971.

Piven, F. F. and Cloward, R. A., *Regulating the Poor*, London, Tavistock, 1972.

Plowden, W., *The Motor Car and Politics in Britain*, London, Bodley Head, 1971.

Roberts, D., *Victorian Origins of the British Welfare State*, New Haven, Yale University Press, 1960.

Rose, H., 'Who can de-label the claimant?', in *Social Work Today*, 4 (13), 1973.
'Up against the Welfare State', in R. Miliband and J. Saville (eds.), *Socialist Register*, 1973, London, Merlin, 1974.

Scheff, T., *Being Mentally Ill*, London, Weidenfeld and Nicolson, 1966.

Selznick, P., *Leadership in Administration*, New York, Harper and Row, 1957.

Seyd, P., 'Shelter: The National Campaign for the Homeless', in *Political Quarterly* 46 (4), 1975, pp. 418-31.

Sharp, E., *The Ministry of Housing and Local Government*, London, Allen and Unwin, 1969.

Shelter, *The Grief Report*, London, Shelter, 1972.

Silburn, R., 'The Potentials and Limitations of Community Action',

248   Guide to further Reading

in D. Bull (ed.), *Family Poverty*, London, Duckworth, 1971.

Simmie, J. M., *Citizens in Conflict*, London, Hutchinson, 1974.

Simon, H. A., *Administrative Behaviour*, New York, Macmillan, 1945.

Sinfield, A., 'Poor and Out of Work in North Shields'. in P. Townsend (ed.), *The Concept of Poverty*, London, Heinemann, 1970.

Sjobreg, G., Brymer, R. A. and Farris, B., 'Bureaucracy and the Lower Class', in *Sociology and Social Research*, 50, 1966.

Skeffington Committee, *People and Planning: Report of the committee on public participation in planning*, London, HMSO, 1969.

Stanworth, P. and Giddens, A., *Elites and Power in British Society*, Cambridge, Cambridge University Press, 1974.

Stevenson, O., *Claimant or Client?* London, Allen and Unwin, 1973.

Supplementary Benefits Commission, *Supplementary Benefits Handbook*, London, HMSO, n.d. (regularly updated).

Szasz, T., *The Myth of Mental Illness*, New York, Hoeber, 1961.

Titmuss, R. M., *Essays on the Welfare State*, London, Allen and Unwin, 1958.

Commitment to Welfare, London, Allen and Unwin, 1968.

'Welfare Rights, Law and Discretion', in *Political Quarterly*, 42 (2), April 1971, pp. 113-32.

Townsend, P. and Bosanquet, N. (eds.), *Labour and Inequality*, London, Fabian Society, 1972.

Townsend, P., *The Scope and Limitations of Means-Tested Social Services in Britain*, Manchester, Manchester Statistical Society, 1973.

The Social Minority, London, Allen Lane, 1975.

Sociology and Social Policy, London, Allen Lane, 1975.

Urry, J. and Wakeford, J., *Power in Britain*, London, Heinemann, 1973.

Vaizey, J., *Scenes from Institutional Life*, London, Faber, 1959.

Vollmer, H. M. and Mills, D. L., *Professionalization*, Englewood Cliffs, N.J., Prentice Hall, 1961.

Wade, H. W. R., *Administrative Law*, Oxford, Clarendon Press, 1971 (Third edition).

Weber, M., *The Theory of Social and Economic Organization*, (trans. by A. M. Henderson and T. Parsons), Glencoe, Illinois, Free Press, 1947.

White, R., 'Lawyers and the Enforcement of Rights', in P. Morris, R. White and P. Lewis, *Social Needs and Legal Action*, London, Martin Robertson, 1973.

Wilson, J. Q., *Varieties of Police Behaviour,* Cambridge, Mass., Harvard University Press, 1968.

Wittfogel, K., *Oriental Despotism,* New Haven, Yale University Press, 1957.

Wraith, R. E. and Hutchesson, P. G., *Administrative Tribunals,* London, Allen and Unwin, 1973.

Young, M. and Willmott, P., *Family and Kinship in East London,* London, Routledge, 1957.

Index

C